Listening to Old Voices

Listening to Old Voices

FOLKLORE, LIFE STORIES, AND THE ELDERLY

Patrick B. Mullen

University of Illinois Press
Urbana and Chicago

Publication of this work was supported in part by a grant from The Ohio State University College of Humanities and the Office of Research and Graduate Studies.

This book is printed on acid-free paper.

Library of Congress Cataloging-in-Publication Data

Mullen, Patrick B., 1941–
    Listening to old voices : folklore, life stories, and the elderly
/ Patrick B. Mullen.
        p.   cm.
    ISBN 0-252-01808-7 (alk. paper)
    1. Folklore—Blue Ridge Mountains. 2. Folklore—Ohio. 3. Aged—
Blue Ridge Mountains—Folklore. 4. Aged—Ohio—Folklore.
I. Title.
GR108.M85 1992
398'.09755—dc20   90-26694
                                                            CIP

For Carol, David, and Linda

Contents

Acknowledgments

The writing of this book was supported by an Ohio State University Seed Grant and a Faculty Professional Leave for 1986–87. The publication of the book was made possible by a grant from the College of Humanities and the Office of Research and Graduate Studies at the Ohio State University. The chair of the Department of English, Morris Beja, and the dean, Micheal Riley, and associate dean, Marvin Zahniser, of the College of Humanities, were supportive of my efforts to obtain the grants and the leave. The original field research was funded by the American Folklife Center of the Library of Congress, the Folk Arts Program of the National Endowment for the Arts, the Traditional Arts Program of the Ohio Arts Council, and the Ohio Sea Grant Program. I thank Alan Jabbour, director of the American Folklife Center; Wayne Lawson, executive director, and Timothy Lloyd, former director of the Traditional and Ethnic Arts Program, of the Ohio Arts Council; and Ed Herdendorf, former director, and Jeffrey Reutter, acting director, of the Center for Lake Erie Area Research, for their support.

Much of the fieldwork was conducted with other folklorists: Carl Fleischhauer, Alan Jabbour, Gerri Johnson, and Harley Jolley contributed greatly to interviews in the Blue Ridge Mountains, and Tim Lloyd and Sandy Rikoon were indispensable coworkers in Ohio. Tim was also my collaborator on another book, *Lake Erie Fishermen: Work, Identity, and Tradition,* and should be considered coauthor of the chapter in this book on Alva Snell. Steve Kelley provided valuable leads during the fieldwork in southern Ohio. Alberta Jackson, Mollie

Ford's daughter, described details of her mother's life that were essential for a full understanding of her story. Jim Winningham, business manager, and Carol Henke, executive secretary, of St. Joseph's Orphanage in Cincinnati also helped me with background on Mollie Ford. Francis Abernethy, Kathy Greenwood, and Sandy Rikoon read individual chapters and helped greatly with the revision process. Paul Smith provided important bibliographical information. Mike Szczepanik of the Ohio State University College of Humanities taught me how to process words and how to link files so that the manuscript preparation was easier and more efficient than it would have been otherwise. Cynthia Cox, Beth MacDaniel, and Martha Sims transcribed many hours of tape; they also provided valuable commentary on several chapters. My folklorist colleagues at Ohio State, Dan Barnes, Amy Shuman, John Stewart, and Sabra Webber, discussed many aspects of the book with me and commented on specific chapters. Roger Abrahams and Janet Theophano read the book manuscript for the University of Illinois Press and made useful commentary; Simon Bronner also read for the Press and provided detailed constructive criticism, which was important in the final revision. My deepest appreciation goes, again, to Judy McCulloh, executive editor of the University of Illinois Press, for her role in seeing the manuscript through all the stages of its development. Bob Baum, Susan Huhta, Jack Shortlidge, and Tony Libby helped with the proofreading. Carl Fleischhauer, formerly of the American Folklife Center, read parts of the manuscript and aided me in securing photographs. Students in my class English 577: Studies in Folklore during the Winter Quarters of 1988 and 1989 had many insights into the material. Participants in the 1990 Fife Conference at Utah State University asked me questions that made me expand some of my interpretations of the material. My wife, Roseanne Rini, read the entire manuscript, helped me through numerous revisions, and, as always, gave me the love and support that makes everything else possible.

I owe the greatest thanks to the people about whom this book is written: Leonard Bryan, Mamie Bryan, Matt Burnett, Mollie Ford, Bob Glasgow, Jesse Hatcher, Bill Henry, Quincy Higgins, and Alva Snell. They gladly agreed to be interviewed, talked openly about their lives, and made the field research an exciting and rewarding process.

It's a new place but you've
always been here
You're just listening to old voices
with a new ear

—John Hiatt

Introduction

Folklore and the Elderly

I was looking for a unifying theme to hold together widely diverse field research materials, and the old age of many of the informants struck me as an appropriate focus. As I began to write, I realized that I was also writing about my own elderly parents and about my own aging. My father died in 1985 at the age of seventy-three after suffering for years with Alzheimer's disease, and my mother died in 1988 at the age of seventy-eight after a series of strokes and a heart attack. They were incapacitated by their illnesses and unable to engage fully in social life. More positive images of old age had come to me from the elderly people whom I had interviewed as a folklorist.

The old people with whom I had worked were often lively and outgoing, passing on traditions in ways that were difficult for my mother and father. The nine elders who are featured in this book were in relatively good health when I interviewed them, although several had physical ailments, as well as other problems. Eighty-four-year-old Mollie Ford (chap. 1) was partially paralyzed; seventy-seven-year-old Matt Burnett (chap. 8) had a heart condition that forced him into early retirement; seventy-eight-year-old Bob Glasgow (chap. 4) had lost the fingers of one hand and was taking care of an invalid wife; and eighty-three-year-old Jesse Hatcher (chap. 2) had lost his wife and undergone major surgery. Despite these various problems and the general infirmities of old age, all the elderly people I consulted with were positive in their attitudes toward life. They were complex people who talked in ways that engaged me deeply in what they were saying. They have something to say to all of us; much of it is directed toward younger generations, but I think their stories will be of interest to other elderly people as well. They are all examples of successful aging (some more than others), and their lives can be taken as models of ways folk traditions can be reshaped and integrated into our lives as a part of growing old. I envision the reader of this book as listening to them tell their stories, seeing the dynamic people that I interviewed.

Folklore is one of the reasons these nine individuals were mentally healthy in their old age; carrying on cultural and individual traditions helped give meaning to their lives. These were not ordinary elderly people; I was attracted to them in the first place not because they were old but because they were tradition-bearers. I was working on field research projects that concentrated on regional or occupational groups, not on the elderly as an age group, but folklorists are drawn to the elderly because they are often more oriented toward traditional life (Hufford, Hunt, and Zeitlin 1987, 69). Not all old people are active tradition-bearers, though; some passively carry on traditions, but the active ones value the past, maintain a connection with it, and often identify themselves as traditional performers and crafts-people. This does not mean that they live in the past; they keep traditions alive by using them as resources for coping with the present. Folklore as an academic discipline is not the study of the past but rather the study of present situations informed by the past. The people who actively bring the past and the present together in creative ways are the ones folklorists seek out in the community, and finding them is not hard because most people in the community know who they are. Folklorists ask for the storytellers, the big talkers, the basket and chair makers, the carvers and the cooks, the quilters and the singers, the banjo and the fiddle players. These are the active tra-dition-bearers, and they are often the oldest people in the community.

This might suggest that folklore is dying out, but it is not. Younger people are often aware of tradition but do not yet actively carry it on. Even folklorists can mistakenly assume that traditions are dying because old people seem to be the only ones passing them on. As Henry Glassie points out, folklorists often predict the deaths of folk arts: "Generation after generation contains the last basket weaver and the last ballad singer" (1982, 63). He then describes the situation in the Irish community of Ballymenone in which young men listen quietly while old men tell the stories. When the old men die, the

listeners, now old themselves, replace them as storytellers and tradition-bearers. Frequently, a tradition learned as a youth lies dormant
during the middle years of life to be revived in old age, especially
among elderly men (Bronner 1985; Jabbour 1981). Matt Burnett
learned how to carve wooden toys as a boy, but he did not engage
in it again until after he retired. He also learned his trade as an
auctioneer, as an apprentice to an old man, and he in turn passed
it on in his old age to a younger man. Folklore is found in every age
group, but the elders of the community will have an accumulation
of traditional knowledge.

Tradition itself is not a static construct; rather, it is a dynamic
ongoing process of interpretation and reconstruction of the past (Handler and Linnekin 1984, 276; see also Bendix 1989). Since folk practices and beliefs are dynamic and adapt to changing circumstances,
traditions learned in youth will not remain the same throughout a
person's life. For instance, the fishing skills learned by retired commercial fisherman Alva Snell (chap. 5) when he started out changed
as technology developed. His stories about his occupational life reflect
the new ways of doing things as well as the old. In fact, one of the
themes of Mr. Snell's stories is the contrast between the old and the
new. The past is viewed from the perspective of the present: when
an old person tells a story about the past, it is not necessarily an
absolutely factual account of the way things were; rather, the story
is filtered through the imagination of the teller and influenced by
what has happened in the intervening years and by the current situation of the storyteller.[1] For example, Leonard and Mamie Bryan
(chap. 3) tell a story about their courtship seen from the point of
view of their relationship after sixty-three years of marriage. He tends
to see the courtship idealistically; she on the other hand has a more
realistic view.

Folklore is a resource through which a person can work out and
then project to others a certain changing self-image; in other words,
stories, crafts, folk beliefs, and ways of cooking and planting project
identity (Dundes 1983). The stories the elderly tell communicate a
great deal about them and their cultures; folklore gives artistic expression to individual experiences of aging and also reveals broader social
patterns of old age. Quincy Higgins (chap. 6) tells legends, jokes,
and personal stories that project his values as an individual within
his particular regional culture in the Blue Ridge Mountains of North

Carolina. Fundamentalist religion is predominant in the region, and Quincy Higgins is a lay preacher in the Baptist church. His stories return again and again to the importance of divine inspiration, indicating its importance for his individual identity and within his culture. Mr. Higgins is seventy-eight years old. His narratives, therefore, are a cumulative view both of one life and of a segment of regional history, progressing from life in a log house with a kerosene lamp to life in a modern farmhouse with electricity and television.

The folklore in this book covers a wide range, from verbal art to customary behavior to material culture. The kinds of folk narratives include supernatural legends, hero legends, jokes, family stories, and personal experience narratives. Folk beliefs are embedded in many kinds of traditional communication, from stories to ritual to planting and medical practices. Many of the beliefs center around some aspect of folk religion: faith healing, conversion narratives, and traditional hymns, for example, all fall into this category. Foodways are a significant part of the lore in one case: Jesse Hatcher talked about family recipes and traditional preservation of foods. Traditional material culture is an element in understanding two of the men: Matt Burnett engages in wood carving, and Bob Glasgow features folk architecture in talking about his life.

All of these kinds of folklore are important in understanding the lives of the nine elderly people, but the personal experience narrative is the most significant traditional form analyzed in the present study. No matter what other kinds of folklore they had, every one of the nine individuals told personal narratives that reveal the meaning of their lives from the perspective of old age. Since personal narratives are based on individual experiences, they may not seem to be a form of folklore, but there are several factors that make them so. They are traditional in terms of their content and structure: people tend to make stories out of incidents that the culture defines as significant and to tell them in traditionally structured ways. Leonard and Mamie Bryan tell a courtship story because courtship is deemed an appropriate story topic in their culture. Their story follows folk ideas about the pattern of courtship behavior at that time and place so that its structure is also traditional. Stories stand out from other kinds of verbal discourse because they are stories: they are distinct units of communication with defined beginnings, middles, and endings.

In a particular conversational situation, listeners will recognize a story as a separate form of communication (Stahl 1977b; Robinson 1981). Personal experience narratives have cultural markers that set them off from other expressions, including other kinds of narrative. For example, when Jesse Hatcher introduces a story by asking, "If I was to tell you that I had had a rattlesnake up in my arms, would you believe it?" he lets us know not only the story topic but also that it will be about his personal experience. After getting our attention with this opening, he proceeded to tell us about tying the tops of corn and grasping a snake in the process. He then used a closing formula to mark the end of the narrative and to make us laugh: "But I haven't tied no more tops since." His story fits Barbara Herrnstein Smith's definition of minimal narrative: "verbal acts consisting of *someone telling someone else that something happened*" (1980, 232; see also Labov 1972), but Mr. Hatcher's story, and most of the ones told by the elderly in this study, are more than minimal narratives; they have complicated plots, developed characters, and rhetorical devices to engage the listener. Finally, the best personal stories are told repeatedly; here again tradition, including traditions of teller-audience interaction, are involved (Abrahams 1976, 195). A story is only repeated if it receives the appropriate response from the audience; the context of storytelling is traditionally determined as is the aesthetic response of the audience. Cultural expectations and traditional aesthetics influence both storyteller and audience in determining which stories will have recurring performances. The personal experience narrative will reveal broad cultural, aesthetic, and practical concerns as well as individual themes.[2]

There is a wide variety of folklore in this study then, but it has a narrow cultural focus and is about only a few individuals. The geographical coverage is not broad. The field research concentrated on two regions, southern Ohio and the Blue Ridge Mountains along the Virginia–North Carolina border. The only chapter about a person outside these regions is the one on Alva Snell, who lives on the shores of Lake Erie in northern Ohio. As the only person in the study who lives in an urban area and has a strong occupational identity in old age, Mr. Snell's story brings a unique topic to the research. Southern Ohio and the Blue Ridge are both rural and considered part of the broader Appalachian region, the Blue Ridge on the far eastern edge and southern Ohio on the western side. This is not, however, a regional study; the people in it live in these regions and they share some cultural traits, but the focus is on them as members of an age group. There are also cultural differences between the two areas and, for that matter, cultural differences within each area. People who live within the same region will have different cultural influences in their lives, such as race, ethnicity, religion, socio-economic level, family traditions, and so forth. Four of the people in this study are black and five are white. African-American cultural traditions have a bearing on the lives of the black people as do Anglo-American traditions on the whites, but these are important for my purposes as they relate to their positions as elders in their communities.

The original field research was not directed specifically at old people. The southern Ohio fieldwork was part of the Scioto Valley Folklife Project, which was sponsored by the Ohio Arts Council, and the Virginia–North Carolina fieldwork was organized as the Blue Ridge Folklife Project by the American Folklife Center of the Library of Congress. Both projects were regional folklife surveys designed to collect a broad range of folklore within a narrowly defined geographical area, four counties in Ohio and parts of seven counties in Virginia and North Carolina. The fieldwork with Alva Snell in northern Ohio was part of another Ohio Arts Council project, which concentrated on commercial fishermen on the Western Basin of Lake Erie. After all of the material had been collected and cataloged and some of it transcribed, I realized how many elderly people I had interviewed and decided to do further research on aging.

The fieldwork methods were similar in the three projects. I or one of the other folklorists conducting the research would hear about a tradition-bearer from someone else in the community. We would then go to his or her house and arrange for a tape-recorded interview, which usually began on the spot. The length of the interview varied from three hours in either a morning or an afternoon session to eight or more hours over a period of days or weeks. In the case of Mollie Ford, I tape-recorded a conversation with her for four hours one morning. I talked to Jesse Hatcher at his home one day without recording him and at his church the following Sunday. A week later I recorded him at his home for five hours. Matt Burnett was recorded on three different occasions. Multiple interviews with the same person were usually conducted over weeks or months, but in the case of Bill Henry (chap. 7) the first interview was in 1980, the second in 1989. He maintained a consistent self-image in both sessions. A three-hour or even an eight-hour interview will not reveal everything there is to know about an individual, but it will often give some significant facts about a person and more importantly project her self-image. The person interviewed will be selective in what he or she presents to the folklorist, often leaving out those incidents that might reflect negatively on him or withholding secrets not revealed to anyone outside the family. It would take years of fieldwork to obtain this kind of information, if it were ever to come out. That is not my purpose here; rather, I am interested in the capsule image that a person projects, how they see themselves, and how they want others to see them.

The elderly people I contacted were eager to be interviewed; older people generally want to tell their life stories, but they do not always have a receptive audience. To the folklorist, it is as if elderly persons are waiting for someone to come along and ask for their stories, and the folklorist had better be a good listener. The interviews were usually nondirectional; I asked some questions but let the individual establish the direction and specific topics to be discussed. Later in an interview, I might ask more direct questions about topics of interest to me. For instance, Quincy Higgins had talked for several hours without any interference before my coworker Geraldine Johnson and I asked him about folklore topics prevalent on the Blue Ridge, such as planting by the signs, moonshine stories, and Daniel Boone legends. The folklorist has an influence on what is said and how it is presented, but folk performers also have a way of getting their points of view across. Mollie Ford resisted all of my efforts to interview her about her life history in order to discuss religious values instead.

This book is, in some sense, collaborative or, to use Kirshenblatt-Gimblett's phrase, "an ethnographic experiment with polyvocal texts" (1989a, 131). The nine elders speak in the first person, and I speak in the first person; we are all there as participants in the creating of the accounts. The significance of this is that the folklorist/ethnographer is not invisible, but is, in fact, self-reflexive about his or her role. Once this self-awareness is accomplished, the researcher can see the process of writing not as a strictly scientific description but as a creative act and the final outcome as a kind of allegory. Anthropologist James Clifford first articulated the idea of ethnography as allegory: "I treat ethnography itself as a performance emplotted by powerful stories. Embodied in written reports, these stories simultaneously describe real cultural events and make additional moral, ideological, and even cosmological statements" (1986, 98). The present study is, in many ways, an example of Clifford's "ethnographic pastoral allegory" (1986, 110–19). I sought out old people who lived in rural areas (my "quest") in order to save their knowledge of the past because when they die that specific knowledge could be lost, although folklore itself goes on. Many of the old people I interviewed had a romantic and nostalgic view of the past. And as part of our collaboration, I worked with them to present that view to the readers of this book. As Clifford points out, the idea of ethnography as allegory is not necessarily bad; the important thing is that we recognize it as such and acknowledge our own underlying moral and ideological goals. I believe that these old people have something to teach us all and that there is something valuable to be retrieved from the past although I recognize that the past as an imaginative construct reflects our needs in the present. Ideologically, I am an advocate for the elderly, for their right to be respected, to be heard.

As part of reflexive ethnography, folklorists need to examine ways in which they influence the material during the interviews, and after they have been completed, folklorists need to investigate the process of transforming field data to the printed page. For one thing, the rendering of an oral dialect in print affects the way the reader perceives the person speaking (Preston 1982). I have transcribed the words and grammar as close to the way it was spoken as possible. I have not tried to indicate pronunciation through dialect spelling, since this can imply social distinctions. There are a few exceptions to this: if someone said "gonna" or "feller," these were not transcribed as "going to" or "fellow," and there are some other minor inconsistencies. I realize that the printed transcriptions represent the way I and my assistants heard people speak, and someone else might hear them differently. I have omitted parts of the transcriptions which were repetitious or not relevant; these omissions are indicated by ellipses. Some repetitions have been left in because they are important stylistically. People sometimes talk in ways that do not make sense when transcribed into print; I have tried to clarify some of these instances with comments in brackets.

I selected stories and other items of folklore from the transcriptions that I thought were significant and representative. I arranged the material, not in the order it was presented, but on the basis of themes that I had discerned. The final presentation of each person, then, is made by me based on my perception of the individual. I think that the characters you read about in this book are accurate reflections of the nine people I interviewed, but choices had to be made in presenting each one: I have left out certain of their traits and enhanced others. One man told a graphic sexist joke, which I chose not to include; it reflected badly on him and it was not relevant to my discussion of him. These are not complete portraits then—that would be impossible with any individual—but they are detailed and complex, reflecting the most important values, attitudes, beliefs, and personality traits of the nine people.

In one sense, their stories have been expanded through the act of interpretation: a story has an immediate surface meaning, but it also has other meanings when seen in relation to other kinds of folklore, to the life of the individual, and to the cultural context and performance situation in which it is communicated. The performance of folklore involves all of these factors coming together, and the folklorist must consider them all in order to grasp the various meanings, recognizing that a full understanding can never be accomplished.[3]

Several folklore studies of the elderly established patterns for me to follow. In a recent article, Barbara Kirshenblatt-Gimblett summarized the development of folkloric interest in old people: "[Folklorists] have come to realize that the elderly are more than custodians of heritage. They are people in their own right, active in the present, and experts on what this period in the life cycle is all about. They are not only witnesses to what once was, they are also individuals with a profound need to be witnessed" (1989a, 138). This development parallels the shift of interest in folklore studies away from texts in isolation to the contexts in which they exist, from the lore to the folk, from static items to dynamic performance. This shift has caused more emphasis to be placed on the performer, and recent folklore research on the elderly has focused more on individual creativity. Bronner's study of older male wood-carvers provides important concepts of the psychological processes involved in folk art for the aged (1985). Alan Jabbour's research suggests some similar basic psychological patterns for elderly old-time fiddlers (1981). Bess Hawes emphasizes the positive uses of folk art for the old, suggesting ways in which a knowledge of folklore can be of value to professionals who work with the elderly (1984). Mary Hufford, Marjorie Hunt, and Steven Zeitlin prepared an exhibition on the folk art of old people, and in their book about this exhibition pointed the way to the use of life cycle and continuity in the analysis of folklore and the elderly (1987). Kirshenblatt-Gimblett continues their concerns by focusing on material culture as elements in life reviews of the elderly (1989b). Dana Steward edited a collection of personal statements by the elderly, which offers evidence of the way creative folk processes are a key to successful aging (1984). Oral historians have conducted research on the elderly that is, in many ways, parallel to the concerns of folklorists except that oral historians focus more on the individual within historical contexts.[4] Finally, the work of Henry Glassie, while not focused exclusively on the elderly, provides many insights into the importance of old people in a community. "Old tellers of tales are not astray in a wilderness of nostalgia. Born in new power, they fill a crucial role in their community. They preserve its wisdom, settle its disputes, create its entertainment, speak its culture. Without them, local people would have no way to discover themselves . . ." (1982, 63). Some of the old people I interviewed fulfill this role in their communities, others do not, but all of them would like to engage an audience by passing on their wisdom in entertaining ways.

Social Science and the Elderly

Up to this point, I have been discussing folkloric aspects of the research—defining terms, describing collected materials and fieldwork methodology—but folklore as a discipline has developed through the synthesis of concepts from other disciplines, from anthropology, ethnography, social psychology, socio-linguistics, and literary studies. In order to establish the analytic focus of this study of folklore and the elderly, I need to refer to how these other disciplines have influenced the present work. Aging has been investigated from many different perspectives, but the ones that most directly inform my work are anthropology and social psychology. Social psychologists David A. Karp and William C. Yoels identify several current theories of aging that have relevance to the study of folklore and the elderly including disengagement theory, activity theory, developmental theory, subculture theory, and age stratification theory (1982, 21); gerontologist James D. Manney, Jr., adds identity crisis theory and continuity theory (1975, 19-20).[5] Research on aging accelerated in the 1950s and 1960s, and some of the theoretical developments from this period are still being discussed in the 1990s.

Disengagement theory was a prevailing concept in the 1960s; it posits that the elderly tend to disengage from the rest of society and to lose continuity with their own cultural past. M. Elaine Cumming conducted some of the original research that formulated the concept of disengagement, and she states that "normal aging is a mutual withdrawal or 'disengagement' between the aging person and others in the social system to which he belongs—a withdrawal initiated by the individual himself, or by others in the system" (1964). As their abilities to achieve decline, some older individuals may voluntarily disengage from society in order to avoid societal pressures to achieve. This could be a part of successful aging, but in other ways disengagement could be negative. According to the theory, withdrawal of the elderly from society is inevitable, universal, and voluntary. Karp and Yoels question the universality and voluntary nature of disengagement when they point out that many old people resist it and others seem exempt from it (1982, 21). Certainly the nine elderly people I worked with did not want to disengage from society. Because they are tradition-bearers, they have a strong sense of continuity, which they use to engage people in the present through their performances of traditional lore. Manney says that most older people want to remain in their social world and that the degree of engagement varies with the individual depending on personal values. When the elderly do disengage, the reasons lie not in their age but in the social environment: "Such factors as work status, health, financial resources, and marital status affect the older person's capacity to lead a satisfying life much more strongly than age does" (1975, 20). Mollie Ford was the most disengaged person I talked to, but she definitely did not make this choice herself; society had relegated her to a marginal role.

Activity theory proposes the opposite of disengagement: "the older person who ages optimally is the person who manages to resist the shrinkage of his social world. He maintains the activities of middle age as long as possible, and then finds substitutes for work when he is forced to retire and substitutes for friends and loved ones whom he loses by death" (Havinghurst 1968, 161). Most of the old people I interviewed at least tried to maintain their social world, but activity theory has only limited application to the study of their lives because it does not account for individual differences. As Manney points out, there are similar problems with both activity and disengagement theories in that neither addresses the complexity of the way different individuals adjust to old age (1975, 18). The study of the folk expressions of the elderly provides a means for examining individual responses to aging.

Other theories of aging also have only limited application to the present study. Identity crisis theory posits that people "undergo a severe identity crisis upon leaving their jobs" (Manney 1975, 19). This has some relevance to the life of commercial fisherman Alva Snell, although he has avoided an identity crisis by maintaining his occupational identity after retirement. Age stratification and subculture theories are similar in their emphasis on the elderly as a separate social group. Subculture theory argues "that the aged form themselves into a subculture with its own distinctive norms, values, and lifestyles" (Karp and Yoels 1982, 28). Age stratification theory posits that "we move through the life cycle with a cohort of persons who experience each major life period at the same time we do. . . . Each cohort, therefore, brings distinctive values, ideas, and consciousnesses to these life periods" (Karp and Yoels 1982, 29). The elderly in this book have, in some ways, identified with other people of the same age, but most were also fully integrated into the surrounding communities and interacted with all age groups. None of them were in nursing or retirement homes, so they did not see themselves as part of a group that had been set aside by society. They did speak of age cohorts, and this concept has some bearing on understanding their folk expressions.

Developmental or continuity theory offers an approach that recognizes variability in responses to aging; it "contends that adaptation to aging can proceed in several directions, depending on the aging individual's past life" (Manney 1975, 20). This observation has direct relevance to the present study since each person's life will be examined to determine individual responses to old age. The elderly in this book are not representative of all the ways of responding to old age in late twentieth-century America (they are not urban or as oriented toward the modern and technological as most people are today), but they do represent a diversity of experience within a fairly narrow cultural range. Although they are mostly rural and Appalachian, they provide examples of some of the class, gender, and race variables that determine the choices people can make about old age.

Developmental theory stresses continuity over the life cycle: "old age itself cannot be understood in isolation from middle age, adulthood, youth, adolescence, childhood, and infancy" (Manney 1975, 11). All nine people under consideration here, in one way or another, have tried to maintain continuity with previous phases of their lives and with their own cultural pasts. Matt Burnett is especially concerned with his childhood, Bill Henry with his adolescence and young adulthood, and Bob Glasgow with his ancestors. The folklore of an elderly person can only be fully understood as it relates to previous stages of development. The developmental approach postulates universal patterns of aging; however, evidence indicates that developmental stages may vary from culture to culture (Karp and Yoels 1982, 25). The lives of the nine elderly people I worked with have to be investigated individually to identify which patterns are present and how they influence that person's folk expressions.

Another valuable perspective on the elderly comes from the symbolic interaction approach of sociology, which argues that "age, as such, has no intrinsic meaning. In concert with others we assign meanings, and often quite arbitrary meanings, to age. Such a view implies that there are *many* aging processes. To comprehend the complexities of growing older, we must consider the subjective responses persons make to their own aging" (Karp and Yoels 1982, 5). The interactionist approach is related to a larger shift in the social science of aging: studies of the life course have shifted from an "explanatory approach," which concentrates on universal stable patterns, to a "narrative" or "interpretive approach," which analyzes flexibility and change. The explanatory approach looks for a predictable pattern in the life course, and the narrative approach focuses on subjective attempts to order life, which is itself essentially unpredictable (Cohler 1984, 210).

Rather than applying some universal pattern from the outside, I shall look closely at the stories, beliefs, foodways, crafts, and other folk expressions of each individual in order to determine his or her subjective response to being old. These expressions will be interpreted in symbolic terms, which may have a multiplicity of meanings (Karp and Yoels 1982, 19). Folklore communicates symbols of the self and thus reflects how individuals view old age and themselves as old. Symbolic meanings may change depending on cultural context; for instance, old age does not mean the same for Quincy Higgins, who is white, as it does for Jesse Hatcher, who is black. Black and white, male and female, high and low, are all influences on the way old age will be perceived by the individual and the community.

Symbolic interactionists stress the importance of multiple meanings of role loss in elderly lives; Karp and Yoels point out that role loss can be negative or positive depending on the values placed on the lost roles (1982, 23). The elderly people I interviewed had various responses to the loss of roles they played earlier in life. Bill Henry's work role was not very important to him, so the loss of it with retirement was not a significant event. On the other hand, Alva Snell's role as a fisherman was central to his identity, and after retirement he maintained a positive self-image as "old fisherman" within his community by telling people about his occupational past. Bob Glasgow no longer fulfilled his role as farmer, but he kept his agrarian values alive through talking about his life as a farmer and by continuing to live on the family farm. Several people did not suffer role loss at all. Quincy Higgins continued to farm his land and serve as a preacher into his 70s, and Mamie Bryan was still functioning as wife, mother, and grandmother in her 80s.

Sharon R. Kaufman's anthropological concept of "themes" in an elderly person's life relates closely to the symbolic interactionist approach and is valuable for identifying both continuity and change through developmental stages:

> In my interviews with many old people who reflected on the course of their lives, I found that the ageless self maintains continuity through a symbolic, creative process. The self draws meaning from the past, interpreting and recreating it as a resource for being in the present. It also draws meaning from the structural and ideational aspects of the cultural context. Thus, I view the self as the interpreter of experience: from this perspective, individual identity is revealed by the patterns of symbolic meaning that characterize the individual's unique interpretation of experience. (1986, 14)

Themes are part of the patterns of symbolic meaning and the means by which old people "interpret and evaluate their life experiences and attempt to integrate these experiences to form a self-concept" (Kaufman 1986, 25). When the narratives that make up a life story and the meaningful objects and rituals in a person's life (personal photographs, memorabilia, quilts, foodways, folk medical practices, etc.) are viewed together, certain recurring themes become apparent. These themes unify the various strands of the story, relating the images, metaphors, and symbols together around the central meaning. Bill Henry tells stories about his childhood as an orphan in a foster home and other stories about his hobo adventures as a young man; throughout both cycles of stories there are recurring images of dominant women and authoritarian men that come together to underscore the theme of masculine freedom. Bob Glasgow's stories about family history, the building of his house and barn, and his personal struggles maintaining his farm are unified by themes of achievement orientation and communal cooperation. Mr. Glasgow and Mr. Henry, like the other seven people in this study, use the perspective of old age to organize and structure their past lives through narrative and other forms of folklore in order to give meaning to their present existence. Themes are dynamic in that certain themes remain the same throughout life while others are reinterpreted based on experience and redefinition of the self. For instance, Leonard Bryan told a story about his daughter becoming a preacher in which it was apparent that his identity as a father had been altered over time.

Many of the approaches to aging share an emphasis on the study of life history, life story, or life review, and these concepts provide a central focus for my book. Although I did not try to elicit life histories as such, the personal experience stories I collected are theoretically related to life history. The people I interviewed did not tell their entire life stories; rather, they told episodes from their life histories, personal experience narratives considered to be part of their life stories. The connection of personal narrative and life history is recognized in the developmental study of aging where the idea of subjective reinterpretation over the life course is stressed: "This concept of the personal narrative as order which is imposed upon a developmental course inherently unpredictable is consistent with perspectives on personality emphasizing the importance both of order and of change across the course of life" (Cohler 1982, 206). Thus, when an elderly person tells a personal narrative as part of the life story, he or she is attempting to impose order on life, and the principle of order can change depending on the particular point of view at the time.

Life history in anthropology is understood to be "elicited or prompted by another person" as opposed to autobiography, which is self-initiated (Watson and Watson-Franke 1985). The situation in fieldwork is actually more complex: a person may present a life story because a folklorist has asked for it, but that person may also tell his life story in other circumstances without being prompted. This was the case with Bill Henry, who often tells about his life as an orphan and a hobo to friends and acquaintances. His life story was at least partially determined by tradition, by the conventional views of orphans as victims, and hoboes as romantic loners. As Linda Degh has pointed out, "We may go so far as to say that tradition contributes effectively to individual life histories and that people themselves adjust their lives to fit the model set by tradition" (1985, 104). Bill Henry and the others tell life stories that blend traditional and individual influences.[6]

More significant than life history to the study of personal experience narratives of the elderly is the psychological concept of the life review. The telling of personal stories from their lives by the elderly is part of the life review process. Robert N. Butler was the first scholar to formulate the concept of life review. "The life review is conceived of as a naturally-occurring universal mental process characterized by the progressive return to consciousness of past experiences, and particularly, the resurgence of unresolved conflicts; simultaneously, and normally, these revived experiences and conflicts are surveyed and reintegrated. It is assumed that this process is prompted by the realization of approaching dissolution and death, and by the inability to maintain one's sense of personal invulnerability" (1964, 266).

Again we should keep in mind that although the process may or may not be universal, the specific ways it is accomplished will vary from culture to culture and individual to individual. Matt Burnett's heart condition caused him to undertake a life review in which he told many stories from his childhood and other stories associated with his occupational life. Bill Henry also concentrated on his childhood in his life review but did not refer much to his occupational life.

Not all scholars see life review as universal, and not all consider every kind of life review as normal and healthy. In their study of a group of elderly men, Arthur W. McMahon, Jr., and Paul J. Rhudick identified four different subgroups on the basis of personal use of reminiscence (1967, 73). First there are those who depreciate the present and glorify the past—"This type of reminiscence not only serves to maintain self-esteem and reinforce a sense of identity, but also appears to allay, if somewhat regressively, the anxiety associated with signs of decline with its reminder of approaching death" (72–73). Second are persons who review their lives in order to justify them—the reminiscences of several of these "reflected themes of guilt, unrealized goals, and wished-for opportunities to make up for past failures" (73). The authors associate the second category with Butler's study, thus suggesting that life review may be abnormal. Although Butler's original study concentrated on those who might reminisce in an obsessive way, his use of the term *life review* suggests a normative and positive process. Third in McMahon and Rhudick's scheme are storytellers who recount past exploits with pleasure—"They seem to have little need to depreciate the present or glorify the past, but they do reminisce actively" (73). Examples of storytellers include elderly tradition-bearers in tribal societies. Fourth are the clinically depressed, who reminisced less than the nondepressed group.

The nine elders in my study do not fit neatly into any one of these categories; rather, each one shows signs of belonging to two or more. Alva Snell and Bob Glasgow tended to depreciate the present and glorify the past, but they were also storytellers who recounted the past with pleasure. Bob Glasgow also expressed a need to justify the past and to make up for past failures, thus placing him in three categories. Matt Burnett's life review was "regressive" in the face of approaching death, but he also was a successful and entertaining storyteller. None of the nine people I interviewed showed signs of clinical depression, and all actively reminisced. Their life reviews fit the positive view of reminiscence stated by McMahon and Rhudick: "a complex organized mental activity" that "is positively correlated with successful adaptation to old age and appears to foster adaptation through maintaining self-esteem, reaffirming a sense of identity, working through and mastering personal losses, and contributing positively to society" (1967, 78).

The terms *life review* and *reminiscence* overlap in the literature; I shall use them interchangeably as long as the process being described involves the attempt to reintegrate the past with the present and to resolve conflicts of the life course. "Reminiscence is no mere escapist desire to live in the past, as some claim; rather, it should be regarded as a major developmental task for the elderly, resulting in the integration that will allow them to age well and die well" (Myerhoff 1978, 222). "Developmental" and "integration" are the key words here that connect the anthropological view to the folkloric, relating reminiscence and life review to personal narrative and other traditional expressions: ". . . the use of traditional materials and skills . . . enables the elderly person to accomplish an important *developmental* task of old age: life *integration*, the pulling together of the disparate portions of a long life into a coherent whole. The synthetic vision, narrative skill, and traditional knowledge characteristic of old age uniquely equip the elderly person for this task, and for a related task, which is to communicate these to others (emphasis added)" (Hufford, Hunt, and Zeitlin 1987, 27).

Elderly people will use reminiscence, personal narrative, traditional beliefs and customs, folk art, and a wide range of expressive culture as part of life review because all of these forms function to integrate the disparate elements of their lives. When folk art is used as part of the life review, it can be thought of as a "life review project" (Hufford, Hunt, Zeitlin 1987, 40). Thus Matt Burnett's wood carving, which he learned in childhood, and Jesse Hatcher's cooking and preserving, which he associates with his long married life, are life review projects. One of the integrative functions of life review is the maintenance of identity: the events and activities that are surveyed are ones that were important in the establishing of the identity of the individual. By telling stories about past experiences or using a skill learned earlier in life, the old person reintegrates that past identity in the present, projecting it as part of his or her present self-image.

An equally important element in the life review process is to communicate it to others, to engage an audience so that everyone comes to a shared understanding, in other words, to perform it as folklore. This has an important function for the individual: "Though taken as a sign of egocentricity, [reminiscence] may be an adaptive move to escape the lethal condition of 'otherness.' As they reminisce, the elders seem to be saying, 'See me not as I am, but as a total *history*, and as someone who was once like you" (Gutmann 1977, 316). Thus, the life review has important personal and communal functions: it establishes the identity of the individual elderly person, and it connects one generation to another, passing on or reconstructing traditions that are important for the survival of the community. All nine of the elderly people in this book, to one degree or another, were engaged in the life review process. Life review can be considered an overarching concept for my study since it provides a frame within which all of the various genres of folklore project identity and maintain continuity.

Several other studies in the anthropology of aging that stress continuity have had a strong influence on this book, especially the work of Barbara Myerhoff and her associates.[7] Myerhoff's emphasis on personal narrative and on ritual in behavior and communication informs my analysis throughout. She applies ritual concepts from the works of Arnold van Gennep (1960) and Victor Turner (1977) to the everyday activities of the elderly. In this sense, ritual involves repeated patterned activity, symbolic enactments that dramatize abstract conceptions (Myerhoff 1984, 305); ritual can be sacred or secular, and it is important in the lives of all nine people in this study. For Bob Glasgow, giving visitors a tour of his farm was a ritual event in which he asserted his identity and his connections with the past. Quincy Higgins's repeated trips to the highest point of land on his property were a secular ritual for him, symbolizing his achievements in life. Bill Henry's telling of stories about his childhood and youth is a ritual experience in which he takes listeners back with him to his past, projecting his core identity into the present. Storytelling is a secular ritual for all nine people; by telling stories about their lives, they connect the present moment, the narrative event, to the past experience, the narrated event (Babcock 1984, 65), thus establishing a strong sense of continuity. "Ritual is an assertion of continuity. Even when dealing with change, ritual connects new events and elements with preceding ones, incorporating them into a stream of precedents so that they are recognized as growing out of tradition and experience. Ritual states enduring and even timeless patterns, thus connects past, present, and future, abrogating history, time and disruption" (Myerhoff 1978, 164–65). Since Myerhoff sees ritual functioning to maintain continuity, her approach is closely related to developmental theory, especially to continuity theory. The storytelling of all nine people being considered here is a ritual process of continuity—healing, correcting, connecting, resolving.

The Elderly as Performers

Bringing all of these disparate theories back to a focus on folklore is the performance-centered approach, which concentrates on the way performers, especially storytellers, use traditional strategies to engage an audience. Thus, the concept of performance has direct application to a study of how the elderly avoid disengagement. Another element that relates performance to the anthropological and sociological concepts mentioned above is the emphasis on symbolism, which is implicit in many of the approaches and explicit in the interactionist approach (Karp and Yoels 1982, 19). As one of the leading performance theorists, Dan Ben-Amos, suggests, "Folklore, like any other art, is a symbolic kind of action. Its forms have symbolic significance reaching far beyond the explicit content of the particular text, melody, or artifact . . ." (1972, 11). There is symbolic meaning in both the text and in the process and situation in which it is communicated. An elderly person telling a personal narrative as part of his or her life review will be performing that story within a particular situation or performance context, and the *way* the story is told will have symbolic significance along with *what* is being said. In one sense, this book is about how we can better listen to the elderly, and the concept of performance provides another way of hearing what they have to say, another dimension for interpreting their expressions.

The focus of the performance-centered approach is on the context of performance and on rhetorical devices and strategies used by the performer to display his or her competence.[8] Performance is, in Richard Bauman's terms, a particular kind of verbal discourse that enhances experience in artful ways, drawing attention to the performer and his or her art, making the audience regard the performance with "special intensity" (1984, 11). The performer displays his or her competence with language, subjecting the performance to the judgment of the audience. "Keys to performance" are those devices used to set off the performance from ordinary conversation, to frame it as artistic communication. Thus, when Mollie Ford changed from a conversational mode to preaching at a point when she wanted to express an important moral value, she had, in fact, shifted into performance and framed that performance by changing the tone and loudness of her voice, the rhythms of her speech, and the intensity of our interaction. I, as an audience of one, was drawn into her performance and regarded her with "special intensity." When Alva Snell said "back in them days," it was a formulaic cultural marker to signal that a story set in his occupational past was about to begin, a frame telling me to pay attention because he was an authority on a time that I knew nothing about. Several storytellers made greater use of figurative language and quoted speech within their stories than in ordinary conversation, thus setting them off as performances. Performance can occur among any age groups that have the ability to communicate with each other (children's rhymes and stories, for instance), but many of the elderly have special performance needs because of their emphasis on engagement and continuity. They have to attract an audience and maintain their attention in order to communicate the elder's wisdom and experience. Performance concentrates on that moment when tradition is being communicated in the present, when received knowledge and art are reshaped and created to fit a particular situation.

The performance context in the case of my research with the elderly is the interview situation, which can be considered a "normal" context in contemporary American society. "The formal interview is . . . a recognized speech event in our society. Members of the society know the rules of speaking for interviews. They expect to be asked a series of questions and to answer them. Although being interviewed is hardly an everyday experience for most people, there is nothing 'artificial' or 'unnatural' about it" (Wolfson 1976, 195). Lee Haring speaks of "performing for the interviewer," recognizing this as a particular kind of performance context in which the fieldworker must take into account his or her influence on the performance (1972, 383). I realize that I influenced the situation in which the elderly people talked to me, but I was in the role of younger person seeking knowledge and thus at least close to their usual audiences. The normality of interviews is especially true in terms of the methods I used: there were usually no preplanned or directed questions, the interviews were open-ended, and individuals were given free rein to talk about anything of interest to them. Also, through happenstance many of the interviews were close to the usual context in which the individual told stories. Bob Glasgow often takes visitors on a tour of the old house and barn on his property just as he took me around as I tape-recorded him, and Jesse Hatcher is used to people dropping by to talk on his front porch, which is where I interviewed him. Therefore we can assume that many of the rhetorical strategies used by a performer in an interview situation are the same ones she or he would use in some other contexts. Still, conclusions about community contexts will be limited by the situation of the tape-recorded interview. For instance,

I do not know if these elders shared their stories or engaged in life review with other people their age or if their rhetorical strategies would remain the same in those contexts.

My aim, then, is to bring two basic perspectives to the material: to interpret the folklore of each person in terms of how the content relates to his or her life as an elderly person within a particular cultural context, and to analyze the communication of the folklore within a specific performance context associated with the performer as an elder in the community. The content analysis is within the framework of the various anthropological, sociological, and psychological theories mentioned previously, especially symbolic interaction and continuity theory; and the analysis of style and rhetoric is mainly from a performance perspective. An example of the dual approach is seen in the analysis of Mollie Ford, who emphasizes the themes of teaching and learning in the content of her discourse while using figurative language, imagery, biblical allusions, rhythmical speech, and so forth to get her message across. The performance approach works well with the anthropological because it relates directly to the patterns of engagement and continuity. It focuses on the ways individuals use their performing skills to engage an audience in order to communicate traditions that establish continuity with the past.

The first person you'll meet is Mollie Ford, who exemplifies many of the recurring themes in the book. She is a folk teacher who actively engages her listeners in order to pass on important lessons from the past; thus, she is a living testament to the value of continuity. Other elders in the book are less self-conscious of themselves as teachers, but they all are tradition-bearers so that teaching younger generations is important to each of them. Jesse Hatcher is next (chap. 2) because he also sees himself as a source of important values for younger people, and he actively passes them on. Chapter 3 focuses on Leonard and Mamie Bryan. Their story picks up on religious themes that are also important to Jesse Hatcher and Mollie Ford. All four are farm people, and their life stories project agrarian values, which are also central to an understanding of Bob Glasgow's life (chap. 4). Alva Snell (chap. 5) has a different occupation—fisherman—but he is like Bob Glasgow in setting himself up as an authority on the past. His central identity is based on being a fisherman even though he has been retired for years. Quincy Higgins (chap. 6) is similar to Alva Snell and Bob Glasgow in his emphasis on achievement and success.

Bill Henry (chap. 7) felt trapped in a factory job and did not have the same opportunity for achievement; he has no occupational identity in retirement; rather, his identity is related to his childhood as an orphan and his adolescence and young adulthood as a hobo. Matt Burnett, like Bill Henry, focuses attention on the early years of his life. He is a fitting subject for the final chapter because he provides an example of the entire life cycle: his heart condition has forced him to confront his own mortality and to conduct a life review from birth to impending death.

The manipulation of identity is a unifying theme among all of them, from the surest in their identities, Mollie Ford and Jesse Hatcher, to the ones still working out identity after a lifetime, Bill Henry and Matt Burnett. Mollie Ford is secure in her role as teacher even though she is marginal in society, and Jesse Hatcher has a local community, which reinforces his role as a wise elder; but Bill Henry still struggles with his identity as an orphan relegated to a low position in class hierarchy, and Matt Burnett must contend with the overall meaning of his life as he faces death. All nine elderly people brought the perspective of old age to an understanding of their lives, and all were engaged in life review. The unifying principle of the book is the way folk traditions are used as part of life review by the elderly. Mollie Ford, Jesse Hatcher, Bob Glasgow, and the rest use storytelling and other folklore processes to engage listeners in the present in order to maintain continuity with their past lives.

In their old age my parents did not have much chance to pass on their traditions because of their illnesses, but the impulse was nevertheless there. My father was still telling stories about his childhood after he was in a nursing home, and my mother was reminiscing with my sisters, Carol and Linda, and my brother, David, and me while she was in the hospital during the last months of her life. They were not able to have much continuity with their pasts, not able to engage fully in the present, but they made a courageous effort. My parents and the elderly people in this book provide evidence that the impulse toward engagement and continuity is strong in the human spirit, and it does not disappear with age.

NOTES

1. See Bauman 1987, 199; Kaufman 1986, 149–50; and Kotre 1984, 142.

2. For more on personal experience narrative, see Allen 1989, Bausinger 1958, Degh 1972, 1985, Dolby-Stahl 1985, Jolles 1965, Labov and Waletzky 1967, Neumann 1967, Stahl 1977a, Sydow 1948.

3. The recognition of the importance of the interpreter in ethnographic research is related to certain phenomenological and hermeneutical concepts (Babcock 1980, 11; Clifford and Marcus 1986; Crapanzano 1980; Marcus and Fischer 1986; Peacock 1984, 97; Ricoeur 1979; Watson and Watson-Franke 1985, 30–57).

4. See Hareven 1978, Morin 1982, Portelli 1981, and Schrager 1983.

5. For another summary of aging theories see Kertzer and Keith 1984, 19-50. Other good overviews on aging are Chudacoff 1989, Clark and Anderson 1967, Fischer 1977, and Neugarten 1968.

6. Other major life history studies include Degh 1975, Joyce 1983, Langness 1965, Langness and Frank 1981, Titon 1980, 1988.

7. See Myerhoff 1977, 1979, 1984, Myerhoff and Simic 1978.

8. See Abrahams 1968, Babcock 1984, Bauman 1984, 1986, Bauman and Sherzer 1974, Ben-Amos 1972, and Gumperz and Hymes 1972.

1

Mollie Ford
How the Old Teach the Young

"Now you can step over, or whatever, and you can take a seat here."

"Okay."

"If you got that kind of time, I mean."

"Oh, I got plenty of time. I don't know if I can get over here or not."

Mollie Ford,[1] an eighty-four-year-old black woman, was giving me directions on how to climb over a wire fence to get to where she was sitting in the shade of a big tree.

"I'll tell you what you do. You sit there, now I'll tell you what's gonna happen. I was certain about—let me see now, wait a minute now, I used to have a—now you sit there, and I'll find me a seat so I can sit down."

"I can find a chair for you. Where is it? I can bring one over here."

"I'm gonna tell you. See, I'm partially paralyzed, you know what I mean?"

"Well, let me run over here and get a chair for you."

"Yeah, but you see some of them over there, some of them if you bring them, I won't sit down on them 'cause if you sit on them, they'll fall with you." Her full high laugh rang out for the first of many times that morning.

I went and got an old rusty metal lawn chair she pointed out, and we started talking. I told her where I had heard about her and why I was there. She said that her farm was a missionary camp where she took care of children.

"I've been taking care of childrens since eighteen and ninety-five, and I been here since forty-seven."

During the course of our four-hour conversation on August 9, 1980, some details of her life emerged, although she seemed reluctant to talk about her life history at length. "My story is so long, but I can make it short, but it's sensible." But I couldn't make sense of it, so in 1990 I contacted Mollie Ford's daughter and officials of St. Joseph's Orphanage in Cincinnati who were familiar with her and who gave me more details about her life, although there are discrepancies in the various accounts.

"How old are you," I asked, "if you don't mind me asking?"

"I don't mind you asking, but I don't like to tell it."

She said that she was born on September 26, 1883, in Bonita, Louisiana. That would have made her 103, although she told me she was ninety-seven. Her daughter had consulted with her mother's siblings and determined that she was ninety-two when she died in 1986, and they said that her birthplace was New Orleans. In terms of her life review, the actual facts are not as important as the way she perceived and presented her life, which was as a struggle from her earliest years. "See, I'm an unfortunate child myself. . . . I'm my mama's unfortunate child. My mom gave birth to me and she wasn't married to my daddy." Later she said, "But my dad was one of them things. That's how come I was got without him being married to my mom. Cause I'm a rape child. You understand what I mean?" During part of her childhood, Mollie Ford was taken care of by her grandfather, an African Methodist Episcopal minister. She was placed in foster homes at other times. "I was given away and shifted from hand to mouth and pillar to post." Eventually her mother married a man who had children from another marriage. Mollie Ford ended up with a family in Arkansas, who subsequently moved to Cincinnati, taking her with them.

In Cincinnati she married a man named Bob Ford. Mollie Ford never talked to me about her marriage or any relationships with men, concentrating instead on her children. She adopted many children over the years and also took in her own grandchildren; therefore, it was never clear exactly how many children she had. Her obituary in the Cincinnati *Enquirer* on July 18, 1986, mentioned that she had reared thirty-eight foster children from 1949 to 1964 and that she

1. Mollie Ford. (Photograph by the author.)

had eleven grandchildren, forty-four great-grandchildren, and nine great-great-grandchildren.

At some point, she began to work for the Catholic church in Cincinnati, and it was through this connection that she came to be associated with an order of nuns from Pittsburgh who had come into the area to establish a school for needy children. In the late 1940s, these Catholic sisters bought land along the Ohio River in Adams County, Ohio, and Mollie Ford went to work for them there. Shortly after they established what she called their "missionary school," they were called back to Pittsburgh by their order; and they left the place in Mollie Ford's name with the understanding that she would continue to take care of children on the farm. No formal arrangement between her and the Catholic church was necessary; she simply found children on her own to live with her; some were her grandchildren and others were children whom she had adopted. Her grandson Sydney Bullucks told me that they were not welcomed by everyone in the community. There were incidents of harassment during the time he lived on the farm. Nevertheless, Mollie Ford continued to take in children until the mid-1970s, and she was still on the same farm when I interviewed her in 1980.

After my long conversation with her, I saw that she was like other old people in her need to communicate. She was also charismatic, intelligent, articulate, and wise in ways that could only come from her many years' experience. As a folklorist, I was not sure how to approach the tape recordings I had made; what Mollie Ford had said did not fit into any conventional folklore genres. She had told a few stories to illustrate moral points and, at times, had gone into a kind of spontaneous preaching; but she was not like any storyteller I had ever heard, and she was not a preacher. Several years later, when I started this project on folklore and the elderly, I went back to transcribe the tapes, and the meaning of our conversation became clear. Mollie Ford was a teacher, not one with formal training and degrees, but a folk teacher. Our conversation was a complex lesson, and I was the pupil. Here was an opportunity to study the folk pedagogy of an elderly, masterful teacher passing on her own learning to the only pupil available at the time, a folklorist trying to do a fieldwork interview.

I say "trying" because she resisted my efforts at interviewing at every turn, establishing her own agenda of teaching a lesson. The clues to her purpose were there in her opening remarks; she gave me instructions on climbing the fence, and then she said, "I'll tell you what you do: you sit there, now I'll tell you what's gonna happen." She had assumed a role of authority, of teacher, from the beginning. At several points during our conversation, I asked her about her life history, but she either did not answer or simply gave a brief answer and returned to her teaching. My attempts to place an interview frame on the proceedings were resisted, as she kept returning to her "pedagogical discourse."[2] In this, she is similar to Arkansas fiddler Absie Morrison when he was interviewed by folklorist Judy McCulloh: "Uncle Absie was not about to be intimidated by visitors from an out-of-state university. He soon assumed—and maintained— the role of history teacher" (McCulloh 1975, 95). There was more evidence in Mollie Ford's speech of her pedagogical purpose, which I shall get to later.

Mollie Ford saw herself as a teacher even though she was aware that society did not recognize her as such. At one time in explaining why she took a circuitous route to make a point, she said, "See, I'm not a read person, and I got to go all the way back around home to come back in," and she laughed. Since she could read, she must have meant that she was not widely read and that she had never studied to be a teacher. Yet, despite her lack of formal training, she saw herself as a teacher. While talking about how some of the nuns she had worked with were called "Sister" and some "Mother," she said about herself, "Me, I ain't nobody, just what you see, me sitting up here now. I was then, and always was, always is up to now, and I don't want to be nothing else." Later she gave a religious explanation for her humility.

"When the Lord puts you up there, He don't say he put you out to stick your chest out. He say, 'Be meek and humble.' So when they, when I do something good to try to help them, and they throw a stone at me, I duck it, and I try to do that much better for Jesus." And later when she was talking about being a "bastard child": "I'm God's creation just like everybody else, but still I use the word [bastard] so that nobody won't try to think I'm trying to pin roses on my shoulder." Despite her own sense of humble origins and a hard life, she still has a strong, positive identity as someone with an important role in life, teaching others.[3]

In her attempts to continue her middle-age life as a teacher's helper into her elderly years, Mollie Ford illustrates the activity theory of aging (Havinghurst 1968). The situation was complicated, however, by the closing of the school and the withdrawal of the nuns. Disengagement theory has some application here, although her disengagement was not voluntary and mutual.[4] Mollie Ford was disengaged only because society had no further use for her. She is part of a larger pattern in contemporary American life in which old people are shut out, ignored, disengaged from the rest of society.[5] But Mollie Ford, like many other elderly people, has resisted disengagement. Although she did not talk much about her life history, she was still using discussion about teaching and learning as a part of life review. By concentrating her discourse on her role as a teacher, she was returning in her mind to her years of actively working with children, the time in her life when she was most productive and fulfilled as a person. She reviewed that part of her life in order to project her image as a teacher in the present. Some recent studies in anthropology and social psychology have emphasized other positive ways in which old people have dealt with disengagment and established continuity in their lives.[6] These works have touched on learning and aging, but have not provided an in-depth view of an individual in a teaching and learning situation. A study of Mollie Ford's folk pedagogy expands the findings of recent positive aging studies. She sees the elderly as important figures in society because they have so much to teach the younger generations.

"It's so many peoples though, that, that's what's wrong with you younger peoples today. Because, in my view, now I'm telling you in my view. I ain't telling about [somebody else's view]. But that's what's wrong with you young peoples today. That's why you all so far behind, it ain't but a few of you is absolutely where you really should be because us older peoples is not teaching. We's setting back and we criticize everything that you youngsters do, but yet, we're not in our places as a leader, as we should be. How in the world you going to learn if we are not learning you when we were here first. And we are what I call the stepping stone, the teachers to teach you-all. You-all is in the world [and] is what you call b-l-i-n-d," she stretched the word out, "feeling your ways. And yet the least little thing wrong that you do, we the first ones to criticize. And I don't believe in that."

"The stepping stone" is a central metaphor in her folk pedagogy; it not only suggests the link between generations but also shows that the accumulated knowledge and wisdom of one generation must be passed on to the next, and that old people such as herself must take their responsibilities as teachers very seriously, even in the face of conditions where the elderly are ignored. Mollie Ford clearly recognizes the existence of disengagment and discontinuity; her teaching addresses these two problems. Old people as stepping stones will engage younger people in the learning process and maintain continuity with their own cultural past in order to pass it on to the future.

"There's so much that you youngsters don't know, and if I started telling y'all, y'all would be amazed. And I'm amazed at how y'all live, and y'all, if I tell y'all how I come up, y'all'd be amazed. But I still love my life back there better than I do y'all's." She laughed.

I think amazement is an important element in her teaching, and as her statement suggests, it is a two-way process: the young and the old can both be amazed by the other, can learn from the other. As much as she emphasized the role of the old in teaching the young, she still believes that the elderly have to continue to learn. They cannot teach if they themselves stop learning. In fact, her use of "learn" for "teach," while common usage, is also a sign of how closely linked these processes are.

"I'm learning too. See, that's what I'm trying to get the peoples to know: nobody knows it all. I had a view this morning, uh, I say a view, a thought of the Holy Spirit led me with something this morning, [something] that I never been led with before, as old as I am. You never get too old to learn. And I'm going to tell you: you young peoples, I learn from you all, and you all learn from me. So that makes us be in the same boat. We all is seeking an understanding and things, why we are existing here in the world together, and ain't— pardon me—and don't no one know more than the other one. . . . As long as you live, you'll be learning."

"I hope I will."

"No, I'm sure. I'm sure. . . . Some of the older people [who fail to continue learning], kinda makes me feel sorry for them. And there ain't, it ain't but a few older than me."

Age alone does not qualify a person as teacher; she must have had experience in the world in order to learn the necessary lessons.

"I been through the world. I been through, that's what I'm trying to tell you. I been through the world, and I've been through everything. I know the difference. Are you understanding me?"

"Yeah."

"And what I'm trying to do is get more older people."

Mollie Ford places the burden of responsibility on older people to teach the young, even though she recognizes that the young are not always receptive to the teachings of the old. Since the nuns have left the farm, she has been isolated from her usual teaching context. The people in the surrounding community see her as an eccentric and therefore do not take her seriously as a person from whom they can learn. In many ways she is a marginal person: a black person in a largely white populated county, a female in a male-dominant society, and an old person in a society that does not respect age. She is, in ritual terms, a liminal person, "betwixt and between," "neither here nor there" (Turner 1977, 95). Myerhoff, too, has recognized the possibility of old people as liminal beings, and she sees it as providing some positive opportunities. "It is not unusual to find old people who are liminal beings, living beyond the fixed and regulated categories. . . . It may be, then, that the often-noted but little studied toughness, fearlessness, idiosyncrasy, and creativity among the elderly in many societies result from this combination of social irrelevance and personal autonomy" (1984, 310–11). Mollie Ford's eccentricity, continuing active mental life, and fierce determination to communicate her beliefs and values can all be explained, at least partially, by her liminality. She is beyond the constraints of the Catholic church, she is geographically remote from her racial cultural group, she is outside the confines of her local community, and she has outlived her own age cohorts.

Because of her liminal position, she has much to offer to those who would pay attention, but as she says, the world is blind to the teachings of the elderly. Interestingly, Myerhoff uses the same metaphor to describe the attitude of the young toward the old. "It is with affection and nostalgia that adults regard the innate creativity of unsocialized children. But usually they are blind to the creativity of *de*socialized elders at the other end of the life cycle, people whose reemerging originality—stemming from social detachment, long experience, the urgency of a shortened future—may be as delightful, surprising, and fruitful as anything to be found among the very young" (1984, 311). Myerhoff does not mean to suggest that the elderly are childish; rather, she uses youth as a metaphor for old age, pointing out how liminality frees an old person to be creative in what we think of as childlike ways. Her use of "surprise" and "delight" certainly describe my reaction to Mollie Ford when I became her pupil for several hours in the impromptu outdoor classroom on her farm.

What was she trying to teach me? What was the content of her lesson plan? Certain values and beliefs were recurring themes in her talk, and these were all based in her religion.

"I don't care what you bring up, if the Lord ain't in my picture, you ain't got no conversation because Jesus created me, and He give me everything. And He give me my thinking faculties, and then He didn't tell me what I *had* to do, He told me what *this* was, and if I do this what the consequences would be. And He told me what *that* is, and if I do that, He told me what the consequences [would be], but He didn't tell me I had to do either. He left the choice up to me.

Well, now I got something to tell you. The Blessed Lover is my God and Angel, I got to tell you."

One of her religious-based values was the equality of all human beings; this came out with great force during an early part of our conversation. Significantly, she was talking about teaching.

"Because I got thousands and thousands of childrens all in various regions, all nations and nationalities, but in my book when I teach my childrens, I try to teach them all, we all the same color, it don't mean nothing. . . . "

"I believe that. We're all brothers and sisters."

She screamed in response, "THAT'S what I'm trying to tell the world, child."

"And I know it."

"It's no difference."

"I know it, and I believe it."

"And I'm here to tell you: I'm a witness to it," she whispered, "the color of your skin don't mean nothing."

"I know that."

And a few seconds later, "It's the truth if ever I told it. I don't care what we call ourselves, what color we are, we are just God's creation, and man, one man ain't made no different than the other one."

"I know it."

"Woman ain't made no different. . . . There ain't but one race created on earth, and that's the human race. . . . And you can tell them I said so."

She is speaking from a liminal point of view here: she knows that the color of your skin does make a difference in the social world, but what she is talking about is a spiritual realm, one that she feels closer to not only because of her advanced years but also because of her focus on leading a spiritual life. At this point, another theme associated with the elderly emerges: many old people who are nearing the end of their lives stress interconnectedness as a major value (Simic and Myerhoff 1978, 232). Mollie Ford suggests interconnectedness when she talks about human equality and whenever she mentions teaching, which is itself a process of establishing interconnectedness. Teaching and learning connect individual human beings on the small scale and generations on the large scale. Mollie Ford's method, teaching, and her message, interconnectedness, are one.

In fact, teaching and learning were dominant themes throughout our conversation. Like the elderly Jewish people Myerhoff studied, Mollie Ford sees learning as "an axiomatic good, an end in itself, but it is also a means, a strategy for appropriate social and spiritual action" (1977, 212). Learning has a similar function for the elderly *Mexicanos* whom Charles Briggs studied. They taught the younger generations through "pedagogical discourse." "Here an elder or elders engage one or more younger persons in a dialogue about the past. The explicit object is to inculcate the basic moral values that exemplify the actions of 'the elders of bygone days' to succeeding generations" (1984). This is also true of Mollie Ford as a teacher; learning itself is valuable because it is a means of passing on values. Learning as a strategy for action has to have detailed rules to follow in order to be effective; one of these rules for Mollie Ford is scepticism about what is being taught and its source.

"I just love to learn life, and a certain position that you get in, it's things that you never know just what life is all about because a lot of people say join them and take them, but they do something. But see, I'm a person like this: I don't believe in doing something for the form and the fashion, I believe in being serious in what you do. Well, it's things in life I like to learn."

Mollie Ford is an individualist, skeptical of groups that seek to teach a certain doctrine. A life-long Catholic, she disagrees with the church on many major issues, papal infallibility for one. From her liminal position, she is able to remain constant to her deeper spiritual beliefs, avoiding current fashion.

"So when these childrens [the ones she taught at the farm] got big enough to. . . cooperate with the doings that these peoples [outside her own belief system] do, it seemed to me like they was making, uh, a contact with these things, and these is not my teachings or my leadership. See, I'm going to tell you what I do. If I teach you something, I believe in it, and I try to lead it. I'm not the person that say, 'Go.' I'm the person that say, 'Let's go.' Are you getting me?"

Her pedagogy demands that she teach her personally held beliefs: she will not tell a pupil to do something that she herself will not do, and her penchant for teaching was so strong that even when she was answering a question about life history, she would turn it into a discussion of learning.

In talking about her father's religion she said, "And he was some of anybody [and] anything. You understand what I mean? Baptist church, anybody's church, and come to find out he turned out to be what you call a Muslim and all of them kind. Well, see all that kind of stuff, I do not avoid listening to it because if you don't listen, you don't learn. That's why you hear me tell you I am of the world. I believe in listening, no matter what. Then it comes to me, it's up to me then to, to, to think of my thoughts, of what I think about whatever is happening or going on."

Her teaching is not all abstract; she mentioned some of the activities in which she was involved with the children.

"In my way, I can't learn childrens too much in the city. I can learn them plumbing, building, and different things, but in a place like this, in my idea, in my view, I can learn them something of everything, because here is building, here is farming, learning you how to provide for yourself, raise your food, do different things. There's something to do here every day. Are you understanding me? It covers everything because we, if we build out here, we got to have materials to build."

One other important lesson came out in our conversation: her understanding of the proper role of women in life.

"Now what the womens is doing, we got a piece in the scripture that can tell you what the womens is doing, how the womens living their life in the toenail, of the heel down in the head of the toenails deep in the ground. We're the last thing, we're the chaff on up, and Jesus didn't tell us womens to, to get out here and take and rule the world. He says man was the ruler of the world, and says he, when He created us, then he wants to know what he gonna do, what he gonna do with that woman? He say, 'That's your helpmate.' And the woman done taken the thing over. It's time Jesus turned over, turned another leaf over." She laughed. "No, I don't believe in all this. I don't do it, don't believe in it, don't approve of it. I believe in us doing things that's proper, that is in our means to do. But that's why things is like this, too many womens is telling the mens what to do. It ain't you mens is dumb. It's just you, you just all, you get back and give over to the womens. Do you see what I mean?"

"Easier."

"That's what I'm talking about. It ain't because you don't know no better. That's why the world is weakening. A woman is a helpmate to a man. If you get out there, start to rolling a log, and it's heavy, and [when] your wife see you straining, if she get out there and give you a hand, push a little bit, that's, that's it then. Man is the ruler of the world, but so many mens don't do it. They, they gets back, get over there, and the womens, we gonna say everything because we know the mens gonna dedicate to us. We know this is wrong. Do you understand me?"

Yes, I understood her, but I did not agree with her. Sometimes the pupil has to disagree with the teacher. I agreed with so much of what she said that I didn't want her to say anything that would undermine my view of her as wise woman. However, because I had been influenced by feminist thought in the 1960s and 1970s, I found myself in basic disagreement with Mollie Ford's views on women; we come from two different generations. Her attitude toward women does have some feminist touches, though. She had said earlier that "women ain't made no different," and her metaphor of rolling the log suggests that women can be equal in ability to work. It also suggests that men and women are a team, the help of one enhances the other. But finally her views reflect the inherent attitudes of her religion and, in terms of age stratification theory, of her age cohorts (Karp and Yoels 1982, 29). She has maintained the basic values she learned as a young adult through all the changes of the intervening years; this is an example of her cultural continuity, how she has maintained contact with her past, resisting the changing attitudes around her.

Up to this point, I have concentrated on Mollie Ford's self-image as a teacher, her strategies for teaching, and the message she was delivering, but a full analysis of her pedagogical discourse involves consideration of the rhetoric she used. I was aware that a performance was going on, but as I said earlier I did not know what kind of performance; later it became obvious that it was a teaching performance with a complex set of rhetorical devices employed to frame our interaction. As I pointed out in the Introduction, performance is a particular kind of verbal art that enhances experience by focusing attention on the performer and the performance, attracting a "special intensity" toward the artistic communication (Bauman 1984, 11). The devices that the performer uses to accomplish this are called "keys to performance," and his or her use of them is subject to the evaluation of an audience. The first keys I noticed in Mollie Ford's performance were her use of repeated words and phrases. She continually repeated the words "learn," "teach," "understand," and "know," suggesting her self-awareness of the teaching process; she was trying to draw attention to the fact of her teaching. Reinforcing this reflexive awareness was the repetition of other key words: "talk," "tell," "listen," "hear," "ask," and "seek," all implying the processes of teaching and learning. These words all have to do with communication and point out her awareness of the importance of communication; they call attention to her speech as a performance and to the relationship between her and her audience.[7] Mollie Ford was telling me with this device that a message was being given, telling me in effect to listen closely. Perhaps she felt a stronger need for these reminders because the context was not an ordinary teaching situation, and the world she lives in does not recognize her authority as a teacher. Elderly people need powerful devices to call attention to their teaching performance. The repeated words—"learn," "understand," "seek," "listen"—also function in a special way for the aged: they reinforce the elder's theme of interconnectedness since they all imply the interaction of human beings in meaningful ways.

She used another form of repetition, parallelism, to achieve her pedagogical purpose. She repeated certain phrases but varied them in a systematic way in order to emphasize significant points (Bauman 1984, 18). For instance, she said, "I was then, and always was, always is up to now, and I don't want to be nothing else." "Was" and "always" are repeated, but she varies their repetition by shifting to "is" the third time. Parallel structure here makes a point about the continuity of a core identity through time,[8] which becomes even more important as people grow older. Another instance of parallelism occurred when she said, "No, I don't believe in all this. I don't do it, don't believe in it, don't approve of it. I believe in us doing things that's proper." The parallel series of negatives sets up a forceful statement of the positive, what she does believe in. There was one more example of her use of parallelism to build up intensity: "I been through the world. I been through, that's what I'm trying to tell you. I been through the world, and I've been through everything." The final variation of "world" to "everything" emphasizes the extent of her experience in the world.

This last example also illustrates another rhetorical device Mollie Ford used repeatedly, the pronoun "you." A shift of pronouns, in this case from "I" to "you," transfers the point of view from internal (the story) to external (the storytelling situation), thus making the audience aware of the performance (Babcock 1984, 73) or, in this situation, the pupil aware of the lesson. When Mollie Ford says, "That's what I'm trying to tell you," she is drawing me into the performance, reminding me that learning should be going on. There are many other examples of this, phrased as both questions and statements: "You understand what I mean?" "You know what I'm speaking of." "And you can tell them." "Are you getting me?" "That's why you hear me tell you." Notice how the pronoun "you" is juxtaposed with the key words "tell," "understand," "know," "speaking," "hear," all pulling the listener into the frame at the very point where the most important message is being communicated in abbreviated form. This device is even more pervasive, though. Many times, she leaves the pronoun "you" out but implies it by asking, "See?" and "Understand?" She also sprinkles "you" throughout her conversation even when it is not linked to a key word.[9]

Mollie Ford uses metaphors in skillful ways to intensify her meaning (Bauman 1984, 17–18). "I was shifted from hand to mouth and pillar to post." She gives a sense of her rootless childhood and marginal existence by using a traditional proverbial saying with which any listener would be familiar. She used the metaphor of rolling a log to make her point about woman being a helpmate to man, making concrete an abstract principle. Her entire pedagogy of the aged is wrapped up in the single metaphor of the stepping stone, and to emphasize her humility she says she does not want to "pin roses on her shoulder." She used biblical metaphors at several points: "If you can go two miles for the devil, well naturally you can stretch one more mile for Jesus." "The womens living their life in the toenail." Here the metaphors are given added power by their sources in the Bible.

Mollie Ford's biblical references and allusions, whether metaphor or narrative, appeal to the highest authority to reinforce a point. The scriptural allusions refer not only to all humanity but also to the specific situation; they connect an ideal model with a temporal event, and a cultural norm with a concrete situation (Briggs 1984, 18–19). For instance, to illustrate how difficult communication is in a world that does not follow God's teachings, she referred to the Tower of Babel twice. Here, the ideal spiritual realm of a universal language is contrasted with the actual present existence of multiple languages and misunderstandings. Contained within the allusion is an implicit reference to the specific situation of the interview: the Tower of Babel was a metaphor for the difficulty she was having in communicating a lesson to me.

Mollie Ford used other kinds of narratives in a similar way. All of the stories are embedded in her pedagogical discourse and are reminders that it is in fact a performance. She told a story about an old woman—"She was old-fashioned and ignorant like myself"—who "shouted" during sermons even if the preacher was not a good speaker. When the good preacher preached, the woman saw Jesus *through* him, and when the bad preacher spoke, she saw Jesus *around* him. "So that's the way it is with me. I'm just the ignorant kind. I don't care what you bring up, if the Lord ain't in my picture, you ain't got no conversation. . . . " As her mention of the "ignorant" woman in this story illustrates, she is perfectly capable of using irony to make her point.

Mollie Ford is an effective orator; my sense of her as a spontaneous preacher came when she shifted from one style to another. She used textural elements of oral delivery such as rate, length, pause duration, pitch contour, tone of voice, loudness, and stress (Bauman 1984, 19–20).[10] For instance, she had been talking at a regular rate and pitch when my statement of one of her major values caused her to scream out, "THAT'S what I'm trying to tell the world, child." And a few seconds later she whispered, "And I'm here to tell you. . . . " She definitely grabbed my attention with the shift of styles; she involved me in a deeper emotional way than she had before and at a point where the lesson was the most significant. Then, juxtaposing the scream with a whisper, she made me pay even more careful attention. The shift of styles is also an assertion that this is not ordinary conversation but a significant performance. Her other use of this shift was not as dramatic, but it was still effective. In describing the condition of young people today she said, "You-all is in the world is what you call b-l-i-n-d," and she drew out the word "blind" at a much slower rate than the rest of the sentence. Again, she uses the shift at an important point of her lesson in order to emphasize it.

Mollie Ford has, I think, a remarkable awareness of her own pedagogical style. Her repeating of lessons in almost the same words could have been taken for the faulty memory of an old person, but turned out to be a conscious rhetorical device on her part. She made the point for a second time about the need for old people to continue learning; then she said, "I just explained that to you. You never get too old to learn." An important point is worth repeating. After her second reference to the Tower of Babel she said, "I just said it before. I said it so don't think that I'm just repeating the whole conversation, but I'm trying to bring your mind to these things, to let you peoples know." By talking about her own pedagogy within a lesson being taught, she is drawing attention to the frame, letting me know again the importance of teaching and learning.

This whole study of folk pedagogy brings up an important issue: the role of folklorist as pupil (Briggs 1985, 303–6). Mollie Ford is removed by age and circumstance from her usual pupils, but she still has this powerful urge to teach. Along comes a folklorist trying to conduct a field research interview, and she skillfully turns it into a pedagogical discourse. Even when I interrupted her frame she always managed to return to it by the various devices discussed above. At a certain point I began to accept her frame and play my role as pupil. The pedagogical discourse is not meant to be a monologue; rather, it is a dialogue (Briggs 1985, 305). For example, when she made her statement about the equality of all human beings, I responded with, "I believe that. We are all brothers and sisters." I fulfilled my role as pupil to the extent that it prompted her to shift styles expecting me to go along, and I did. After each of her subsequent statements I responded, "And I know it," "I believe it," and "I know that," affirming the truth and validity of her values as a good pupil should in a form similar to the traditional African-American call-and-response pattern. When I said the right thing, she called me "child," making me in effect one of her children, one of her learners. I was drawn into her discourse so much that I lost some of the objectivity fieldworkers are supposed to maintain. This loss of objectivity occurs frequently, though, to a fieldworker who is involved in his or her work. Perhaps more surprisingly, as I analyzed her pedagogy, I became even more subjective about what she had to say. The distance that usually comes with analysis did not occur; rather, I found myself seeing correspondences between her pedagogy and my own in the far different arena of college teaching.

The process of fieldworker becoming learner seems to be cross-cultural. Myerhoff certainly accepted this role among the elderly Jews she consulted with in California, and Briggs began to study the process whereby the elderly *Mexicanos* of New Mexico turned him into one of their students (Myerhoff 1978; Briggs 1984, 1985). In these cases, as with Mollie Ford, the impetus came from the persons being studied, and the fieldworker had to shift from his or her usual role. In Myerhoff's case, she was a member of the same cultural group; Briggs and I were not. Myerhoff seems to have had an easier time qualifying as an appropriate student; Briggs had to prove himself worthy over a period of time. Mollie Ford deemed me worthy after only a few minutes of conversation because of her situation as a teacher without anyone to teach. The *Mexicano* elders are part of a culture that respects their wisdom and that comes to them in order to learn from them. Briggs had to learn a complex set of rules and establish trust before he could join this group. I came into a situation where Mollie Ford was ready for someone like me to come along.

Given her religious beliefs, it is not surprising that she saw my visit as providence: God had provided me as a means for her to deliver her message to a world much in need of it. When I asked her about the past she said, "Now you remind me of them days; now you're seeking something for the Lord. . . . " She also said, "If you hadn't a come here, I wouldn't have knowed there was such peoples like you. . . . There should be lots more of you seeking somebody to work for the Lord and things like, you know what I'm speaking of." She assumes from the beginning that I am a seeker after her word, and of course, she is right, although my motivation was secular and not religious.

Mollie Ford clearly stated my function when she said, "I'm trying to bring your mind to these things, to let you peoples know. And a person of your ability, I admire you. I ain't gonna tell no lie. Because some things, when you're talking about the Lord, I believe you're gonna take it to somebody else, and somebody's gonna give somebody else a different thought." Yes, I am her pupil, but I must become a teacher myself in order to carry on the message. Finally, she articulated her hope for my ability as a pupil. "I just hope you can see it, the way I see it and feel it." Teaching and learning require the deepest, most spiritual kind of interconnectedness, for one human being to see and feel with the eyes and emotions of another.

NOTES

1. I am grateful to Adams County historian Stephen Kelley for telling me about Mollie Ford.

2. My experience with Mollie Ford is similar to the situation described by Charles L. Briggs in his role as fieldworker/pupil with "the elders of bygone days" in *Mexicano* New Mexico (1984, 1985).

3. In this she is similar to Barbara Myerhoff's informant Jacob, who was a teacher and model right up to the moment of his death. The difference is that Jacob had a community to teach; Mollie Ford does not (Myerhoff 1978, 171).

4. For disengagement theory, see Cumming 1964, and Karp and Yoels 1982, 21.

5. See Clark and Anderson 1967, Neugarten 1968, and Fischer 1977.

6. See Manney 1975, Myerhoff and Simic 1977, Myerhoff 1979, Keith 1977, Fry 1980, Fry and Keith 1980, Amoss and Harrell 1981, Karp and Yoels 1982, and Kertzer and Keith 1984.

7. Barbara Babcock and others call these reflexive rhetorical devices "metacommunication" (1984, 61–79; Bauman 1984, 15–24).

8. This is what Erik Erikson calls "selfsameness" in his seminal study of identity (1959, 102).

9. Briggs notes a similar pattern in the pedagogical discourse of the *Mexicano* elders he studied in New Mexico. They called for a response from the students with "you see?" or "you know?" (1985, 304).

10. Bauman calls these "paralinguistic features" (1984, 19–20).

2

Jesse Hatcher
Shaping a Life through Religion

Like Mollie Ford, eighty-eight-year-old Jesse Hatcher of Patrick County, Virginia, sees old age as an opportunity to pass on to succeeding generations knowledge learned through experience. I interviewed him on the front porch of his farmhouse at the foot of the Blue Ridge Mountains in 1978. At one point in talking about the old ways of doing things, he said, "Now old things like that is something you-all don't know nothing about, but they are true."

Mr. Hatcher, who takes pride in his position as an elder in the community, explained the origins of his church in 1902, adding, "Only two, only two of us living now, you know, that knows back, back them times I'm talking to you about now."

"You, and who was the other person?"

"Mrs. Reynolds. Nora Reynolds."

"You're the oldest people in the church?"

"The oldest people in the church, and the oldest black people in the community. And so, you see, our days been very well, don't you think so?"

Mr. Hatcher chuckled softly, as he often did after stating a truth he expected to be affirmed. He counts on respect from younger listeners, just as he respected his elders when he was young.

I asked him how he learned all of the folk cures he talked about, and he replied, "Well, you know, I was always, I would take notice of the older people as I growed up years ago." Like Mollie Ford, he sees himself as a link between generations, passing the wisdom of one on to the next.

"I always have people come by here almost all of the time. A fella stopped here the other day—mail carrier—and he had a runaway boy, and he only had the one child. And I thought that he, you know, had such a happy home. He come and wanted to know, . . . did I have any experience of that kind, and what must he try on his sixteen-year-old son? Now, you see."

"What did you tell him?"

"Exactly. I only had two boys, yeah. There's so many things that I've experienced, you know, in life. I only had two boys, and they never, they would tell you if they were here—no they never saw Daddy take a drop, never heard Daddy curse a oath, never used no slang language around my family. But you can still, they got a little bad about this here drinking, but they tell you, no, not Daddy. And so that's what I told this young man. I told him, only thing I could tell him to do, never quarrel with him when the boy come in a little out of the way, wait till he got sober and talk to him. If he could coax him and could get him to go back to school—he said he'd dropped out of school—could get him to go back to school, the Lord was able to handle him. And that's all he could do because he can't make him do anything now, you know. When one gets that age you can't make him, because when he gets out he's just like that."

Since Jesse Hatcher is used to having people seek him out, he was not surprised when I contacted him about doing a tape-recorded interview. I talked to him first on August 11 without doing any taping and then saw him a few days later at church; I returned to his home on August 17—several other people were with me—to record an interview. The field research was sponsored by the American Folklife Center of the Library of Congress, and often several folklorists ventured out as a team. On this particular day, I was accompanied by Carl Fleischhauer, who recorded and photographed the interview; Harley Jolley, a historian from Mars Hill College who was a summer intern with the National Park Service; and a man and woman from a local television station who were scouting our activities for a possible news story. (Unless otherwise attributed, I am the other speaker in the following.) I was apprehensive that this crowd might intimidate Mr. Hatcher, but he seemed pleased to have an audience, and he spoke freely to all of us as younger people who were there to learn from him.

2. Jess Hatcher with the author. (Photograph by Carl Fleischhauer, American Folklife Center, Library of Congress, BR8-1-20205 / 33.)

Jesse Hatcher was born in Patrick County on February 22, 1890, and was educated in the local schools until the age of sixteen. Except for trips to work in the coal mines, he remained in Patrick County all his life.

"Now, I used to, I rambled a whole lot when I was young."
"Traveled around?"
"No, I didn't go far, you know. Rambled around a whole lot. And I used to be a miner. I've loaded a many ton of coal."
"Where'd you go to do that?"
"Out in West Virginia and Pennsylvania. Loaded a many ton."
"Did you ever work in one of these sawmills?"
"Sawmills, rock quarries. I never did work on the railroad though."

For most of his life Jesse Hatcher was a farmer growing tobacco and other crops. He was married for fifty-five years and reared several children who have all moved away. He spends the winters in Richmond with his children but returns to the Blue Ridge in the summer. "Always come back home," he said. "This is home." His family has lived in the same area for three generations; his parents and grandparents were slaves on plantations in Patrick County. He belonged to the Clark's Creek Progressive Primitive Baptist Church since childhood and is now a deacon.[1]

As he talked about his life, family history, and beliefs, certain ideas kept recurring, and upon further examination I realized that he had been shaped by his religion. He uses it now, in his old age, to order his past and to secure his present place in the world.

Within Mr. Hatcher's religious belief system are *themes* that give meaning to his life history. I use that term in the sense Sharon R. Kaufman does in her study of aging (1986), where she emphasizes identity and continuity in the lives of the elderly. Kaufman says that a person's self-concept is ageless, that continuity is maintained through a symbolic and creative process. The self uses the past as a basis for identity in the present, but this process is not static: the past is reinterpreted based on changes in the culture and the individual. Each individual has an interpretation of experience that is expressed in symbolic ways (1986, 14). Themes are part of the patterns of symbolic meaning and the means by which old people "interpret and evaluate their life experiences and attempt to integrate these experiences to form a self-concept" (1986, 25). Themes are both unique to an individual and culturally shared.

Although Jesse Hatcher shares his religious beliefs with most of the other people in his community, he has applied those religious values to his own experiences to form unique personal themes in his life story. These themes are also the major concerns of his life review. As he talks about his past, Jesse Hatcher returns to a consciousness of past experience which is then directly related to his present self-image; his emphasis on religion is associated with the past and the present.

"Well, have you always been a religious man, or did you go through a period of life—?"

"From a child. Never drank no liquor, never knowed anything about any liquor, don't know how it makes you feel. And I always— never hit a man in my life after I got to be grown. I just wasn't a rowdy fella. Began my first Christian work when I was sixteen years old. I was added to the church as a superintendent of the Sunday school, first superintendent ever at Clark's Creek Church. And I just, you know, worked on, worked on, worked on. And you know I get a lot of enjoyment out of it."

"Oh yeah. I can tell that when I see you, when I saw you in church last Sunday, I could tell you enjoyed it. You were right down there in front."

"No, they don't put me behind. I don't sit on the back seat."

This last statement indicates Jesse Hatcher's present self-image: a highly regarded leader of the religious community who doesn't take a back seat in church or out. Clearly this image goes back to his childhood and is part of his feeling of continuity. He has spent his life trying to live up to the ideal that religion has established— paraphrasing the gospel singer Mahalia Jackson—to live the life he sings about in his song. He recognizes, though, that people do not always live up to the Christian ideal.

"What I want to say, what I want you to understand I'm talking about, you know, you hardly ever run across anybody now but what they don't belong to the church, say they're Christian, say they belong to the church. But I don't look at it that way. You could belong to the church and then not be no Christian. You see what I'm talking about? But *borned again* Christians, and you have been born of the spirit. You don't find many of them don't take time to get that duty."

Once a person has been born again, he or she must still deal with the presence of evil and suffering in the world. Mr. Hatcher told a long, detailed personal story that symbolically represents his struggle with evil.

"And you know all of these things, takes all of that, I guess, to make up a world. We all suffer one way or another, one way or another, sooner or later. And then lastly, that zone in the flesh will strike us. Did you ever think of that?" He paused. "That zone will strike us. And it's a stumbling block to you too if you let it." He laughed.

"Well, your religion has been important to you; I know that from hearing you talk."

"It's been everything to me. Lord, Lord, if I, I can't begin to tell you what that has been to me and is to me now. That has strengthened me and enabling me to stay here. If I was to tell you that I had had a rattlesnake up in my arms, would you believe it?"

"I don't know. Have you?"

"Yes sir."

"How did that happen?"

"Well, now that's our mode of farming, you know. We'd save feed. We'd pull fodder off of corn from the ear down. That was blade fodder. Leave the top standing, and we'd go back later then and cut the top, that's called tops, you see. Well them things's burning you when you're in hot weather, you know, tying them tops. And I would cut tops early in the day and tie them at night, cool, you know. See? Now you understand?"

"Yes sir."

"Alright. Well I had my tops cut, and I had supper. I went back tying tops, get the tops tied up that night, you see. And I guess maybe I tied from here about like past to the woods. And now I'm under, hand under the tops, you know, to raise them up, hug them up and tie them. I felt something real cold moving."

We all laughed.

"Now y'all think this is, this is no joke. Lord, no, it's a fact. I turned him a-loose, and when I throwed the tops down he began to sing. Then I knowed where he was. Now this is true. I could carry you to this very place right where I was. And I didn't kill the snake then. I went over there to a white fella, right across the river from me, I was on one side, he was on the other. And I told him I wanted his shotgun. He said, 'What you gonna do with a shotgun tonight?' I said, 'Rattlesnake over here.' And so he got it, had a double-barreled shotgun. I went back over there and shot him sure enough. But I haven't tied no more tops since."

We all laughed again, but this time it was an appropriate response. "How come he didn't strike you?"

"They can't, they can't strike you unless they're coiled up. They can't strike, not anymore than when he's stretched out. No kind of snake that can bite you, they got to be coiled up. But anyway in the world you look at a rattlesnake, he's looking at you. You know anything about—?"

Harley Jolley answered, "No, not much."

"Anyway you look at him, he's looking at you. He always sees you first."

This story is significant in Mr. Hatcher's life review because it is a concrete representation of his Christian confrontation with evil and of his ability to overcome evil in the world. The narrative is grounded in concrete details to indicate that it is true, that spiritually significant events can take place in the everyday world. If the story is not told in the context of how important his religion is to him, the meaning might not be clear; but when he prefaces the story with the statement that religion is "everything to me," the religious meaning is inescapable. Even though he says that rattlesnakes cannot strike unless they are coiled, the evidence of God's grace is still there: events can have both spiritual and mundane explanations. The snake is evil, and Mr. Hatcher has to confront it and eventually destroy it. The snake represents the devil and is a powerful adversary who sees what you are doing before you are aware of his presence.

Jesse Hatcher sees existence in terms of opposing forces: nature and culture. This is his personal adaptation of a widespread cultural pattern in which nature is seen as the elemental forces and raw materials of the universe, and culture as human thought processes such as art and technology. Thus, culture is associated with human endeavors that take nature and shape it into products. Sherry Ortner makes the point that "the culture/nature distinction is itself a product of culture" and is found across cultures and age groups (1974, 84).[2] Besides its seeming universality, the culture/nature dichotomy has specific application to the study of the elderly: Jesse Hatcher uses this theme in his life story and as a structuring device in his life review. The culture/nature concept also has a bearing on the understanding of gender roles in the elderly, which I shall discuss later. Ortner establishes the dichotomy in hierarchical terms: "[culture can] transcend natural conditions and turn them to its purposes. Thus culture . . . at some level of awareness asserts itself to be not only distinct from but superior to nature, and that sense of distinctiveness and superiority rests precisely on the ability to transform—to 'socialize' and 'culturalize'—nature" (1974, 72-73).

For Jesse Hatcher, nature is superior to culture, thus placing him at odds with the prevailing beliefs of society. But he recognizes that humans cannot exist totally within the realm of nature, that culture is necessary to transform nature into usable products. Nature is seen as closer to the spiritual realm, while culture is viewed as removed from that realm. In the implied spectrum from nature to culture, Mr. Hatcher sees nature as the source of spiritual truth. Nature is usually good, a means to understanding spiritual ideals, while culture is often antithetical to nature, a worldly source of corruption of spiritual ideals. Being in nature leads to a good religious life; getting away from nature causes the loss of goodness. The snake story indicates the complexity of the distinction: the snake as a symbol of evil is found in nature, so that nature is the source of good and evil. Culture, then, is not the source of evil, but corruption from the forces of evil is more likely to occur within the realm of culture. Although Mr. Hatcher does not perceive his ideas as going against Christian belief, his view of nature as essentially good is in conflict with traditional Christian doctrine, which sees man in nature as a fallen creature (original sin). His attitude toward nature is actually closer to nineteenth-century romanticism. Another complicating element in the snake story is that Mr. Hatcher must use a product of culture (the shotgun) in order to control evil, but it is understood that the shotgun can also be used for immoral purposes. Mr. Hatcher's role in the story, and in others which follow, is as a mediator between nature and culture. He commented directly about the moral and spiritual benefits of living close to nature.

"You know you get a lot out of life reading, meditating, even just to yourself. You get a lot out of life, I tell you. Yeah. Sounds a little strange, don't it? Don't you see people just running, running, running, running now? Who's satisfied? They go, go, go—go, go. But who's satisfied? You get way, just out in the bushes, kinda to yourself. Get out there where nature is, nature's out here." He chuckled. "See? Now my children, they all in the city. I ain't got a one, not a one, not a one. But that's not Daddy. They want me to come and live with them, but they won't come back here and live with me."

This statement indicates the interdependence of culture and nature: his reading and meditating as processes of human consciousness are associated with culture, but they achieve their highest meaning within the realm of nature. In Mr. Hatcher's scheme of things, then, reading and meditating mediate between nature and culture; they are a means of transforming inspiration from nature into thoughts that act as moral guides in the cultural realm. Nature and solitude are available on the farm, in an environment conducive to meditating and reading. Mr. Hatcher implies that the city is the opposite, a place where people "run, run, run," a representation of culture, crowded and antithetical to the contemplative spiritual life. In his mind, sacred ideals and nature are linked on one side, and secular life and culture are connected on the other.

"And you know, there's a better way to live. Now go back to talking about drinking. Did you know there's a better way to live than to get out here and guzzle that stuff down and get so you don't know what you're doing, and getting knocked up and beat up and all like that? Don't you know that? Lord didn't aim for a man to do that. That's what He suffers him to do. He shouldn't do that. It's not intended for him to do that, but that's what he does."

Drinking alcohol is an activity associated with culture and is unnatural and against God's wishes. This nature/culture or sacred/secular dichotomy runs through everything Jesse Hatcher talks about; it is the basic structuring idea for his life review. I elicited many kinds of folklore from him, and the nature/culture theme is found in all of it, in his discussion of foodways, folk cures, faith healing, the history of his church, family slave narratives, and in his means of understanding race relations. This controlling frame provides a context for analyzing the way folk traditions fit into his life review.

Mr. Hatcher emphasized the importance foodways had for him;[3] indeed, he cooked and preserved food more than most men in his culture. In doing so he placed himself within the domestic realm, which is traditionally associated with women's activities, but he also placed himself closer to nature. Ortner says that women are traditionally seen as being closer to nature than men because, among a complex of biological, social, and psychological reasons, giving birth, child rearing, and domestic pursuits associated with women are viewed as natural processes. On the opposite side, men are more bound up in culture because their usual realm is public, not domestic, oriented toward achievement in the outside world rather than toward the emotional inner life (1974, 73). This anthropological concept is paralleled by the sociological principle of men as "instrumental" and women as "expressive" (Zelditch 1955, 313-14). Women's expressive roles connote responsibility for nurturance, interpersonal relations, and emotional life, thereby providing for internal home life. Men's instrumental roles suggest more goal-directed, problem-oriented activities, thereby providing for external worldly states. Women's expressive roles are thought to be based in nature; men's instrumental roles in culture. In Ortner's application of this dichotomy, women are not seen as being totally cut off from culture; rather, culture as a masculine-oriented concept "recognizes that women are active participants in [culture's] special processes, but at the same time sees [women] as being more rooted in, or having more direct affinity with, nature" (1974, 73). Jesse Hatcher's discussion of his interest in foodways illustrates this association of culture with the masculine and nature with the feminine.

"I can can just as good as the madam can," he laughed.

"When your wife was around, did she do all the canning, or did you do it together?"

"No, we did that together. That's the way I learned. And I cooked. . . . I can cook just as good a apple pie as you can."

"I'll bet you can."

"And I can make just as good a cake as you can."

"You wouldn't have to do much to do better than me."

He laughed and said, "Yeah, well, I cooked, I washed. I can run the washing machine just as good as she could. You know, she was sick for a long time, and we just stayed here, you know. I'd cook, help her cook all the time. And then so much of the time, I'd cook myself."

In his orientation toward nature, Jesse Hatcher has also oriented himself toward traditional women's expressive roles—washing, cooking, and canning. However, since cooking involves the transformation of raw natural materials into culturally usable products (Levi-Strauss 1969b), isn't cooking more closely associated with culture, and thus is a masculine endeavor? Ortner addresses this question when she points out that "higher" forms of cooking (*haute cuisine*) are associated with men, but domestic cooking remains a part of the woman's world (1974, 80). The basic domestic cooking and canning that Mr. Hatcher does place him within the women's realm, which is itself not totally within nature. Ortner states: "At the same time [woman's] socializing and cooking functions within the domestic context show her to be a powerful agent of the cultural process, constantly transforming raw natural resources into cultural products. Belonging to culture, yet appearing to have stronger and more direct connections with nature, she is . . . seen as situated between the two realms" (1974, 80). Thus, in his role as cook and preserver of food, Mr. Hatcher can be seen as mediating between nature and culture in the ways usually associated with women as mediators.

Jesse Hatcher's statements show him and his wife to be equals in their domestic chores. He learned how to cook and can from her, and his pride in his domestic accomplishments is clear. He has moved from an outward instrumental role as coal miner and farmer to more inward expressive roles as domestic cook and nurturer, from an association with masculine culture to feminine nature. In doing this he follows a pattern of the elderly that is cross-cultural: "older men, whether traditional-urban or rural-preliterate, move towards values, interests and activities which are no longer stereotypically masculine" (Gutmann 1977, 306). According to David Gutmann, as men get older, they tend to be less aggressive and become more passive, and hence in cultural terms, more feminine. Barbara Myerhoff extends this idea to the expressive/instrumental gender roles of the elderly: "roles allocated to the elderly are predominantly of the expressive kind" (1978, 261). Retired men and women are expected to pass their time socializing and taking care of themselves, not being active in the world. Yet retired men lose their links to the instrumental dimension with the loss of work. Myerhoff tells us: "The expressive concerns that men are expected to devote themselves to after retirement are usually areas in which they have had little experience, and often which they regard as demeaning, being associated with female ('not serious') concerns" (1978, 262).

Having made the move from instrumental to expressive, Mr. Hatcher does not see it as demeaning, probably because he was already more "feminine" in his orientation toward nature than most men are. His close relationship with his wife and her infirmity in old age caused him to become more involved in domestic pursuits. It seems that there was a transition period when he helped her and learned how to cook, then he took it over completely as primary nurturer. This was an easy role for him to assume because of his desire to mediate between nature and culture. Cooking and taking care of his wife were "natural" roles for Jesse Hatcher. And he has managed to avoid the problems most men encounter in shifting roles as part of aging.

Most of the food Mr. Hatcher prepares comes from his own farm, so he has a sense of the source in nature of what he eats every day. Orchards and grapevines surround his house, and he continues to make preserves from apples, peaches, and grapes. I asked him what his favorite dish is.

"Well, I'm not so particular about what I eat. I eat most anything, like it pretty well. I never complain. But now the fact about it, ham tastes pretty good, don't it?"

"Yeah, sure does. What about your favorite dessert?"

"Steak pretty good. And dessert, peach preserves. I ain't showed you that. I made me a glass. I made me a glassful just, I don't know, Saturday or Monday one. What do you think of that? A glass of peach preserves."

"You made it?"

"Oh, yes, been eating on it. Really that does taste good too."

"What are you cooking in there now?"

"Oh, I was just stewing some apples in there."

"You got plenty of apples around here."

" . . . There's just plenty of apples and peaches."

Jesse Hatcher's tone of awe when he said, "What do you think of that? A glass of peach preserves," is an indication of the meaning certain foods have for him, especially those that come from his own farm and that he has prepared himself. Again, we can see his role as mediator between nature and culture: nature provides the raw fruits, which he processes into cultural products. When we walked around his house, he pointed with pride at the things that were growing.

"Now you didn't notice my grapes, how they was beginning to ripen since you was last here. Looky there, over on the other side, real pretty."
"Oh yeah, they're really ripening."
"Just look how they're hanging down there."
"What are you going to do with these?"
"Make grape juice and jelly. Just looky there."

He repeated "looky there" several more times as we walked. His wonder at the bounty of nature is clear; the proximity of fruits that he can prepare and eat is a part of this wonder. Traditional foodways symbolize Jesse Hatcher's direct and satisfying relationship with nature. They also provide a link to his past, which in turn gives meaning to the present. Myerhoff says, "In a modern world of pluralistic cultures, first experiences of nurturance set in the context of domestic life are often associated with ethnic origins, bound up with first foods, touch, language, song, folkways, and the like, carried and connoted by rituals and symbols learned in that context" (1984, 327). In this sense, the picking and preparing of peaches is a ritual for Jesse Hatcher, one associated with his childhood and with his deceased wife, one that connects him spiritually with her and with nature.

The plants that grow in his yard are also useful in the making of folk cures, an area of expertise for Mr. Hatcher and one that again shows him to be a mediator between nature and culture. Folk medicine is widely practiced in the Blue Ridge; I talked to many people in 1978 who were knowledgeable about the use of herbs, roots, and barks as cures.[4] Mr. Hatcher's cures are products of nature, and his explanation of their use places them within the nature/culture dichotomy. We walked out into his front yard to see the balm of Gilead tree (Brown #1215, #1926),[5] and this led to a long discussion of other kinds of folk medicine.

"We'll go out here and show you now about the balm in Gilead bush. Now I'll show you here about the buds. Now right yonder you see at that post, that's a big one. There are more buds on that than there is this. But now these are what you get now. See?"

"The buds."

Carl Fleischhauer asked, "The little thing that sticks out, that little part that sticks out?"

"That's right. That's the bud."

I asked, "What'd you use that for?"

"Well, you use that to make a salve, also to make a cough syrup."

"How'd you make the salve?"

"Well, I made that salve, or my wife, she did. She blended mutton's tallow, honey, buds, and stewed that down to a thick, heavy salve. And that will heal a cut quicker than a doctor's medicine."

Carl asked, "Is that right? So it's good for any kind of a cut?"

"Any kind, any kind. And then not only for that—this is among the best medicines for asthma."

"Is that right?" Carl wondered. "Do you rub it on or—?"

"No, you take it kinda like a cough syrup."

Carl responded, "Now, do you-all make cough syrup in this country from black cherry bark sometimes?"

"Oh, you mean wild cherry [Brown #1214]?"

"Wild cherry bark," Carl emphasized.

"Oh, years ago that's all we ever had was, we didn't know, wild cherry and end of white walnut. They grow down on the bottom, you know, white walnut. You take them and put it together, and sassafras [Brown #788, #895], that's a little old vine grows on bottom land. That makes one of the best tonics. In the spring of the year we didn't think about going to the doctor. You get some of that, you know, and use it, you didn't need no doctor. You just needed that."

I asked, "Sassafras tea?"

"Yeah."

"You said this," I pointed to the tree, "was mentioned in the Bible."

"It really is. Oh yeah, yeah, balm in Gilead. Man, ain't you read all this?"

Harley Jolley intoned, "There is a balm in Gilead—"

"This is it, yeah. But people just got so they won't use it, you know."

I said, "And they even knew about it back in Biblical times as a cure."

"Oh yes. Oh years, years ago. When I was a boy, you know, a lot of times you get cut, cut your foot with a ax, you know what I'm talking about."

"You also told me a way, if you cut the end of your finger off. What was that?"

"Well if you cut your finger—try not to cut it off," he laughed. "But if you *do* cut it off, while it's yet warm, just take it and put it together and put some brown sugar, wrap it up, put your splint on the bottom and on top, wrap it up [Brown #969, #1268]. Just as good as going to the hospital, only you don't have to pay for it. . . . Oh yes, that will heal. Oh, why didn't you mention that to me. I didn't think about it. I would have showed you the fella, and you could've looked at his finger, that I told you about, he cut it off, you know."

"Oh yeah. He was at church Sunday?"

"He was at church Sunday. . . . Now these things are like gummy, but they're great large in the spring of the year when they're large and ready to bust out. And they're right gummy. And it's got a yellow-looking gum in it."

"What were some of the other cures people used to use?"

"Well, black snake root [Brown #1213, #1451]. Did you ever see a black snake root plant?"

"I don't think I know that one," Carl said.

"Ain't you never, really? You have ain't you? Black snake root. I've got down there at my old place; down there on the river I had a patch of them that I knowed where to go and get it in the winter, you know. Yeah, it's good for sick stomach, good for children."

"How did you use it, how did you prepare it?" Harley asked.

"Oh, just get a little bunch of it, just a lot of little bitty fine roots there is, you know, just little fine roots. You wash them right clean, and you take them and boil your water and put it in a cup, boil your water, and pour your water on it. Let it set a little while, put a saucer over it. Take it and drink it. The best thing for a bad cold and a whole lot of other things."

As he touched the buds on the balm of Gilead tree, Jesse Hatcher was reconnecting with the powers of nature. Throughout his discussion of cures, he emphasized both the natural object in nature and the cultural process whereby it was transformed into a product that could cure. Like cooking and canning, making folk medicine is seen as a mediation between nature and culture, but here culture is also represented as being removed from nature. Everytime he says, "you don't need no doctor," "it will heal quicker than a doctor's medicine," or "just as good as going to the hospital," he is suggesting that medical technology is a cultural product that is too far from nature. He believes that folk cures based in nature are more effective in many cases than medical technology. This is not to say that Mr. Hatcher does not use doctors at all: he has been in the hospital for surgery and speaks highly of his surgeon. He believes, however, that certain problems can be more effectively dealt with using nature's cures. The folk cures can also be seen as closer to his feminine expressive side; he associates them with his wife—mentioning that she was the one who made the balm of Gilead salve—and cures are linked to nurturing.

He also talked about cures for dental problems, and again they were illustrative of the nature/culture dichotomy. We walked around to the back of his house to see horseradish growing (Brown #1297, #2003).

"We'll go right around this way."

"Now what was the horseradish used for?"

"Well, you can use turnip greens, just like you use turnip greens if you want to. . . . Then it's good for headache, good for toothache, use it for neuralgia, and I don't know, a whole lot of other things."

After we found the horseradish I asked him, "Now what would you do? You'd just pick those leaves?"

"Just pick you a leaf and lay it on a warm stove, and it'll turn right greasy looking, just right greasy."

"You need to put any oil in with it or anything?"

"No, don't do anything, just lay it where it'll get good and hot, and it'll turn right greasy. And you put that to your jaw if you got the toothache, to your finger if you got any kind of rise or anything, and to the back of your neck, and I will assure you it will give you relief. I will assure you it will."

A little later I asked him, "So you mean even after doctors and dentists were more available, you still would use these things?"

"Well yes, because they want to, want to numb it, want to numb your jaw. Well, I don't believe in that stuff. If you just let that jaw alone and take that tooth out. About the only time it'll hurt you [is] just when you're putting them clippers on there. Putting the [clippers] on your tooth, that's the last of it. . . . 'Cause I had, the first I ever had pulled out, the fella went and shivered my jawbone, and then I had to go back and let him, you know, probe and get that out of the tooth. That's when I had a time. Just pull mine without it."

The novocaine used by a dentist is removed from nature and is, for Mr. Hatcher, therefore harmful; horseradish leaves, on the other hand, are from nature and are more effective. He values the horseradish on his property to the extent that he said, "I wouldn't get rid of this. I wouldn't take nothing for this. I don't think you're going to find another bunch of, that I know of, nowhere." The use of traditional cures is similar to foodways for him in that they are both ritualistic; both function in Mr. Hatcher's old age in even more important ways than they did in his earlier life.

As much as he practices folk cures, he relies even more on faith healing. "The best remedy is talking to the Father above. I live by faith." Faith healing is a Primitive Baptist ritual that he has experienced directly and about which he tells a personal narrative.[6]

"But I study the Bible more now than any one thing for the past thirty, forty years. I had an experience with that. I, I promised the Lord if He would do one thing for me what I would do, and He done that. And I've done my best to live up to it, what I told him that I would do, and that is—can you see anything on my neck excepting the skin?"

"Uh, where?"

"Anywhere on my neck, anywhere on it."

"No, I can't. What do you—?"

"I really want to make plain to you now. I told that young man about, about what I promised the Lord and what I told Him I'd do and what the Lord done for me. I had a large goiter on my neck, a large one. Couldn't even fasten my shirt over it. And my family all was at home then. Pretty tight times, you know. But I promised the Lord if He, if He wouldn't have mercy on me, and, and remove that, what I would do. And I remember one morning, I never will forget that, that knot went away, to my knowledge it just seemed, it just all just disappeared and went down. I've got a son in his sixty-seventh year, and I've got a daughter that's sixty, but if they were here, they all would witness to what I've told you. They *know* it to be fact. Now, would you doubt a God like that?"

This was a transcendent experience for him, a rite of passage from one stage of life to another, a moment that changed his life forever: "I never will forget that" (Van Gennep 1960; Turner 1977; Clements 1976a; Mullen 1983). As he recalls the experience he relives it. "These numinous moments carry with them their original pristine associations and feelings" (Myerhoff 1984, 327). Recalling such transcendent ritual experiences is especially significant for the elderly because it gives them a sense of a consistent core identity through the changes of time (Myerhoff 1984). Jesse Hatcher was forever altered by his healing; he kept his promise to God, and he became a better Christian. As a sacred experience, it put him into closer contact with nature and the spirit, and further removed him from the secular world.

Mr. Hatcher's membership in a church community has given him support for his beliefs; he has testified about his healing during church services. His relationship with the local church can be likened to an extended family, and his relating of church history is mixed in with family history. His family helped to build the first church, a log building, in 1902. I asked him, "Where did you meet before you had the log cabin?"

"Well, we met out there under a large oak tree, much larger than that [one], a white oak tree. That's where we held service at, and you know we had slab benches, four-legged benches. Split a chesnut log, you know, cut it up so long, eight, ten foot long. Split them, take a auger and bore four holes in them, two in each end, you know, and we cross that, and put trimmed sticks, you know, and put in that for legs. And we sat on that, that is, as many as we could get, and then we'd sit on logs, and a good many sit about on the ground, around a tree, you know."

"How long did the meetings go on outdoors like that?"

"Oh, about three years before we got it completed. You see the top of that little building right down there? Right there. Well, now, right straight down there is a branch, and there set a sawmill down there, among one of the first sawmills that was settled in here—ever. And my grandfather, he had a oxen, we called them steers, you know. Well, there was another old brother up here at the foot of the mountain, and he had one. And so they put them together and they had a yoke of oxen, then, see?"

"Oh yeah."

"All right then. Well, my grandfather owned that land right there just the other side of me right here. Well, he give timber, you know, from one to another, and I recall me and my brother, we were small, and they'd take these oxens and uncouple the wagon and use the two front wheels, the front end, and they'd pull that log up, you know, and put one end of it up on this, these two wheels, you know, the wagon, hook them two steers, and they'd snake them up, what we'd call snaking them out of the woods, all the way, right down there to that sawmill."

"It must have been hard work."

"Oh, people don't know anything about work now. They just don't know anything about work. And then hard work don't hurt a man if you took care of yourself."

"Well, after the church left, moved inside the log cabin, what was next?"

"Well, after we got the building up, of course, covered with boards, you know. Back in them mountains, had fine oak timber, what we call board timber. . . . And so we finally got it, finally got it, you know, the top on it. And it had wide doors, you know, made out of rough oak lumber, and the pulpit, we called it, was just built with four boards, two up here and two across here, this way."

"And then you finally—? So it was a board church?"

"Then, later on then, we built then a weather-boarded church, framed. And then that one, the church began to grow, and at that time, a good many of the younger ones, you see, was coming up. And so we built, then we remodeled that one and made it still larger. And then thirdly we built, lastly then we built the one that was destroyed last year by a storm. And now you see what we are in now."

Although Mr. Hatcher was twelve years old when the log church was built, he remembers it vividly. When he discusses church history, instead of talking about the people—the early preachers and church leaders—he talks about the process of constructing the buildings, going into a long digression on how they "snaked" the logs out of the woods to make timber for the church. This recollection demonstrates again the nature/culture theme. The image of meeting under the large oak tree places the congregation in nature. The emphasis then is on the cultural process whereby nature is transformed into a place of worship, the using of trees from nature to make a spiritually appropriate church building. He describes in detail how logs were made into benches, doors, and the pulpit. Even the image of the oxen suggests a process very close to nature. The emphasis on process suggests mediation again, but this time the gender roles being projected are more traditionally masculine, builders who are interested in the cultural product. The building of the church is a public community activity, and it was engaged in by his male forebears. Since it was his grandfather who used oxen to pull logs for the church, family and church history intertwine.

Family history also involves stories that his parents and grandparents told about slavery.[7] "Some of those stories your parents told you from back in slavery, were there any, was it all kind of bad stuff?"

"Oh no, [but] there was some. Now my grandparents, they never was [traded], they never did exchange hands. Just my grandfather, he exchanged hands from the Smiths to the Hatchers back and forth. But you see he married, my grandmother was, you see, was a Hatcher slave, but that was the way, worked it by some means, you know. Some called him Jerry Hatcher, some called him Jerry Smith, but you see, they belonged. They were freed with the Hatchers, you know, by [them], they went by that name. What a pity. But that's the best we know. I don't hold no grudge against them, but I say that's the best they know. And I guess in one respect, it was better on my people."

"Well, I think it was like you said, it was ignorance on the part of white people."

"That is all. That's the way I look at it. Well, the way I look at it now, but sometime [it] make you get a little sort of ticklish up your back every once in a while," and he laughed.

Later he said, "But to treat them like stock was bad. Now don't you think so? That was bad. Stock." He also talked about the attempts by slaves to learn to read and to escape.

"Now understand it wasn't just only the [white] folks that could read and write. My parents would tell me about how they would steal off in the cabins at night and try to learn how to read. And she said the old mistress would catch the old master out, and she would try to show her mother how [to read] because she was a housegirl, what they call, and she would slip and learn them the alphabet. But now, . . . old man David Hatcher didn't know, unh, unh. If they catch [you] going around the cabins, and you'd be there with a book, you were punished and severely punished too. Yeah. And you know, kind of make you feel a little, to think they're trying to [read]. I've had that to happen right here to me, but you know, not bad."

"If they tried to run away, there was nowhere to get. But anyhow, they would, occasionally they would break away. But when they got them, they would punish them, beat them just unmercifully, and then sometime punish them, put them to work. . . . But, you know, there was nowhere for them to get, you just could go from one plantation to another one, and it was all the same thing, every bit of it was slave. Under slavery, you see, and you had nowhere you could go."

For Jesse Hatcher, slavery as an evil institution was not natural; it was a product of culture. When he says that "in one respect, it was better on my people," he is referring to the fact that his slave ancestors were not sold outside of the region, but were traded between local plantations. Otherwise, his statements are a clear condemnation of the entire system. When I first asked him about slave narratives, he told two personal experience stories that suggest his understanding of slavery as part of the nature / culture dichotomy.

"Do you remember anything they told you about what slavery was like?"

"Oh, they told a whole lot about slavery. I don't like to think about it. Some of it was very sad, you know, but it was done. I considered, I try to consider it was done through ignorance. I'll tell you why I say that. Now you see I rent my land to white and colored too, it don't make no difference. Sometimes I rent it to white, sometimes to colored. But there was a young man, a neighbor of mine lived right over there just across the hill, and he had land over on the other side, right down there on the river. And he had three little children, and of course they'd come here, you know, eat their dinner, stay around here and cool off, you know. And them little children— I didn't have no little children, I had grandchildren. Well, it was just remarkable to see how them little children would roll and tumble and play, and they, they just didn't know anything in the world [about race], they was just children. And me and my wife would talk about it. . . . But it was just remarkable to see them little childrens. You know the way I looked at it. It wasn't in the child, it was in the parents, wasn't it? I remember right back out the road here, a boy that I growed up with, like I was telling you about Harry [another white neighbor], we all just growed up together, and we played and stuff like that. But now, listen, we would do that out here in the yard or anywhere around, but now you go in the house, they went in the house, I stopped. Now just as good a friends, and they would do you any kind of favor, but I stopped, they went in the house." His soft laugh seemed ironic here.

"What about into your house, would they come into your house?"

"Oh yes, yes, yes sir. They'd come into my house, and thought my wife was one among the best cooks they'd ever, well said it was the best chicken pie ever they eat in their lives. They'd just laugh and talk, you know, but that's been years ago, it's been fifty, sixty years ago. That's on back before then. And so I just think about it and how pitiful and how cruel it was."

Black and white children can play together because they are closer to nature; they have not yet learned the prejudices of their parents, who as they grow older get further away from their natural state of innocence. Children are traditionally thought of as being closer to nature, not completely socialized (Ortner 1974, 78); therefore, race prejudice as an adult attitude is associated with culture. Mr. Hatcher's stories also suggest the irony of race relations: the children can play together, but their parents cannot; he was not allowed in his white friends' homes, but they could come into his. The house is a cultural product and associated with the segregation of races; significantly the children are playing outdoors, in nature. The irony seems to be a result of going against our own natural inclinations, of learning attitudes and behavior that are antithetical to the order of nature. This irony becomes even more acute in the way racism influenced church activities.

"We had more white preachers than we did colored, our own people. But we'd go, and we'd sit around, stand around beside a tree, set on logs, you know, and hear them [white ministers] preach. Well, I have wondered, and can either one of you just explain? Wonder what did them ministers, what, do you reckon they ever did read the Bible any? Now just think about it."

We talked a little about how white ministers could interpret the Bible to support their beliefs, and then Mr. Hatcher went on.

"You know, well now, I have always, that is what got me, wonder, do you reckon they really think, you reckon they really thought they [white ministers] were doing right? Now I had an uncle that was a preacher, and now this is back down here in the Hatcher settlement. You know that was a rare thing, he was a slave too; he was my old, yeah he was my oldest uncle, and he was a slave. But he become to be a Primitive Baptist preacher; of course, he couldn't read. But anyhow, the old Hatchers and Mildrens, another old family down there, they wanted to hear Green, that was his name, wanted to hear Green Hatcher preach. And I recall, you walk right out across the mountain over there and went over to Red Bank to hear him preach. And it was just like an association, but all was white excepting him. And a fella Robinson, he was a Primitive Baptist preacher, and treats him just as nice, just as nice. That is before, there weren't no cars then. You know they rode horseback, we walked. Wasn't nothing more than nine, ten miles to church. That wasn't anything at all, just good exercise," he chuckled.

The ironies of racism are implicit in his statements and in his story of Preacher Green Hatcher. The white ministers would preach to black people, but they still had racist ideas. The racist white people wanted to hear a black minister, and they "treats him just as nice." Black and white would both travel to hear a preacher, but whites rode horseback and blacks walked. Mr. Hatcher's tone of incredulity arises from his conviction that the truth is in our nature and should thus be obvious: "You reckon they really thought they were doing right?" To him, the truth is plainly stated in the Bible: "Do you reckon they ever did read the Bible any?"

The Bible also explains the suffering that black people endured during slavery.

"But I tell you, the children of Israel, you know, . . . look how they suffered. But they suffered over 400 years. But we see in the course of time this was ordained [as] it should be. And in the course of time, the Lord just attracted Moses with a bush, and a fire in the bush. . . . And so that's the way it was, you see. We were that way, we were held that way, we didn't know any better."

The history of black and white people in the Blue Ridge is closely intertwined because of slavery; black and white families often had the same names.

"Then, all the families then that you named have been here since slavery times?"

"That's right, on down. Oh yes, all together. Just as the whites, so was the colored, you see. When we were turned aloose, some of the older masters—slave owners—they would give a slave a little plot of land."

Later he told of an experience that indicates that the relationships of blacks and whites on a local basis are still bound up with family.

"But after all, all the Hatchers now, we have a cemetery down here, and they have a large plaque for their slaves. And I tell my people here—we're short of land, and our cemetery's not large enough, and it's hard to buy any more—and I told them I wasn't worried about it because I had a burial ground." He laughed. "Any of the Hatchers can be buried down there."

"Family burial ground."

"Yeah. They keep it way up, keep it up real well, and they got the Hatcher plaque, that is [for] their slaves. They recognize us now. I was over here in Mt. Airy one day, and I gave a check. And there was a [white] lady standing there, I wasn't paying any attention, and she was standing there, and she kept looking at me and just kept a looking at the check. And when I went out of the store, she come right out after me. She said, 'Which one of the Hatchers are you?' And I told her. But she says, 'I'm a Hatcher,' says, 'you're my folks.' That's the way they claim. Any of the Hatchers, yeah. And I mean they speak to you too. And so she was telling me about the plaque that they had put up, asking me had I been down and looked at it. And she, whenever any of the old Hatchers passes, they always prepares for their black folks, right there with them. They're real nice, but yet we were just slaves and we couldn't help ourselves."

This reminds me of Faulkner's fictional account of the McCaslin family in *Go Down, Moses* (1942): blacks and whites in the south are bound together through generations. The meaning for Mr. Hatcher is similar to the meaning for Faulkner: despite the existence of suffering, racism, and hate, the ideal of interconnectedness as expressed through the metaphor of family gives some small sense of hope for race relations in America. Mr. Hatcher's emphasis on the interconnectedness theme places him with other elderly people, and is similar to Mollie Ford's concern with race relations as an expression of interconnectedness.

The rhetoric through which Jesse Hatcher articulates his major ordering themes is also similar to Mollie Ford's: they both use scriptural allusion to support their major points and second person address, "you see," to draw the listener into the performance (Bauman 1984; Briggs 1985). In addition, Mr. Hatcher uses imagery, concrete details, contrast, and an emphasis on process to effectively present his message. He cites the Bible several times: the balm of Gilead reference to reinforce the healing powers of balm of Gilead salve, a comparison between the children of Israel and black slaves to explain the sufferings of slaves, and New Testament verse to support the concept of being born again. When he wants to make sure his listener is paying attention to the performance, he says such things as, "Man, ain't you read all this?" "Did any of you ever see horseradish?" "Just looky there." "Now just think about it." "Now you understand?" and "You see?" As with Mollie Ford's use of "you," this is a reminder that a mesage is being given, highlighting it by saying in effect, "pay attention."

Jesse Hatcher uses concrete visual imagery throughout the conversation; this is perhaps his most effective rhetorical device. The major images are, of course, from nature: the balm of Gilead tree standing in his front yard, the big white oak tree under which the church congregation met, the cluster of grapes, and black and white children rolling and tumbling in play. Some images depict the cultural process of transforming nature for human use: the oxen snaking the logs out of the woods, making the benches and pulpit, frying horse-radish leaves as a cure, pulling fodder off the corn, and making the glass of peach preserves. Although he often went into long digressions that did not seem relevant to a story, he was following a pattern; the digression used detailed concrete images of process to help the listener visualize the underlying abstract point.

Mr. Hatcher, in telling about church history, concentrated on the building process: "four-legged benches. Split a chestnut log, you know, cut it up so long, eight, ten foot long. Split them, take a auger and bore four holes in them, you know, and we cross that, and put trimmed sticks, you know, and put in that for legs. And we sat on that." These images of process fit the theme of the story; the church is close to nature since both are based in the spiritual realm, and humans have to use nature, turn it into a concrete representation of that spirit. Thus, his rhetoric also emphasizes the importance of mediation between nature and culture.

The other rhetorical device he uses extensively is contrast, and this fits neatly with the underlying nature/culture dichotomy that runs through his discourse. Contrast is explicit in his discussion of folk medicine: "And that will heal a cut quicker than a doctor's medicine." He contrasts the horseradish cure for toothache with the dentist's novocaine. He contrasts the natural play of black and white children with the learned prejudicial behavior of their parents, and the way of life in the country with that in the city. Finally, he contrasts religious life with secular life: "And you know there's a better way to live." He is not as self-conscious as Mollie Ford about teaching a lesson, but the presence of these rhetorical devices is an indication that his discourse is a teaching performance, and that like her, he is an elderly person with something valuable to teach the young.

One final image, which I have not dealt with until now, kept recurring in his speech: his wife who has been dead for a number of years remains a strong presence in his life. His bond with her in life was so close that death could not sever it. They shared a secular and sacred relationship; they helped each other in household activities, and they had both been "born again." Their closeness may account for the ease with which he seems to have assumed the more expressive feminine role associated with old age. Mrs. Hatcher was a model of the ideal spiritual person, more so than anyone he knew in his lifetime.

When I asked him about his conversion, his response included a reference to his wife.

"When did that [religious conversion experience] happen to you?"

"Years ago. Me and my wife both. I believe I told you about the incidents, you know we both have the same name, same initials, same birthday, same month. You ever hear of that? Yeah. We never had a [quarrel], never had a quarrel in fifty-five years. My name is Jess Lee, her name was Jennie Lee. My birthday is the twenty-second of February, her birthday is the twenty-second of February," he chuckled. "That's what you'll find in these woods around the foot of the Blue Ridge." We all laughed.

"So both of you had your religious experiences at the same time?"

"Oh yes. Lord, young man, you ought to have heard my wife talking before she went away. What I mean, she'd talk to anybody come, white, black, rich, poor, anybody'd come, she'd tell you where she was going. And do you know when she went away, it was just me and her. I was the only one there, just me and her, just me and her when she went away. You talk about a trying experience, and trying. You know, a lot of people they talk about I can't do this, can't do that. Oh don't say you can't do that, you just don't know. You just ain't tried. That's what it is. Whenever it comes around your way, you'll do it, won't you?" He laughed again.

Being alone with her at the moment of her death was a ritual experience for him, one of those transcendent moments that provide "connectedness to the present and to the collective, even sacred symbols of the culture" (Myerhoff 1984, 321). Jesse Hatcher feels that his connection with his wife is mystical; having the same initials and same birthday is related to the fact that they never had a quarrel in fifty-five years of marriage. Somehow the place they lived, at the foot of the Blue Ridge, is also connected to their marital bliss; perhaps this arises out of his conviction that in this location they are closer to nature and thus closer to a spiritual realm. His wife is clearly a spiritual person; she embodies the ideal of interconnectedness: "she'd talk to anybody come, white, black, rich, poor." She had a sense of her own spiritual destiny: "she'd tell you where she was going," and she appears to have accepted death as a part of life although her death was very difficult for him. "You talk about a trying experience." His use of "she went away" instead of saying "she died" is not a euphemism, but rather it represents his religous views. She has gone away to another level of existence; she is not dead, and he will join her someday. It is this knowledge that helped him to survive the trying experience of her death. "Oh don't say you can't do that, you just don't know. You just ain't tried."

NOTES

1. For more on religion in southern Appalachia, see Brewer and Weatherford 1962; Jones 1977; Sutton 1977, 1988; Titon 1988; Titon and George 1978; Tyson, Peacock, and Patterson 1988; and Mullen 1983. For folk religion in America, see Yoder 1974; Titon 1978; and Clements 1983. The Primitive Baptist church is well established in the Blue Ridge among both blacks and whites; the Progressive Primitive Baptists are an offshoot formed by blacks who wanted to have Sunday school as part of their meetings.

2. Also see Levi-Strauss 1969a, 1969b.

3. Recent folklore foodways studies include Jones, Giuliano and Krell 1981; Camp 1982, 1989; and Brown and Mussell 1984.

4. Relevant works on folk medicine include Hand 1976, 1980; and Hufford 1977, 1983.

5. Brown numbers refer to Wayland D. Hand, ed. 1961, 1964. *Popular Beliefs and Superstitions from North Carolina,* vols. 6 and 7 of *The Frank C. Brown Collection of North Carolina Folklore,* edited by Newman Ivey White. Durham: Duke University Press.

6. On faith healing, see Clements 1977b, 1983; Gopalan and Nickerson 1973; and Mullen 1983.

7. For a historical background of slavery, see Genovese 1974, Joyner 1984, and Levine 1977. For other examples of slave narratives, see Botkin 1945; and Perdue, Barden, and Phillips 1976.

3

Mamie and Leonard Bryan
Looking Back on Sixty-Three Years of Marriage

Mamie and Leonard Bryan, a black couple who live on a farm in the Blue Ridge Mountains of North Carolina, have been married for sixty-three years. When I interviewed them in 1978 (one other person, Boris Weintraub, a reporter for the Washington *Star*, was present; he only spoke once during the interview), I wondered if they recalled details of their courtship after so many years. The first question I asked them as we sat down on their front porch was, "When did you first meet?"

Mr. Bryan replied, "We been together a long time."

Mrs. Bryan, thinking her husband might not have heard me, repeated the question, "He asked you how did you first meet?"

"How did we?"

"I don't know."

Mr. Bryan suddenly remembered, laughed, and began the courtship story. "There used to be an old poorhouse up here, and her and her Mammy, and she had a sister that'd been to that poorhouse. And I'd been to White Plains to a meeting, and I met them coming in the road, her and her sister and her Mammy. And told her Mammy— she's fourteen years old—I says now—"

Mrs. Bryan corrected him, "No, I was nine years old."

"Just nine?"

"Wait a minute, I was nine years old when you met me."

He continued, "Yeah. I told her, I told her Mammy, I says, 'You see this one here?' She says, 'Yeah.' I says, 'I want you to give me her for my wife.' I says, 'I want this one for my wife.' She's just nine years old. And she says, 'Alright,' says, 'You can have her.' And boy, I never did forget it. And I just kept working, I was always thinking about her. Went to West Virginia, back over in there working. I, I, I, and I'd come back in to see her, and she'd just soothe me. And boy, sure enough I got her. Now, I told her when she was nine years old that I wanted her. The good Lord sure must've fixed that for me. Yes sir. I'll tell you, when He puts two together, buddy, they'll stay. When He joins two together, they'll stay. Now, I married when I was twenty-one, and she was about fifteen, wasn't you?"

"Along about sixteen."

"And look how long we been married. And I think as much of her today—or more—than I did when I married her."

"We married the first day of May, 1915," she added.

"Yeah. And I could eat her when I married her; now she's getting too old, I can't eat her." He laughed uproariously.

I asked, "Well, what happened between the time you saw her when she was nine and the time you got married?"

She answered this time, "Well, he stayed in West Virginia all the time, and I stayed back here."

"I stayed in West Virginia mostly all the time."

"Now he stayed in West Virginia near all his life."

"Then after I married her, I stayed with her here about a month or two, then I went to West Virginia. I just bought this farm, and then I went to West Virginia and stayed *twelve months* before I ever come back home."

"I ought to have left him right then." We all laughed.

"Ah, you couldn't leave me."

A few minutes later, I asked him, "You didn't see her in between that time she was nine and fifteen?"

"No," she replied for him.

"No. I didn't see her and, no I didn't see her at all, did I?"

"No, he stayed in West Virginia."

"I stayed in West Virginia."

"And then, when he did come out, we got married."

"I wouldn't hardly know her. And when I come home, why, I told my brother I wanted to go see these two girls, and he says, 'Alright,' says, 'I'll go with you up there.' That was her brother, and he lived

3. Mamie and Leonard Bryan. (Photograph by the author, BR8-3-20398 / 24.

over here, and he was here and I was in West Virginia. He carried me up there, and I showed him which one I picked out. I knowed her just as soon as I seen her. Her and her sister was—I knowed just the one. She was standing there rubbing an old coal Thomas stove, had a rod to it. And she'd put in some cornbread, and she's just setting there rubbing that stove with it. She wouldn't let me see that cornbread; she took it and throwed it out."

"I never did."

He laughed. "Cooked biscuits after I went," he said, and laughed again.

I asked him, "You didn't like cornbread?"

"Sure. I was raised on cornbread. I loved it."

"How come you threw out the cornbread then?"

"I didn't throw it out," she explained, "I just started back, and my mother told me to bake biscuits, says go ahead and bake biscuits; what we had to eat, we wanted biscuits."

My opening question brought about the telling of a story that can be seen as part of a mutual life review, a review by both partners in a married life. Although I elicited the courtship story, it started a process in which they both spontaneously told stories from their life experiences, some of which were also told in family contexts, not just during an interview. The life review is an important concept in the study of aging, yet it has not been applied to a married couple reviewing their lives together. From the perspective of sixty-three years, Leonard and Mamie Bryan looked back to the beginning of their relationship and sorted through a variety of events that made up their lives indicating ways they have changed and ways they have remained the same.

The courtship story is obviously personal, but at the same time it is traditional, an expression of courtship patterns of the early twentieth century and an indication of cultural values and ideals regarding courtship (Mullen 1981, Zeitlin 1980). Their courting takes place within community and family contexts, on the way back from a meeting and at home. The story depicts an ideal courtship: they may have had private moments, but these are not mentioned because they may be considered improper.

Other kinds of folk expressions from the Appalachian region, such as Anglo-American love songs and ballads, reflect an idealized view of love and courtship (Belden and Hudson 1952; Davis 1929), and the Bryans' courtship narrative seems to be part of this tradition. The idealization of love is widespread in folklore, popular culture, and literature and is ultimately based on conventions of medieval courtly love (Lewis 1936). Some of the elements of courtly love which are found in courtship customs and narratives depend upon gender roles. The woman is presented as an untouchable object of desire to be pursued from a distance until her heart has been won and the marriage takes place. She plays her part by not committing herself, and he plays his by having perseverance and dedication in his pursuit. These idealized elements are maintained to varying extents in the Bryans' story. There is love at first sight on his part; he is so smitten that he cannot forget her. Mrs. Bryan was young at the time, but she could be thought of as playing a role since her passivity fulfills cultural expectations. Also as a very young girl she fits the ideal of virginity. The description of her striking physical beauty made her an appropriate object of desire according to cultural standards.

The Bryans' courtship story relates directly to the larger cultural context, but the story also reveals the individuals involved; it tells us something about their relationship and the way they view their married life. In order to interpret the personal meanings, we must view the narratives within the specific performance context of the interview. The story projects an ideal of courtship and marriage, but since it is being told from the perspective of sixty-three years of married life, the experiences of that life affect the way they view their courtship. Dual narrating takes place so that two perspectives are presented, and the two points of view are sometimes in conflict: a state of tension exists in the storytelling event. There are disagreements about dates, ages, and specific details (more on this later), but there is also conflict about the ideal of love itself.

Mamie and Leonard Bryan do not agree consistently on the ideal: Mr. Bryan holds onto it in his narrating, but Mrs. Bryan interjects contrary opinions. He emphasizes his certainty about his choice of her at such an early age and offers the longevity of their marriage as proof of the correctness of his decision; their marriage exemplifies the ideal. From his point of view their marriage was ordained in heaven, and his narration never brings in any element to contradict the ideal. Mrs. Bryan, on the other hand, sees their relationship more realistically, acknowledging problems and conflicts in the courtship and marriage.

Later in the interview, I tried to determine exactly what her attitude toward their courtship was by asking her, "Well, what'd you think of him when you first saw him?"

"I don't know. I was too young to know much. So now we went to get the license, and the license man wouldn't let him have them. Told him no, I was too young. Couldn't get no license, had to go see Mama. Didn't have no license."

I persisted, "Well, what about, uh, when you saw him later, what'd you think of him then?"

"Well, I don't know, I's just, I's just too young to know much about it. You take a girl way back then, I was young, just fifteen years old."

"So?"

"I just married."

Mr. Bryan interjected, "Oh, she liked me; she wouldn't take nothing for me. She wouldn't."

I asked him, "Even back then, huh?"

"No," he laughed.

"How do you know? I mighta just sat there."

He seemed to ignore her comment by saying, "Boy, I sure have had a time all my life. The good Lord has blessed me."

But she returned to the topic, "We had a, I had a lot of boyfriends, and he was afeared I'd get married before he got me. That was the reason he came home. He should have stayed away."

Her contrary opinions are not part of the self-contained narrative; they were only given at my insistent questioning, but they give another picture of courtship in addition to his idealized story. Back then, she followed the traditional passive role of the woman, but from the perspective of sixty-three years later, she seems to have grown somewhat dissatisfied with it.

His working in West Virginia while she stayed in North Carolina seems to have been a central conflict in their marriage. Not only was he gone for the first year of their marriage, he continued to work in the West Virginia mines for thirty-two years. In their behavior, they followed the traditional gender roles of the society: she was "expressive" in staying home and attending to the children, and he was "instrumental" in going away from home to work. Details of this period of their lives are important to an understanding of their relationship and their concept of it.

"When I first went to the coalfields I believe I was fourteen years old."

"Thirteen."

"Huh?"

"Thirteen."

"Thirteen?"

"With your brother Lester."

"No, Emment Choate carried me."

"I thought your brother Lester."

"Emment Choate carried me to the coalfields when I was thirteen or fourteen years old. And he got me a job on the coke yards, got a mule and a cart. He got me a job on the coke yards, a mule, and I had a mule to drive a cart, to haul brick and ashes to these men that was building the coke yard. And I was getting me a dollar and a half a day. Boy, way back then, boy that was money. Dollar and a half a day, that was money. Sure was." He laughed. "They give me dollar and a half a day. But boy that was money then."

I asked him, "How come you first went to West Virginia?"

"I went to make money, to live. You know my mother stayed here with me then, then I wasn't married. Mother stayed here with me, and I'd leave her and go there to work to make money to help pay for my farm and first thing and another. I just bought ten acres of land there the first time, and then when I got it paid for I bought about twenty-five or thirty more, more acres just joined it. That put me more in debt, and I had to get out to pay for it."

"Couldn't find a job to make any money here in North Carolina?" I asked.

"No. Didn't have no jobs, they didn't have nothing around here really."

"And he had three brothers to take care of," Mrs. Bryan emphasized.

"Yeah. And didn't have no jobs, didn't have no factories or nothing." She added, "And his father died."

He continued, "Just make it on the farm, or just work for these here big farmers, had big farms. They'd give us fifty, seventy-five cents a day to help them. And boy that was big money. I worked for twenty-five cents a day. Down here at Frank Falk's when I first commenced to hiring out, worked for twenty-five cents a day. This is a new world from what it used to be."

"Yeah. Well, when you went over to West Virginia, how long did you stay the first time?"

"It was about three or four months, and then I come back and go back again. I'd go in the winter time and stay, then summer I'd come here and farm, raise corn, wheat, and stuff. Then gather up in the fall of the year, I'd pack my old suitcase and go back to West Virginia work that winter. And when you come back the next spring, I'd come back and do the same. Boy, what a time I've had. But the good Lord, 'Len, I'll let you pull through if you go back what you have out there.' No, and I knowed I'd pull through. I wouldn't want to go. I've had such a time. . . . Going and coming, wife back here, my mother back here, and I just had to stay out there to make it, to get things so that I could pay out."

I asked, "Well, how often would you come home after you got married?"

"Let's see, when I first left I stayed a year before I come back. And then when I come back home, I bought me an old Model T

Ford car, and then I bought that old car, I'd come home every two weeks. I stayed that year. I'd come home every two weeks. Come home on Saturday nights, come out of the mines at one or two o'clock, take a bath, get my old car, and by daylight I was here at home, waking up Mamie, hollering at her." He laughed. "And I stayed till Sunday evening about three or four o'clock, and I'd hit the ball back. I'd rather take a whipping than to live [like that]. The Lord stood right by me. Boy, I've been well blessed. Never had no wrecks on the road. The good Lord helped to [keep] that coal—that old slate— up off of me. I've been here a long time. You take, you take eighty-seven years, there's a long time."

Economic conditions forced him to lead a hard and disagreeable occupational life, but his religious faith enabled him to endure it and to look back on it now with acceptance. Mrs. Bryan's interjections— "And his father died" "And he had three brothers to take care of"— suggest that she understands the circumstances that led to the disruption of their married life, but this does not mean that she was happy about it. I asked her, "Mrs. Bryan, how did you feel about that, about him having to work over there?"

"There wasn't nothing I could do about it. He just stayed out there. After we married I stayed here and took care of the children. We had, well we had six children; we lost three of them. We had, a boy, two boys and one girl, we lost them, and we had a team of mules, milk cows. Somebody had to take care of that stuff, so I stayed here and took care of it."

"Well, you couldn't do anything about it, but how did you feel about it?"

"How would you feel if your husband was in the mines, expecting them to tell you any time he was dead?"

"I wouldn't like it."

"Nobody wouldn't like it."

"That's what I thought."

"Every time you'd hear any news, you'd be scared to death, scared that one of them had been blowed up in the mines."

Her statement here seems to summarize her position in the family and in the culture: "There wasn't nothing I could do about it." At the same time, there is a sense that Mrs. Bryan realizes the importance of her role: "Somebody had to take care of that stuff, so I stayed here and took care of it." This is in keeping with a pattern in elderly women's attitudes noted by Myerhoff: women's work may be seen as unglamorous, trivial, and transient, but women still recognize the value of their conventional roles, although they may not communicate it directly (1978, 267). The elderly women Myerhoff worked with communicated a "quiet conviction and satisfaction with themselves" as they looked back on their lifework (1978, 268). This, I think, describes Mrs. Bryan's attitude perfectly. She was quiet and self-effacing, expressing a sense of her accomplishments only when directly asked. She might express it more readily in family contexts or with other women. As part of her life review, this awareness of her significance as nurturer of the children and caretaker of the family farm is an important part of her mental health in old age.

She did express her resentment at her husband's absence, and related it to men's behavior in general by pulling me into the discussion on a personal level.

She asked me at one point, "Are you married?"

"Yes ma'am. My wife's in Ohio; that's where we live. She came, visited me for a week, and then she went back home."

"You mean you don't stay with her either?"

"Oh yeah, I do."

"You're just like Len, you stay out. He stayed out."

We all laughed.

"You know I ain't got no use for these men that won't stay home," she added.

I meekly replied, "I know."

But Mr. Bryan defended men, "Sometimes they can't stay home, can they? They have to work and get out and get jobs, and sometimes that job just won't let them stay at home all the time. Just can't do it."

As with their courtship story, Leonard and Mamie Bryan's talking about their married life reveals different attitudes; they offer two different versions of the story. He is more positive and forthcoming about expressing his views; she seems more reluctant, but when she does state her more negative view, she does so forcefully. In giving two different accounts of their marriage, they follow a widespread pattern recognized in sociological research and summarized by Jessie

Bernard as "his marriage" and "her marriage." Researchers "have found that when they ask husbands and wives identical questions about the union, they often get quite different replies" (Bernard 1972, 5). "There is a very considerable research literature reaching back over a generation which shows that: more wives than husbands report marital frustration and dissatisfaction; more report negative feelings . . . [and] marital problems . . . [and] have considered separation or divorce . . ." (1972, 26–27). Mamie Bryan's negative attitude could spring from the same general reasons Bernard offers to explain the pattern: going into the marriage she had high expectations and was disenchanted by the actuality. She had to make greater adjustments in terms of her self-image, including the difficult adjustment to the occupation of "housewife" (1972, 37–53). Mrs. Bryan's statements during the interview support this interpretation. Another factor was her inability to change the conditions of the marriage; the culture expected her to accept the expressive role of staying home, raising the children, and doing domestic farm work while he was away. The hard economic times in the region suggest that Mr. Bryan also did not have much choice; however, his time in West Virginia also fulfills a cultural double standard. This was viewed as a time of male freedom for him; he spoke of being "wild" in his younger days, of attending dances and getting into fights when he was working in West Virginia.

The marriage is even more complex than this though: she is not a victim; she negotiated for power so that it grew during the course of the marriage. In this gaining of power, she follows a pattern identified by anthropologists: "As men and women age, their relationships vis-à-vis each other are gradually transformed, and overt power as often as not increasingly masks the locus of other kinds of authority and control" (Myerhoff and Simic 1978, 237). Being left in charge of the farm for long periods of time was one source of power that was there almost from the beginning. She was also the main parent in the raising of the children. According to Myerhoff and Simic, "The roles of men and women are determined not only by formal position, but are also the product of sentiment and happenstance, and in each are embedded different kinds of power" (1978, 239). For instance, men might control property and women have control over the children; however, the power relationship can change and one partner could gain power as the other loses it (240). Mamie

Bryan maintained power in running the farm and rearing the children, and she also had a say in the ownership of property.

Leonard Bryan told me, "I sold all the land, just kept the—well, I sold the house and everything. The old woman wanted the house back; I bought the house back, and this lot all around the house here and the sheds out yonder, I just bought them back. Mamie wasn't satisfied till she got them back. Just the house, I bought it back."

Mrs. Bryan added, "Well I had some children, and some in Jarrodsville, and I got some in Baltimore, and I decided that we should let this house stand as a summer home, so that if anything happens to me and Len, if we was to pass out, why, the children might want to come in here, you know, as a summer home. And they could come in here on a vacation. It'd be nice for them to have a home."

The areas of her power are clearly defined here: in her old age she has assumed the authority to decide about property because it impinges on her area of expressive responsibility concerning the children. Note that she says "*I* had some children" and not "*We* had some children." Again, this indicates a way that elderly women have traditionally gained power. Men are traditionally outside of the home while the children are growing up, and women come to be recognized as responsible for how the children turn out (Myerhoff 1978, 266). It is Mrs. Bryan's concern for maintaining a home for the family that prompts her to assert her authority. She was the one who kept a home all of those years he was away, and now she is assuring that a home will be there for the children even after she and Mr. Bryan are dead.

The folk traditions they share also reveal the negotiation of power within the marriage and how this changed as they grew older; in fact, most of the patterns of their relationship are reflected in their discussion of planting signs, slave narratives, stories about race relations, and in conversion and other religious personal experience narratives. I asked them about planting by the signs of the Zodiac (Barker 1957; Passin and Bennett 1943) because this belief system is so widely found in the Blue Ridge.

"Did you use the signs, planting signs, like—?"

"Yeah," Mr. Bryan responded, "most of the time, most of the time."

Mrs. Bryan said, "Nobody don't go by signs but me."

"She'd tell me, you know, and I'd plant."

She said, "Plant my garden, set my flowers, and things like that I go by signs."

He said, "I go to plant my corn, I say, 'Mamie, where are the signs?' She'd go get the old almanac there, say, 'It's a good time now. Plant.' And say, 'Oh, the signs is so and so, bugs are up, better wait.' And I'd wait until she told me to go, and then I'd go plant. Some people wouldn't pay no attention to signs, but there's a whole lot in them signs. Did you ever try it?"

"No," I answered.

Leonard Bryan continued, "A whole lot. Sometime you plant in the secrets, some bugs and things will eat you up, work on it. And you plant in the right time, and they wouldn't touch it. Whole lot in them signs. Now, I never did go by them until she got to going by them, then I'd tell her look, and then I'd plant."

She explained, "Well, you had to keep the bugs and the worms, if you don't they'll eat it out" [Brown #8342].

I asked her, "What almanac do you use?"

"The Blum's" [Barker 1957].

"Where do you get it?"

"Well, it comes from Winston. I just buy it up here at the store. They bring them in here."

Mr. Bryan added, "They buy them up here at Sparta."

"But it's made in Winston?" I asked.

"We used to could get them there Blum's Almanacs for a dime," he commented. "Now they've gone up to seventy-five cents. Yeah."

"The last one I saw was a dollar," I remarked.

"Yeah. See. It just keeps going up. And you used to get them for a dime."

"Your garden right now, did you plant it by the signs?"

"Yeah."

Mrs. Bryan agreed, "Ever foot of it planted by the signs."

"Well, what were some of them that you used?"

"Well, I use cancer, signs in the cancer [Brown #7995]. In the head."

"For what?"

"The twins. I planted cucumbers when the signs in the twins" [Brown #7994, #8167].

"What about corn?"

"When the sign's in the cancer [Brown #8125]. And on new of the moon."

"And beans?"

"I plant all my beans by cancer [Brown #8069]. Signs in the thighs. I don't plant nothing when the sign's in the heart. Potatoes, they'll be ripe, they'll be hollow all the way through if you plant when the sign's in the heart."

"So you've tried it, and it works."

"Yes, I've tried it, I've tried it all." She laughed and said, "See, I'm pretty old." He laughed.

"How old are you?"

"I'm seventy-eight, seventy-nine. I'm seventy-nine years old."

"So you've tried it without the signs just to see what would happen."

"Yeah, I've tried it. You have to try different signs, didn't do well, dig it up, and plant again."

"How did you learn about the signs?"

"My mother and my grandmother, old folks. Len's mother."

"So they all used to do it, and you've just been carrying it on."

"Yeah."

Leonard and Mamie Bryan believe in the efficacy of planting signs, but Mrs. Bryan is the family bearer of knowledge concerning the Zodiac; Mr. Bryan defers to her expertise. "Nobody don't go by signs but me," she said, and he responded, "She'd tell me, you know, and I'd plant." You would think that a farmer who believed in the signs would know the details of their application. Why is his wife the main bearer of tradition in an area that is at the heart of his occupational life? Her testimony that she learned the signs from her grandmother, mother, and her husband's mother suggests that it is a female tradition; however, my research in the Blue Ridge indicates that men and women equally believe and practice planting by the signs. Either the husband or the wife will take responsibilty for learning when to plant what. Mrs. Bryan learned the system because her husband was away working in the coal mines. She has taken over responsibility and gained power in the relationship over the years because "happenstance" created a "vacuum" that had to be filled (Myerhoff and Simic 1978, 239–40).

In knowledge of signs, Mrs. Bryan is clearly the dominant person in the relationship because of her experience. In terms of historical knowledge of slavery they are equally informed. The parents and grandparents of both passed on information about the conditions of slavery. Mr. Bryan's mother was born after emancipation, but she told him about slavery.

"She did talk about it. I heard her tell that way back yonder how the old people pray, they wouldn't let them pray; they had to slip out, steal away and pray; if they didn't, they'd whip them. Old slaves."

Mrs. Bryan mentioned her grandmother, who was a slave, "That's what Grandma always said."

Mr. Bryan continued, "They'd slip out anyhow. If they caught them praying, they'd land on them. I heard Ma tell it, but Ma wasn't a slave."

Mrs. Bryan said, "Praying for the world to change. It sure changed, didn't it?"

I agreed, "It sure did. You mean they wouldn't let them have church?"

She answered, "No, oh no. They wouldn't do nothing but work."

He agreed, "Unh unh, way back yonder, unh unh."

"What else did you hear? Do you recall anything else that parents or grandparents said about slavery?"

Mrs. Bryan said, "Yeah. They sold their children. They'd take women, my Grandma said, they'd take their children. . . . They'd take their children, and they'd sell them. That they raised children, they raised children by them, and then they'd sell them. Sell them off at auctions, just have them up on blocks and things, and just sell them off on auction. It's awful. I don't like to think about it."

Mr. Bryan added, "Well, they'd sell a man and a woman too, put them both up on blocks."

She said, "Yeah, they sold them."

A few minutes later, Mrs. Bryan said, "Lord, I don't like, I don't even like to think about it, but I've heard it. Sat down on the floor flat, and hear my Grandma sit and tell it. She was old, she was awful old, my grandmother was."

"And she would talk about slavery?" I asked.

"Yes, she'd tell us younguns about them a praying, they would be a praying for the Lord to fix the world so their children and their grandchildren wouldn't have to go through what they went through with. Well, see the Lord changed [it]."

Mr. Bryan interjected, "He fixed it too, didn't He?"

"The Lord changed it," Mamie Bryan added.

"He heard their prayers, He fixed it."

"And if they caught them a praying, said if they go out to pray and they caught them a praying, they'd whip them for it. This world, this world's been something. Now this world has been something."

Mr. Bryan came back to the difference between whether God "fixed" or "changed" the world. "See, it hasn't been the world, Mamie, this world's like it's always been. It ain't never changed, but the people the ones that's changed. The world, in this world, it never has changed. God never has changed the world. It's the people in the world. That's right."

"Well I said God changed it all," Mamie Bryan disagreed. "He changed it."

"He fixed it," said Leonard Bryan, getting the last word in. "He fixed the world that start just like it is now."

They may disagree on a theological interpretation, but they agree on all of the facts concerning the conditions of life under slavery. On this topic they shared equally in the interview; neither deferred to the other. Both of them are descended from slaves; both heard slave narratives from older family members, and both think that as painful as this knowledge is, it is important to remember and pass it on. Talking about slavery is one way they maintain continuity with their own cultural past. Two remembered images are especially vivid: slaves slipping away to pray and being sold on auction blocks. One small difference in their testimony is apparently based on gender. As a mother, Mrs. Bryan emphasized the fact that children were sold away from their mothers, and Mr. Bryan added that men and women were sold too. The image of slaves praying is strong for both of them because of their deep religious convictions. An implied religious moral of their discussion of slavery is that God helped the slaves endure hardships, and that if God had not changed or fixed the world, black people might still be in slavery.

Their emphasis on dependency on God could suggest that the Bryans are simply accomodationists who do not believe in resistance to racism; however, the stories they tell about race relations indicate that they advocate personal action as a response to bigotry. Mr. Bryan told a story about his father.

"But the people are so much different way back yonder than they are now. Why, a colored man, I used to—my daddy, and they used to couldn't hardly go up here in Sparta, what the white folks would run them out. Had to call them coloreds, you know, wouldn't allow them to go into Sparta. I saw, I saw my old Daddy grease his pistol and rub it up and grease it up and work it and put cartridges in it. And say, 'I'm going into town today.' And he had a buddy, Rufe Brown would come up and go with him, and Rufe Brown, he had a double-barreled shotgun. He'd put it on his shoulder, and then Pa and Rufe Brown would go to Sparta. And boy there's two they wouldn't fool with. They knowed death was coming." He laughed, "They didn't mess with my Daddy and Rufe Brown. They knowed death is coming. They wouldn't try to run them out of town either. They knowed if they did what they'd get; Pa—my daddy—and Rufe, they had lots of good white folks too would stand by them. Yes sir, they wouldn't tackle them, they knew it would be too bad."

His personal reminiscence of his father has the qualities of a hero legend; here is a man who stands up for his rights, and Mr. Bryan clearly admires him for it. His father is a hero whose values and actions should be emulated by other black men. He was ready to fight prejudiced whites, but he also maintained friendships with whites who treated him fairly, the "good white folks" who "would stand by them." Even in this confrontational story, the possibility for interconnectedness between the races exists. Even though this story is about Mr. Bryan's father, it can still be thought of as a part of his life review since it establishes continuity with his family past. His identification with his father is strong, so that telling the story reinforces his own attitudes toward racism and his own identity as a black man. Another story he told makes racial harmony the central theme.

Mr. Bryan started out, "We raised, we raised a boy here. [From the way they speak of him, I concluded that he was not one of their sons but a child they took in.] I bought him a guitar."

"I bought it," Mrs. Bryan corrected him. "I had to buy it."

"Didn't I help you?"

"No, you wouldn't help me. You helped me buy the gun, rifle."

He continued, "I know we bought him a guitar, and two white boys up here at White Plains. . . . They run with him. We raised a boy here. He was born here, and we raised him. And he got with these Sexton boys, and these white folks would have music and have dances. Larry would go with these two Sexton boys and go help make music. And I was afraid that he would get in trouble, but he never did. Them there boys took care of him just the same as [if] he was just as white as they was. They'd go together and make music up here in town, and around everywhere they'd have dances. Larry would go right with these two white boys [and] help make music. And they never, Larry never did get in no trouble. They stuck right by him. White folks liked him."

Mrs. Bryan said, "They stayed [here], he stayed there; when he wasn't there, they was here. They stayed together nearly all of the time."

He went on, "Yeah, they'd come here and play. And even if they had a dance, Larry and them'd go together. I love to see, I love to see white folks and colored folks get along with one another. I always did. I never did believe in no fighting and a messing."

Mrs. Bryan said, "They have to get along cause there ain't but the one heaven."

Mr. Bryan agreed, "That's right."

She said, "They've got to get along. If they don't get along here, they ain't gonna be together when they leave here."

"That's right."

"Now that's the truth. There ain't but the one, two places, two places to go to, just choose, no matter the one you want."

"Lord, white folks is a sight better now than they used to be here. White folks was awful hard on the colored folks around here. When they would see them. Had to go to town, but Lord, they had a terrible name. They'd say, 'Yonder's a nigger, yonder's a nigger.'" He laughed.

She said, "A lot of them says it now."

"No they don't. I ain't heard one say 'nigger' now in—"

"A lot of them still says it."

"—I don't know—if they do, they don't let you hear it."

"I've heard it. They catch themselves."

The fact that Mr. Bryan remembered buying the guitar and Mrs. Bryan says that she bought it is revealing. People have a tendency to remember things the way they want them to be if the actuality counters their present world view. "Psychologists who study memory have come to emphasize that it is a constructive process. Long-term memories in particular appear to be creations that depict what happened after a remembered event as much as or even more than the event itself" (Kotre 1984, 142). The fact that long-term memory is especially susceptible to this process makes it relevant to the study of elderly reminiscence and life review. The tendency toward constructive memory is complicated by the fact that in a married relationship the spouse is there to correct these alterations of memory. In Mr. Bryan's case, after the event took place and a story was made about it, the guitar became an image of interconnectedness between the races music brought the white and black boys together. At the time that the boy wanted the guitar, however, it did not have this meaning for Mr. Bryan, and he refused to pay for it. Interestingly, he did buy a gun for him; perhaps the counterimages can be explained by Mr. Bryan's admiration for his father carrying a gun. Even though he says, "I never did believe in no fighting," his story about his father and other stories he told about fights he had in West Virginia indicate otherwise.

At one point, he told a story about threatening a man and then said, "I used to be mean as a devil." Mrs. Bryan said, "You can say that again." And he did. "Yeah I used to be mean." The gun and the guitar represent two different ways of dealing with race; earlier in his life, Mr. Bryan may have preferred the symbol of the gun, but later music better expressed his attitude toward race relations. From the perspective of the present he remembers himself in a better light as having bought the guitar. Even after Mrs. Bryan contradicts him, he still continues the story, "I know *we* bought him a guitar [emphasis added]." The life review process, then, involves the reinterpretation of events to fit the self-image of the elderly person in the present.

Again, given their religious beliefs, it is not surprising that they both agree completely on the religious morals drawn from this story. Heaven is the ideal: there will be no race prejudice there, and people who are prejudiced on earth will go to hell. Mr. Bryan sees more of a fulfillment of the ideal on earth than Mrs. Bryan does in terms of the use of "nigger" among whites today. He seems to have a more idealistic view of life than she: he sees race relations and their marriage as mainly positive, and she sees negative aspects in both.

Religion permeates much of their conversation, and several other stories project religious morals directly. Mr. Bryan told another story that had a religious point about his father.

"And my daddy used to have a church, the old Macedonian, not this church. This is another one way on down further. He went to a communion meeting one Sunday, and him, and there was another colored fella, him, my daddy and Charlie Edwards got into a racket. And my daddy, he always carried a .38 Smith and Wesson pistol, and they, and when they got into this racket—this man that my daddy was with, he was a great big man, he was stout too, he was a man like, like my daddy was. They got into it—the church about something, and when they got into it, my daddy throwed, got out his pistol and throwed it in his, and snapped it five times. Boy, it wouldn't shoot a'tall."

Mrs. Bryan laughed softly.

"It just wouldn't fire. And he, Isham Wagner was a white man, a big white man; he had a farm, I think. He got, coming home, he told, says, 'Jeff, get on behind me,' and says, 'and I'll carry you home.' And Pa got on behind him, and they had to cross the creek before they got home. And my daddy says, 'Mr. Wagner, I don't know what was the matter with my gun.' Says, 'It never have misfired. It never had failed on me until today.' Says, 'It just snapped and didn't shoot a'tall.' Says, 'I want to see what was the matter with it.' He reached down and got it and just throwed it down into the river, and he was on top, he was behind Isham on the horse. He throwed it down, and boy, she shot five times just as clear." We all laughed. "He says, 'I don't know what was the matter.'"

"See, God had it. That's what had it. See, God wouldn't let that gun go off. It got it down and fired it five times. First time it ever had failed. He throwed it down in that water, and it shot five times just as fast as he pulled the trigger. And him coming home out there after having that racket. See, God can stop things. Yes sir, He's got all the power. Yes sir, He's got all the power. If he wants to stop a thing, He can stop it. Now see, Pa would have killed him, [but] He just wouldn't let that gun go off."

This story can be related to the one about his father going to town with a gun and the one about the guitar. The two opposite concepts of those stories are contained in this one: the tendency toward violence is contrasted to God's desire for harmony. Mrs. Bryan's responses to the stories make it clear which side she prefers: she did not react at all to the story of his father going to town carrying a gun, but she shared in the telling of the story of the guitar and was the first to make an explicit moral from it, and she laughed at the point in the last story when the gun did not go off. The three stories taken together represent a struggle between these forces in Mr. Bryan's own life: his father as a man to be emulated represents someone who has been through the same conflicts he has. A black man must stand up for his rights, but on the other hand, God commands, "Thou shalt not kill." Here again, because of his identification with his father, Mr. Bryan uses the story as part of his life review emphasizing a self-image that extends from his father's time to his own old age.

Mr. Bryan went through a period in his life when he was "mean as a devil," but the Lord intervened and saved him. His conversion story details this turning point in his life.

"If I hadn't belonged to the church, I'd done been dead and gone. I used to be wild as a buck, had an old thirty-two twenty pistol, put it under my arm, and I couldn't go to church without [being] half-drunk with that old pistol buckled on me, didn't care for nothing. It's a wonder I hadn't a been dead. I've got that same old pistol right in here now, thirty-two twenty that I used to carry when I was wild as a buck."

I asked, "What made you change?"

"Good Lord, I got a blessing, and I just changed." Both of them laughed. "I just, when the Lord blessed me I throwed away all this old stuff. Throwed away drinking, and carrying pistols, and got to serving the Lord and living a better life. If I hadn't, I'd a been dead and forgotten, I'd a killed somebody or somebody'd a killed me."

"Did you have an experience that made you change?"

"Yeah."

"What happened?"

"I just—"

Mrs. Bryan set the story for him, "We had a meeting here, we were having a revival."

"Went to a revival," he continued, "and I just got to praying and wanted to change. I seen I was on the wrong road. Commenced to praying, and used to be woods right out here, all this out here, there was woods, and we had this cleared right down here. And I'd go out there at night after I'd come from the church and say, 'I'm gonna go out here and pray in the woods out there.' And seemed like the boogerman," he laughed, "get me out there and I couldn't pray. I had to come out of them woods. I'd come out of the woods and come down here in the field. I was afraid, just kinda afraid that the boogerman was trying to get me, and run me out. I was scared, and I come down here in the field, down here and prayed. And you know when I'd go up to church, I'd just feel something run all over me that I never had felt, and I'd been a praying for two or three weeks. And I come down here that night and prayed, and went back, come back out—I was sleeping upstairs here, I sleep upstairs—and I just laid there and cried and prayed all night, I couldn't, I couldn't sleep. And I said, 'Good Lord, if you'll just let that spirit, that feeling hit me like it's been a hitting me, I'll get up and shout.' Now I says, 'Then if I ain't right, I'll tell them I ain't right.' And boy, you know, when I had it made up in my mind thataway, and went to the church, they couldn't hardly commence singing soon enough. It commenced raining, and I thought we may never start. And boy when they did start singing, well I'd been up and shouting all over the house, and I didn't even know much when I got up. Boy, I had a time there. See, I'd done, I'd done made it up in my mind, 'Now Lord, you do so and so,' and He done it, and that was the Holy Spirit, and I didn't know what it was. I didn't know how to own it."

A few minutes later he described the feelings he gets in church now.

"I don't know what I'd do if I couldn't go to church. I enjoy going to the church. I get a blessing. He gives me a feeling that nobody can give me; nobody in this world can give me a feeling like God can give it to me. I don't care how old you are and how stiff you are, you'll move." He laughed. "When He gets a hold of you." He laughed again. "Yeah, you'll feel like a young man. Yes sir."

"I noticed that when you were leading the singing in church, you said when you worship it should be a joyful experience."

"Yes sir. Yes sir. It should be. Yeah sure, it should be. You serve the Lord, serve Him, and he'll give you a feeling, boy. You can't help but to move, do someway."

His conversion experience follows patterns widely recognized in the scholarship on sacred ritual among American fundamentalists.[1] Being saved is dependent on God's grace, and conversion narratives often contrast the lowly state of the sinner with the exalted state of the saved. Mr. Bryan's conversion was a highly emotional experience, characterized by disorientation, which is subsequently relived at certain points of worship in church. He must confront the devil directly in the form of the "boogerman," who is associated with the woods. The setting of the story reinforces the contrast between good and evil: he cannot pray in the woods because of the presence of the boogerman; he must go to the safer setting of the cultivated field in order to pray effectively. Unlike Jesse Hatcher, Leonard Bryan associates untamed nature with the devil and the tamed farm land with God, security, and control. In this, he is clearly on the culture side of the nature/culture dichotomy; he is more oriented toward a traditional masculine role in his old age than is Mr. Hatcher.

His new spiritual state came at the exact moment that his life radically changed, and the change is permanent. This experience is especially significant in the study of old age because the change that is undergone establishes a new identity, which is then the basis for continuity. More immediately, his experiencing of the spirit enables him to feel young again: "I don't care how old you are and how stiff you are, you'll move. When He gets a hold of you, yeah, you'll feel like a young man."

The continuity between his new self at the moment of conversion and the person he is today can be seen in the way his identity as a spiritually saved person colors everything else he talks about. His marriage has been good because the Lord brought them together. He survived the dangers of coalmining because of God's grace. His slave ancestors endured and were eventually freed through prayer. Racial harmony depends on following God's commandments. The way he views his life history is shaped by his religious belief in much the same way that Jesse Hatcher's is shaped by his. The conflict within himself between his tendency to be "mean as a devil" and "wild as a buck" on the one side and to experience transcendent joy on the other is expressed in his conversion narrative and in stories about his father, which take on new meaning when viewed in the context of his conversion. He carried a pistol in his youth much like his father, and if he hadn't been saved, he would have "been dead and gone." When he "throwed away drinking, and carrying pistols" it was a symbolic act. In some ways he relived his father's experience: God intervened to save his father by keeping the pistol from firing, and He intervened by giving Mr. Bryan a chance to be saved. These stories are all linked thematically, related together as part of the life review process.

Mrs. Bryan did not tell a personal conversion story, the implication being that she was never "wild as a buck" and thus not in need of such a dramatic reversal. She has belonged to the church since childhood, and they share the same religious beliefs. I collected more religious conversion stories from men than from women in the Blue Ridge, and although this is not conclusive evidence, I suspect that the pattern would be born out by further investigation. The explanation seems to lie in culturally learned expressive/instrumental gender roles: the woman was expected to stay at home and be a housewife; the man was expected to go out in the world to work. The opportunities for a sinful life were greater for him, and he was expected to sow his wild oats; she, on the other hand, was expected to remain virginal until marriage. The cultural double standard may explain the preponderance of conversion stories among men. A related explanation could lie in the pattern in elderly behavior noted by Myerhoff: old women tended to quietly communicate their understanding of their strengths in intimate situations, and old men were more apt to make public expressions of their accomplishments (1978, 268).

The Bryan family has followed cultural expectations in gender roles with one significant exception: their daughter became a minister in their church, and this event is important in understanding the changes that have occurred as they aged. Mrs. Bryan was the first to mention it. "Now our daughter that was with him a leading that service, she's a preacher . . . that sat with him a leading that devotion, she's a pastor herself. She's a preacher herself." There have been some women ministers in the history of the black church in America, but generally, despite the fact that women represent seventy percent of the church, they have been relegated to support rather than leadership roles (Grant 1982, 142). When women were "called" to preach, they had to prove their calling to an extent not required of men (Grant 1982,

143–44; Lawless 1988a, 1988b; Peck 1988, 143–44). This seems to have been true in the case of their daughter, as Mr. Bryan pointed out.

"Some people here don't believe in it, but I tell them I ain't got nothing to do with it. I says, if God calls them, I says, man or woman can't stop them. I say, I don't know what God had done calling them or who He's called to preach. And I ain't got nothing to do with it. I say, if you're called to preach, preach. I'll never fight them; I don't know who I'm fighting. You know God can call a woman to preach just the same as He can a man. What does the Bible say?"

Mr. Bryan seems supportive of his daughter's decision to be a minister, but his story about when she first got the calling indicates that his attitude is more complex. After Mrs. Bryan said, "She's a pastor herself. She sure can preach," he told the story.

"Yeah, she was a—God called her to preach. And when we go off, far off to meetings, she lives, she drives a car, I tell her come by, and I just leave my car. I always give her a dollar, and she carries me way off [to] Galax, or [other places in] Virginia, around; I just let my car set here, and I give her a dollar. And when the Lord called her to preach, she's telling me, says, 'Daddy,' says, 'the good Lord called me to preach, and I'll know what to think about it.' And I never did said a word; I just let her go ahead and talk. She talked, and I never said. I said, 'Well,' I says, 'if God really has called you to preach,' I says, 'you'll know it.' I says, 'If God calls you,' I says, 'you needn't be ashamed, you needn't be afraid. If God's behind you, almighty God,' I says, 'there's somebody behind you,' I said, 'tain't like man nor woman here in this world.' I says, 'If God's called you,' I says, 'you'll know it.' I never said [a word], and she's looking at me and says, 'Go ahead and preach and do this, that, and t'other.' I didn't say a word, but I knowed if God had called her, she'd go. Yeah. She come back and tell Mamie, says, 'I told Daddy about it,' and said, 'and Daddy never said a word . . . Daddy wouldn't say a word.' No use in me saying, if God called her, she'd know it. No use in me saying it. I was hoping he had, but I wouldn't tell her."

Mr. Bryan's narrating of the experience is another instance of a discrepancy between what happened and what he wishes had happened. Hearing the story, the listener thinks that he told his daughter of his support for her calling. "I says, 'If God calls you,' I says, 'you needn't be ashamed, you needn't be afraid.'" Even though he prefaces this statement with "I never did said a word," his repetition of "I says" throughout this part of the story leaves the impression that he spoke out loud to her. The contradiction can be seen at the point where he starts to quote himself: "... and I never said. I said ..." Only at the end of the story is it clear that he never said a word. He rationalizes at the end, "No use in me saying it. I was hoping He had [called her], but I wouldn't tell her." This is a good example of what Sharon R. Kaufman calls reinterpretation of themes in life stories. "The sources of meaning which themes integrate are continually reinterpreted in light of new circumstances. A person selects events from his or her past to structure and restructure his or her identity. Thus, themes continue to evolve from and give form to personal experience—making identity a cumulative process" (1986, 149–50). Mr. Bryan's narrating of this story shows the reinterpretation of themes in process, not as a finished product. I suspect that at the time his daughter came to him he had doubts about a woman being a minister, which he indicated by his silence. Like most men of his generation, he required more proof of a woman's calling than he did of a man. Since her calling has proven so successful, he feels the need to reinterpret the event to conform to his view on women preachers now. Her calling is analogous to his conversion, although he may not have realized it at the time and still may not. Since the theme of religious conversion is central to his life story, he had to have some way of reconciling his earlier doubt of her; his attempts at reconciliation are clear in his telling of the story.

Mrs. Bryan's attitude toward her daughter's calling, on the other hand, was positive from the beginning. As the primary nurturer in the family, she was closer to the children and thus in a position in her old age to take credit for their accomplishments. Older women, in general, are better able to use the success of their children as a positive attribute in life review (Myerhoff 1978, 266). The successful daughter reflects favorably on the mother's job of child rearing. Even in Mr. Bryan's telling of the story, Mrs. Bryan is shown as having known about the calling before her daughter went to tell her father and of being sought out afterward to explain why he had remained silent. She expresses her pride in her daughter's achievement at every opportunity.

"She sure can preach. And they call on her far and near to come pray for the sick, and they get better. And she went this week. Was it Monday or Sunday? No it was Sunday she went over there. They called her to come plumb to—where was it she had to go? Had to go plumb to Baron, pray for a man, have a meeting with a man in a hospital. Expecting him to die. But he's still alive. She went over there to preach for him and to have prayer with him. And he's still alive, she said this morning, still alive, and they was expecting him to be dead."

And later she said, "Our daughter really can sing too, the one that preaches. Boy, she can sing."

Mr. Bryan agreed, "Yeah boy. She can really sing."

Mrs. Bryan was even more emphatic, "She can *really* sing."

There is more identification between mother and daughter than between father and daughter. Perhaps Mrs. Bryan's pride in her daughter is partially based on the daughter breaking through the restrictions that the culture had placed on women of Mrs. Bryan's generation. As she said of herself, "There wasn't nothing I could do about it. . . . Somebody had to take care of that stuff, so I stayed here and took care of it." But her daughter, although she met resistance, did not have to stay; she could leave the expressive realm and become successful in an instrumental domain that was dominated by men. Clearly though, she was able to take some of her expressive traits such as caring for others into the masculine world of preachers. Just as Mrs. Bryan was outspoken in her criticism of men who left home for long periods of time, so too is she vocal in criticizing male preachers. Significantly, she interrupted her husband in order to make this statement.

"Well I believe the reason the Lord is calling women to preach is because men, there's lot of men preachers, they got to where they do everything they're big enough to do. They drink, they go to dances, they do everything they're big enough to do, and then they go right in the pulpit and preach."

Mr. Bryan agreed, "That ain't right."

"And I don't think it's right," she continued. "I think if they're gonna be a preacher, be one. And I think that's the reason that God's calling women now, on account of men. The men is not living the life, a clean life like he's supposed to live. And He's calling women.

Ain't nothing that they can do about it. And most of them, they're preaching for money anyhow, the big salaries."

She is outspoken in her opinions, and so is he. They shared the stage during the interview, sometimes taking turns, sometimes interrupting each other, sometimes finishing each other's sentences, at times disagreeing and at times agreeing. Their style of narrating can be seen as a metaphor for their marriage: their sixty-three-year relationship is reflected in the way they talk and tell stories. An instance of this can be seen in their telling of the courtship story. In the middle of his narration, Mr. Bryan said, "And told her Mammy—she's fourteen years old—I says now—"

Mrs. Bryan interrupted, "No, I was nine years old."

"Just nine?"

"Wait a minute, I was nine years old when you met me."

"Yeah. I told her, I told her Mammy. . . ."

Her interruption does not advance or support the story, but she considers the mistake in age important enough to justify breaking into the story. Even though he is telling the story, the subject is *their* courtship, so she has the right to interrupt. He is the major storyteller here, but the possibility for mutual storytelling exists in the content of the story and in their usual interaction in conversation. He acknowledges this later in the story when he asks, "And she was about fifteen, wasn't you?"

"Along about sixteen."

"And look how long we been married."

He invites her to take part in the narrating right at the point where he wants to emphasize the longevity and solidity of their marriage. Their disagreements are at times couched in humorous terms, which helps to resolve them. He especially uses a teasing tone as he said she made biscuits instead of cornbread and when he said he couldn't "eat her" anymore because she was too old.

They both have "entitlement" to the courtship story (Shuman 1987), but he seems to hold the storytelling rights to the narrative about his first trip to West Virginia. He started out, "When I first went to the coalfields I believe I was fourteen years old."

"Thirteen," Mrs. Bryan disagreed.

"Huh?"

"Thirteen."

"Thirteen?"

"With your brother Lester."

"No, Emment Choate carried me."

"I thought your brother Lester."

"Emment Choate carried me to the coalfields when I was thirteen or fourteen years old [he continued with the story]."

When she corrects him this time, he turns around and corrects her thus establishing his right to tell the story. He also never gives in completely to her correction of the age; instead, he says, "when I was thirteen or fourteen years old." She must feel some right to take part in the narrating of the West Virginia story because of the conflict this caused in their marriage. The disruption of the telling of the story parallels the disruption of the marriage. Later, in the narrating of the same story, she interjects statements that support his point of view by justifying his actions: she mentions that his father died and he had to help care for three brothers.

At the end of the discussion of the West Virginia experiences, they supported each other in both content and interaction.

He said, "When I come back, I had me this farm payed for, and I bought me some cows, and had that silo out there built, and went to milking cows—"

"And raising cabbage," Mrs. Bryan continued.

He repeated, "And raising cabbage."

The conflict is resolved, he is back home to stay, and their mutual style of narrating reinforces the sense of resolution. When she finishes his sentence for him, it is an example of what Katherine Young calls mid-sentence starts, or citing Harvey Sacks, a "chime in" (Young 1987, 167–68). With the Bryans, the chime in functions not as an interruption but as a supportive utterance and hence a part of "mutual construction" of the story (Young 1987, 168–69). Their competitiveness at the beginning of telling the story has turned into collaboration at the end, after the conflict within the story has been resolved. Their dual narrating is similar to the married couple studied by Karen Baldwin in that their corrections and interruptions are ultimately resolved in a collaborative weaving together of family stories (1985, 150–51).

The analysis of the Bryans' interaction in storytelling and conversation gets even more complex when we consider their talk about slavery and religion. She was talking about how children were sold at auctions. [Simultaneous or overlapping speech is indicated by braces.]

"Sell them off at auctions, just have them up on blocks and things, and just sell them off on auction. It's awful. I don't like to think about it."

Mr. Bryan: "Well, they'd sell a man and a woman too, put them both up on blocks."

Mrs. Bryan: "Yeah, they sold them."

Mr. Bryan: "Back there in slave times. Colored folks—"

Mrs. Bryan: "They'd bid them off just like, just like people selling {cows} around here now and horses and things like that."

Mr. Bryan: "{Cows.}"

Mr. Bryan: "They'd put them up and sell them, {and the highest}—"

Mrs. Bryan: [overlapping with his last words]: "{They'd have an auction,} you know, and sold them."

Mr. Bryan: "—the highest bidder would get them."

Mrs. Bryan: "That's right."

Mr. Bryan: "They're smart and all of that would go, some of them would go way high, and some of them, you know, just like cows."

Mrs. Bryan: "Lord, I don't like, I don't even like to think about it, but I've heard it." [She goes on to tell about hearing this from her grandmother.]

The entitlement to tell stories about slavery seems to be equally shared because they are drawing on the same tradition of parents and grandparents, so that this is another example of mutual construction. The series of chime ins and simultaneous speech indicate how mutual the storytelling is (Young 1987, 166). Mrs. Bryan finishes the sentence Mr. Bryan starts, and in the middle of her sentence they have simultaneous speech on the word "cows," and without a pause she finishes the sentence. After he starts the next sentence, she starts another one, they overlap for a few words, he pauses, she finishes her sentence, he returns to the same point in his sentence at which he paused, repeats one word, and finishes the statement. She agrees with him; he repeats the point about slavery and cattle, and she comes full circle by repeating her statement about not liking to think about it. This could be viewed as competition for the floor, but the effect is of two voices telling one story. It is collaborative rather than competitive. Katherine Young points out, "Chiming in to complete another person's utterance, whether competitive or collaborative, discloses shared understanding" (1987, 184). The Bryans' telling of slave narratives is certainly based on shared understanding. My role in this exchange is similar to that of Young's in her interview with a married couple. "The Browns on this occasion take up the same alignment toward the events in the story, as privy to [the same] realm, in contrast to my own attitude as an outsider" (1987, 184). An elderly black couple talking to a younger white person about slavery see themselves as a group with an understanding that the white person did not share.

Finally, in their talk about religion they exhibit an intertwining of themes on the level of discourse matched by turn-taking on the level of interaction (Young 1987, 161–63). Mr. Bryan concluded his conversion narrative in the following way. [Thematic links are indicated by **boldface type.**]

"See, I'd done, I'd done made it up in my mind, 'Now Lord, you do so and so,' and He done it, and that was the Holy Spirit, and I didn't know what it was. I **didn't know how** to own it."

Mrs. Bryan said, "A lot of folks **don't know what** it is."

He continued, "Then I owned it. Huh?"

She repeated, "A lot of folks **don't know what** the spirit is."

He agreed, "No. But I owned it, boy. When I owned it, I, I, I **didn't know when** I come to myself. I **didn't know what** I'd done. I'd been shouting all over that church. He sure laid His hands on me."

She said, "Now a lot of them **don't get changed** like that either. Some of them just get up and **give their hands.** They don't think they have to pray for it."

He agreed, "Just **a handshake** ain't worth two cents. You've got to pray and let God, let God get in your heart, and boy you know it."

She repeated, "A lot of them **don't do that.**"

He agreed, "No, they **don't.**"

She added, "They just go up and give **their hand** and say they're going to do better, and that's it."

He followed up with, "And when they go to church, they just sit there, can't sing, open their mouth, or **nothing.** How do they expect to **feel anything?**"

She answered, "They **don't feel nothing.**"

He said, "If you don't put **nothing** in **nothing** you get **nothing** out."

She concluded, "**They don't know nothing** about the spirit. **They don't know, they don't know** about that. **They don't** really believe that God'll give them a spirit."

Mrs. Bryan makes a statement during his story that is both competitive and collaborative, since she interrupts to make a point that is supportive of his moral. She repeats a phrase from his story, "didn't know what it was," to establish a thematic link, and repeats it since he did not hear it the first time. He then finishes his story, and she picks up the same thematic thread with "don't get changed" and introduces a second key phrase, "give their hands." He continues the linking with the hand image, "a handshake ain't worth two cents." She then repeats the first phrase with "don't do that," and he also repeats "no they don't." She then returns to the second phrase "give their hand," which he elaborates on with "they just sit there." Finally, he introduces a third linking phrase, "to feel anything." She alters it slightly to "feel nothing," and "don't know nothing" becomes the key phrase for the next two statements. These key phrases establish thematic links and transitions between their separate utterances so that again the effect is of mutual construction. At the beginning there is a sense of competition; she has to repeat her point before he relinquishes the floor, but once he has finished his story, the conversation that ensues is collaborative. The linking phrases give unity to two people speaking. Here again, the style of speaking, the participants' interaction, and the content of what they are saying are all complimentary. He was telling *his* conversion story, but once that was concluded, their basic agreement about religious beliefs provided a foundation for mutual construction of conversation.

In their conversation and storytelling the Bryans reflect on their long life together; they engage in a mutual life review: they consider their courtship and the conflicts of marriage, their relationships with their children, their work, and their play. They project their view back into the past and the world of slavery their grandparents knew, and they project into their own spiritual future when they talk about their religious beliefs and experiences. The conflicts they have experienced are dealt with in storytelling and conversation in ways that express what they have learned from the experiences. At times they attempt to correct mistakes that were made by verbally reliving and reshaping the events being narrated. The interaction and style of their talking and storytelling reveal underlying concerns of their marriage which are only indirectly touched upon in the content of their speech. We can see some of the process involved in their making the marriage into what it has become; we can see the construction and reconstruction of their shared and separate identities. By looking at content, style, and interaction in the presentation of themselves as old people, we can better appreciate the richness and complexity of their lives.

NOTE

1. See Clements 1976a; Mullen 1983; Sutton 1977, 1988; Titon 1988; Titon and George 1978.

4

Bob Glasgow
Folk Architecture and Family History

Bob Glasgow[1] was showing me through his barn in Adams County, Ohio, in 1980, and telling me about how the barn was built for his grandfather, Robert Glasgow, in the nineteenth century.

"Grandfather hauled the pig iron, and the man down here took an old-fashioned forge and anvil, and hammered all the hinges and nails out for this barn. Made the nails. Now he cut off forty dollars if he didn't have to make nails for the top end. So they set the plate out over, and they had a, like a double shovel plow, and they cut the tongue and groove, and they used the wide one, and put the boards up in that."

"When was this barn built?" I asked him.

"1858. House was built in '42. Now this man [Sam Laird, the carpenter who built the barn] had an axe with a sixteen-inch blade, weighed twenty-five pounds. I'd like for you to see a man today take an axe—look up through there, man, how smooth that is."

"Yeah, hewed that out."

"Yeah, with an axe. Look here at this piece, the width of it and how true it is. He was a craftsman, honey, he wasn't no ordinary carpenter. There's fifty-three pieces of timber in this barn. It's forty feet long, eight by eight, nine by eleven, and twelve by fourteen. It's forty feet long."

"And all of it hand-hewn? All of it was hewn out by hand?"

"Oh yes, oh yes, oh yes."

"And wooden pegs?"

"Oh yes. All morticed in. But now listen, honey, there's hewing."

As he showed me around, he shifted from description of the barn to the narration of several stories about the barn and Sam Laird, so that the barn itself acts as a reminder of the narratives. In fact, Mr. Glasgow often shows the barn and the old house to visitors while he talks about the buildings and family history. The built landscape becomes the context for reminiscing and storytelling; physical artifacts become elements in the life review, not only for Mr. Glasgow's life but as connections to his ancestors' lives as well. The expressions of elderly people often go beyond their own lives to include their fore-bears (Hufford, Hunt, and Zeitlin 1987, 45). In Bob Glasgow's case, the house and barn are physical links to his grandfather, whom he never knew, and to his ancestors before his grandfather. Mr. Glasgow was seventy-eight when I first interviewed him in 1980 (I conducted a second interview several months later); he had an excellent memory and enjoyed telling personal experience narratives and family history filled with detailed names, dates, and places. He has been a farmer or employed in agriculture all of his life; he has raised sheep, hogs, and cattle, and run a dairy farm; he has grown tobacco, corn, hay, and other crops, and he operated a threshing machine for over twenty years. He lost the fingers of his right hand in a corn-shredding machine accident at the age of thirty, but he continued to work and even took up woodwork recently.

After we toured the barn, we went inside his present home and sat at the dining room table. I asked him, "Now could you give me some information about your family history going back to Scotland and how they came over and all that?"

"Well, my grandfather, great, great-great-grandfather Robert came [to Ohio] about 1796, and there was five of his boys came with him. And they, then my great-grandfather [Joseph] went back [to Virginia from Ohio] in 1805 and married his first cousin, Arthur's girl, his uncle. And they came [back to Ohio], and let's see, they had I think eleven children, and when my grandfather [Robert Anderson Glasgow] was six months old, he was the second child, and his mother decided she wanted to go home and visit. So she took a pack horse and a rifle, six months old baby, and went back to Rockbridge, Virginia, by herself, had a little visit, come back. Then they, grand-

4. Bob Glasgow. (Photograph by the author.)

father came, well my great-great grandfather came, he bought out two generals and got two thousand acres of land there for services in the War, the Revolutionary War. And then he divided that up among his children and grandchildren."

"You were telling me about the brothers in Virginia, what was it, three brothers?"

"There was three brothers, and John went to Kentucky, and as near as we know he settled at Glasgow, Kentucky. And Arthur stayed there [in Virginia], and his family are mostly there. There's, my sister contacted an attorney at a place, Marlboro, I believe was the name of the town and talked to him, but he wasn't interested in any family history. He told a little bit about what was there. And the Greenacres in Rockbridge County is where the old estate is, and part of the family still holds that."

"So one brother went to Kentucky, and where did the other two go?"

"Arthur stayed there, and Robert came here."

"To Ohio?"

"The three brothers."

"Why did they split up? Why did they go in separate directions?"

"Well, they just had a little family argument, and John was left with no contacts, but the other two made up and corresponded back and forth later."

"So the Robert that settled here was your grandfather or your great-grandfather?"

"My father's name was Gilmer, his father's name was Robert Anderson, his father's name was Joseph, his father's name was Robert and he was the one that came. Five generations."

Mr. Glasgow's great-great grandfather, Robert Glasgow, came from Scotland and originally settled in Pennsylvania; from there the family moved to Virginia. Then, Robert Glasgow came to Ohio in 1796 and established his farm in northern Adams County. His son Joseph, Bob Glasgow's great-grandfather, settled on an adjacent farm. Joseph's son Robert Anderson, Bob Glasgow's grandfather, was born in 1813, and when he came of age settled on the present Glasgow farm. I continued the interview. "And what about the name Glasgow, how did your family get that name?"

"Well, it was, we was, when they left Scotland and went to Ireland, they was first known, the old family name was Cameron. And they was known as the Camerons from Glasgow, and then they dropped the Cameron and took the name Glasgow, and their name was Glasgow before they came to this country. They settled first for a few months in Pennsylvania, and then went to Virginia. And they were there then for, oh, I would say, approximately fifteen, twenty years, at least. Because they were there before the, they were all in the Revolutionary War."

I later asked him, "How did you find out all this information about family history?"

"Well, they, in 1926, there was a fella that came in here, and his grandmother had been a Finley, a sister of my great-grandmother, and he got us interested. And well, we got to writing stuff down and one thing and another, and going to the cemeteries and getting the old records. And it was still at that time, there was a lady and she died when she was in her late eighties, but her mind was clear as a bell up to the last. Her name was Ometa MacIntyre, and she was a granddaughter of this Nancy Glasgow that my, that Joseph went back to Virginia and married. And she lived to be ninety-three, and this Ometa, who was her nursemaid for several years, well she got that assignment she said when she was sixteen, and she was, I think four or five years that she had that assignment. And this old lady had this mind like an elephant, memory. And that was their folklore and talk and everything else. And there wasn't a [motion] picture then on every corner, and people didn't, that was more their pastime. And so she had it and had all that history, and I got it from her."

"What about from your father or grandfather? Did you used to sit around and talk to them about the family?"

"Well, my grandfather died twenty years before I was born."

"What about your father and the rest of your family?"

"My father was never as much interested in history as one of his brothers, Arthur, but he had two brothers that was interested, Arthur and John. And John had a nervous breakdown and his health, and he came here and lived with our folks for about two years. And that was all he could do, just talk about the old things. I got a lot there."

This family history, which Mody Boatright calls the family saga (1958), has become even more important to Mr. Glasgow as he gets older.[2] Ancestors are an important theme in his life story (Kaufman 1986, 25–26); he reaches back to before he was born to find a source for his own identity. In telling stories about his grandfather and great-grandmother he is affirming who he is as a Glasgow. Their characteristics and values represent who he wants to be, an ideal that he has tried to emulate in his own life and now wants to pass on to the next generation. Talking about his ancestors is his way of establishing continuity between himself, the past, and the future. The length of time, five generations, his family has been in America and the fact that his ancestors fought in the Revolutionary War are sources of pride for him. He clearly admires the courage of his great-grandmother, who traveled alone with a six-month-old baby from Ohio to Virginia on horseback. Her trek was motivated by her need to maintain contact with family separated by great distances. The baby she carried was Mr. Glasgow's grandfather, so that his link to this episode is even more direct. Even though he does not stay in touch with his family in Kentucky and Virginia, he still feels a connectedness to them; they are all Glasgows.

The way he learned about his family history is also significant, I think. A key figure was Ometa McIntyre, who was the granddaughter of Nancy Glasgow, Bob Glasgow's great-grandmother. Ometa

McIntyre had a mind that was "clear as a bell" and a memory "like an elephant," traits which Mr. Glasgow is proud of in himself. He identifies with Ometa McIntyre as a family tradition bearer and as a direct link to his great-grandmother, whom Mrs. McIntyre tended to in her old age. Her pastime was talking about family history and folklore, an activity that Mr. Glasgow sees as preferable to modern entertainments such as going to the movies.

After I had interviewed Mr. Glasgow on two separate occasions, I did some research of my own into his family history. There was quite a lot of information about his grandfather, Robert Anderson Glasgow, who had the house and barn built. I read about him in *Caldwell's Illustrated Historical Atlas of Adams County, Ohio:* "In 1834, he was married to Dorcas Finley, by whom he had five children, all of whom died in infancy, except one son Joseph, who died at Memphis, Tenn., while serving his country in the War of the Rebellion. He was married again in 1843, to Jane Smiley, who was born March 20, 1818, near Hamilton, Butler county, O. Her father, John Smiley, was a native of Pennsylvania. Mrs. Glasgow died Sept. 17, 1879" (1880, 59). Mr. Glasgow tells a family narrative about how his grandfather met his second wife, Jane Smiley. This is a courtship story in which the building of their house is a central concern. Bob Glasgow heard the story from his father, since his grandfather died before he was born. During the second interview, Mr. Glasgow, Tim Lloyd (a folklorist who accompanied me on my second visit), and I were walking from the barn to the house when he told the story.

"My grandfather had a fancy for cattle, and his first wife died, and he was riding around one evening looking for some more cattle. And he went above Hamilton [and bought some cattle from a man there]. So the man said, 'Where you live?' And he told him. So he said, 'You better stay all night,' and he said, 'and you can go home in the morning.' He said, 'Appreciate it.' So he stayed. Well, there was a young lady there looked pretty prosperous. So he went back in a couple of weeks, and by golly he talked something besides cattle.

"So the old man asked him, says, 'What kind of a house have you got?' Well, he said he had, described it, had a log house right in there, four rooms and by a spring, told him about it, tried to brag it up pretty nice. 'Ah,' he said, 'my daughter's used to a nicer home than that.' Said, 'You let me draw the pattern for a house, plan, and,'

said, 'you build the house and alright.' So Grandpa come home and built the house."
Tim said, "So he got the plans from his father-in-law?"
"Uuhh, huuhh."
"And this is it?"
"And this is it. And he built the house, and they got married, and she had ten children. There's been twenty-two births, four weddings, and, I believe, it's five deaths in that house."

The house plan drawn by the father-in-law and subsequently built by Robert Glasgow in 1842 was a folk house type, an I-house, which is geographically widespread and common in southern Ohio. The I-house is a folk type in which the basic form remains the same as variations in it occur. In one of the original studies of this house type, Fred B. Kniffen gives a description of the basic characteristics. "But these qualities all I-houses unfailingly had in common: gables to the side, at least two rooms in length, one room deep, and two full stories in height" (1986, 8). The house could be frame or brick, usually had chimneys on one or both gable ends, and was generally symmetrical. Variation could come in the number of upstairs front windows and in additions on the back.

Folk architecture, such as the I-house, is a cultural expression and as such can have symbolic meaning, can be interpreted much as a narrative or other verbal expressions can.[3] Bob Glasgow's narrative about his family house illustrates the social meaning mentioned by Kniffen and reiterated by Henry Glassie that the I-house connotes the economic success and "agrarian stability" of the middle-class farmer (Glassie 1971, 99). The story suggests an additional related meaning for the house: "They [traditional houses] are metaphors of the traditional Western concept of marriage, as the founding of a landed family in a *joint* enterprise" (Gowans 1986, 382). Bob Glasgow's description of his grandmother as looking "pretty prosperous" links human and house together symbolically and supports the visual metaphor of marriage. The story is clearly from the masculine point of view in making the woman part of the man's property. It indicates that Robert Glasgow had to have physical proof of his agrarian stability, of his middle-class status, before his prospective father-in-law would give him permission to marry his daughter. The replacing of a log house with a frame one at a certain point in the growth of a family farm was a traditional pattern (Gowans 1986, 375; McMillen 1974, 21–25). The house had symbolic value as an ideal even before it was built; behavior and object affected each other in planning, building, and living in the house. A status symbol of that society is reflected in the courtship behavior, which is in turn symbolized by the house itself and then carried down in family tradition in verbal form by the oft-repeated story.

Bob Glasgow's comments about the house show his pride in it as a symbol of his family even though the house is now abandoned and in disrepair (see figs. 5 and 6). The house has become a symbol in his life review; in his old age it is a reminder of the status of his family in his youth and before he was born. As we walked to the house on my first visit I asked him, "You were born right here in this house?"

"Yes, and all my sisters, and my father and all his brothers and sisters. One of his sisters was married there in the house, and two of his daughters and one of my daughters were married here. But everything is nice. It was a showplace once, I'd say. Nobody's lived here now for three years. This house is one of the first three farm houses that had electricity in this community. 1921."

He twice remarked, "There's been twenty-two births, four weddings, and five deaths in the house, and it's seen a lot of history." Births, weddings, and deaths, the cycle of life for his family is contained in the 138-year-old house. As David Lowenthal has pointed out, "the past is not only recalled; it is incarnate in the things we build and the landscapes we create" (1975, 6). Since Bob Glasgow never left home, he has a strong tie to the landscape of home, to his "personal landscape" (Lloyd 1982; Sopher 1979, 136). Because his family has occupied the same place continuously for five generations, the objects on the landscape, which were important to his grandfather, are also important to him and hence subject matter for his stories. The house and the barn as containers of the past have personal meaning for him because they connect him with his ancestors and give him concrete evidence of the status of his family and are thus significant in his life review. The buildings are physical symbols of his own family identity.[4]

The barn is a large traditional Pennsylvania bank barn, and its size also symbolized the affluence of the owner (Glassie 1971, 55;

5. The Glasgow I-house showing the el addition on the side.
(Photograph by the author.)

6. Bob Glasgow by the side entrance of the family I-house.
(Photograph by the author.)

Hutslar 1981, 236). William I. Schreiber says of the Pennsylvania barn in Ohio: "Its sheer size, length and towering height . . . make it unique and command respect. It indeed seems to make the farm; it is the center of activity, it forms the axis of the farm's existence" (1967, 18). The bank barn is a two-level structure with cattle kept in the basement level and hay and grain stored on the upper level, which is cantilevered over the lower on the barnyard side creating an overhang, or "forebay" (see fig. 7). On the opposite side, the barn is built into a bank providing access to the second level for vehicles (see fig. 8). The Pennsylvania barn is constructed of stone, brick, log, or frame with a stone basement (Glassie 1971, 55). The Glasgow barn is a type H, since the basement walls are built out under the forebay to support it (Dornbusch and Heyl 1958, 153–215; Glassie 1966, 18).

Bob Glasgow tells a family story, which explains a unique status feature of the barn.

"Well, the barn, Grandfather was pushing his thoroughbred stock, and he built it more as an advertisement. He had, well, barns almost adequate for the farm, below, but they were all log, and log pens and not much of a show. And at that time this was a pretty much used road from, a shortcut from May Hill to Cherry Fork, so in order to be, really be seen, he contacted the commissioners, and they allowed him to build the barn in the road, and to put the road around the barn."

As travelers came down the road from town, they saw this large bank barn in the middle of the road and the house just beyond and set back from the road. The house had an el addition on the side facing town so that it appeared to be even larger than the ordinary I-house (see figs. 5 and 6). No one could miss the fact that the Glasgow farm was one of the most prosperous in the county. *Caldwell's Illustrated Historical Atlas of Adams County, Ohio*, published in 1880, has a picture of this very scene with fat cattle and woolly sheep in the foreground and insets of Robert Glasgow and his wife at the top (see fig. 9), another means for Robert Glasgow to "show off" his place and another visual metaphor for prosperity and marriage (1880, 146). The *Atlas* also states the meaning of the metaphor directly: "Mr. Glasgow's farm is one of the finest stock farms in the county, containing 270 acres. A view of the residence, surroundings

7. The Glasgow barn from the forebay side. (Photograph by the author.)

8. The barn from the bank side. (Photograph by the author.)

9. The Glasgow family farm as depicted in *Caldwell's Illustrated Historical Atlas of Adams County, Ohio* (1880).

and fine cattle is seen in this work" (59). People approaching the farm from the opposite side would see the forebay side of the barn including the barnyard piled high with manure, another visual (and olfactory) metaphor of agrarian success (Glassie 1986, 415). According to Alan Gowans, this need to display prosperity was part of the agrarian frontier experience throughout America. "Families who have the same recent origins as their neighbors but believe themselves superior, require the visual metaphor of a building similar in type to their neighbors', in the traditional style of their common race and region, but proclaiming superiority by being larger, solider, and above all showier" (1986, 385). The barn, like the house, functions symbolically in Bob Glasgow's life review in old age; it is a means of recalling the past glories of his family and a reminder of prosperous times in his childhood.

The barn was built by a local carpenter named Sam Laird who takes on legendary proportions in the stories Bob Glasgow tells about him. Knowledge of the builder/designers is important to a full understanding of folk architecture (Upton and Vlach 1986, xxiii).[5] As Mr.

Glasgow showed Tim and me the barn, he emphasized Sam Laird's authority as builder.

"My father, grandfather was to hew, put the timber on the ground, hewed, rafters, everything, all the timber. So he [Sam Laird] come to start working and brought the gang. And he looked at it, 'Uummph. We can't use that stuff. Go on home boys,' said, 'I'm sorry, but I ain't got no job for you.' Well, there was a few stayed, and he stayed. He cooled off directly. He was a high-tempered man. And one man said, 'Mr. Laird,' he says, 'you know, if we took a half inch off of every side,' he said, 'we'd get a frame on that barn yet.' He said, 'Yes, we could; it'd make a nice light frame, stand a few years.'"

"He was right," Tim said.

"So grandfather asked him what he'd take to finish the hewing. Grandfather was pretty good at hewing, but a little bit rough. Well he said to finish it and smooth it he'd take so much; I don't know how much that was. But he took the job, and he had his axe, Dad said, was twenty-five pounds, sixteen-inch blade."

Tim commented, "That was some axe."

I said, "He must have been a real big man then."

"He was a big husky man."

This conversation took place inside the barn, and again, as he had on my first visit, Mr. Glasgow pointed out details of the barn's construction and related them to stories about Sam Laird. "Oh the way them braces, note how them braces fit up there. . . . Now it had to be pretty near a craftsman that could frame that and put them mortices, look how them mortices fit, them on the end of that post."

The hand-hewn beams and mortices in the barn are a reminder of the skill of the man who made them (see figs. 10 and 11). "[The folk builder's] signature is in the details, in the care, and in the craft of building (and while the modern observer might not see this signature you can be sure his contemporaries saw it)" (Hubka 1986, 431). Bob Glasgow is a modern observer, but he sees the signature the way a contemporary of Sam Laird's would. The beams create an image of the legendary carpenter with his twenty-five pound axe, who then becomes the major character in a narrative. Mr. Glasgow's reaction to the beams and other construction details of the barn is an aesthetic one. He is aware of the skill required to make rough

10. "Look up through there, man, how smooth that is."
(Photograph by the author.)

11. "But now listen, honey, there's hewing." (Photograph by the author.)

timber into smooth beams with only a large axe as a tool. His aesthetic response is based on his admiration for a human being establishing control over nature by creating something fine out of raw materials. Unlike Jesse Hatcher, Bob Glasgow's emphasis here is on culture, not nature; he stresses the masculine task of transforming nature into usable objects rather than the good inherent in nature. Mr. Glasgow used the phrase "he wasn't no ordinary carpenter" several times in talking about Laird. His narratives about Laird are all associated with the barn; the barn symbolizes the qualities of the man and stands as a monument to his craftsmanship and personality. As Henry Glassie has said, "The house carved out of the forest contains the narrative of the battle. It teaches its occupants continually about their position in the universe and surrounds them with a sense of their capabilities. From it they learn the validity of their culture" (1985, 49). Thus the barn symbolizes more than an aesthetic response; it also projects values, values that have become even more important in Bob Glasgow's old age because he sees them slipping away.

One story about the legendary carpenter has special relevance for the value system of Bob Glasgow. I asked him during the interview in his present home, "What else did your father tell you about this Mr. Laird? What kind of man was he?"

"Well, he was a sarcastic man. And at that time, well that far side of the barn was all framed, and a bank barn, you know. And the back part of the post was up on the frame, or the basement, and the other part there, the eighteen foot out was down below. Well, they had the folk dances, and, at that time, and the one caller, and he called, and these people had to have their minds alert, quick of mind; nobody talked but the caller. Well, it was just the same way on these barn raisings; the one man talked, nobody else said anything, and everybody was alert, and when he said lift, everybody lifted, and when he said pike, they put the props under; lift, they lifted; everybody had to work together, cooperation. And they lifted on the far side and turned that up over; think what a lift that would be of all them heavy timbers. Then there's five posts across there that are ten by fourteen, eighteen foot, and then all your braces and everything else. Well all that weight, and it lifted up over.

"And when they came up over, and it was coming out and coming into the mortices, and it didn't come in, and he looked over, and one of the fellas wasn't prying his to make it hit the mortice. He says, 'Look what you're doing, you lazy lout.' And the kid pushed the bar over, and ummm, ummm, and everybody pushing, and it came together. Well when he turned and he put his hand over the end of his mortice, and the thing come together on his [hand] and cut his thumb off. And he sat there for, they said for over twenty minutes and give orders on how to pin and everything, put the braces, before he come down. So he had a little bit of grit in his craw."

I asked, "That was Laird?"

"Laird."

"And he lost a thumb?"

"Lost a thumb. But he never, they didn't take the mortice apart; they left it [his thumb] in there."

"He must have been some kind of man."

"Yeah. Grit and backbone. But he was demanding and impulsive, but accurate to the last notch, and just look at those mortices and how they fit and all the joints and everything just, well, immaculate you might say."

The story and the barn are bound together; the barn is often the setting for the storytelling, and it is referred to in order to illustrate certain points. In this particular telling of the story we were not in the barn, but had been there earlier so that he still referred to it. The story is a model for a set of values central to Bob Glasgow's life, values that have been important throughout his life, but ones he holds on to even more tenaciously in his old age. Cooperation was important in many of his agrarian endeavors; barn building and other cooperative ventures depended on one strong man at the center to unify the effort. Sam Laird is the heroic man who is so dedicated to his job that he overcomes personal injury to accomplish his goal, and not only does he finish his task, he also makes a final product which is "immaculate." The completion of the job seems more important than the man: the man is permanently disfigured, but the barn is perfect. The physical loss in the story links Bob Glasgow and Sam Laird together. The injuries that each man suffered came about while working with other men and was beyond their control. Mr. Glasgow's injury was worse, but he too has continued to work to see the job through to completion. The legend of Sam Laird not only reflects the personal values of Bob Glasgow, it also functions as an inspiration for overcoming hardships in his own life. As he reviews his life from the perspective of old age, no event is more central than the loss of his fingers, and by symbolically connecting himself to Sam Laird, he can show that he too has grit and backbone to survive.

There is another sense of loss in the story: changes have taken place since that time, and certain qualities of life have been lost. Pride in workmanship, attention to detail, craftsmanship itself seem to have declined. Like many of Jesse Hatcher's stories, and others in the chapters that follow, Bob Glasgow's story expresses his nostalgia for the old days and the old ways of doing things. Several times he said, "Them old fellas knew." This is another widespread pattern in the elderly: older folk artists are said to be "spokespeople not only for themselves, but for an era. They commemorate a pre-industrial, rural past" (Hufford, Hunt, and Zeitlin 1987, 52). Henry Glassie's theory about technological change and the effect on the human imagination helps to explain Mr. Glasgow's feelings of nostalgia.

> The key to vernacular technology is engagement, direct involvement in the manipulation of materials . . . and active participation in the process of design, construction, and use. . . . The product of engagement is knowledge. As technologies evolve to indirect techniques for the manipulation of materials and to isolation of segments of the creative process, the major loss is the experience of engagment that produces the awareness of connectedness that enables people to evaluate their situation in the world and thus to be ambivalent about historical change (1985, 52).

Bob Glasgow not only yearns for the engagement of turning raw materials into finished buildings, he also misses the connectedness to his environment and to other men engaged in a common technological endeavor. His taking up of woodwork in his old age seems to be an attempt to recapture the directness of experience that Sam Laird had. One of his responses to old age and the change he sees around him is to go back to the past in terms of values and behavior.

Mr. Glasgow's nostalgia is not just for the old ways of building; he seems to yearn for the whole way of life associated with the agrarian past. For instance, he told one story which contrasted life today with that on farms in 1918.

"Now you take today, people have to go to the store to buy everything you can imagine. Now think how little those people bought."

"Oh yeah, everything they provided for."

"Used to have family dinners all through the country. Farmers always had a lax time after Christmas. And well, there was one family, Joel Troutman's, let's see there was Edith and Alice and Florence and Chloe, and there was three boys, Ralph and Edgar and Sam, and the father and mother. And we was there for dinner. I'm telling you they had everything on that table; now it was loaded to the finish. And the family always did eat good as far as that goes. Well now they made their own maple syrup; they made their own sorghum. They baked their gingerbread and everything that way. And they was talking at the dinner table. Well, Mrs. Troutman said she just didn't know what they was gonna do. Groceries was just getting so high. She said, 'Of course, George trades flour, wheat for flour for meal.' And she said, 'We've got our own grist mill; we grind our own buckwheat, and we grind our own cornmeal.' And she said, 'The flour from the flour mill is better for baking.' And said, 'We make our own mustard; grind our mustard seed down. And we have our own horseradish and our own sage, had our honey, and sorghum, maple molasses, and we pickled the pears, and we have our own meat and other things.' And had turkeys and geese and chickens and ducks, hogs and beef. They had a variety. She said, 'You know last year our grocery bill, we had to buy salt, we had to buy pepper, and there was twice we got tired of scorched wheat for coffee,' and said, 'We bought some coffee.' And said, 'You know last year our grocery bill run almost nine dollars.'"

This story shows Mr. Glasgow yearning for the abundance of a farm family's dinner table and for the self-sufficient way of life that made that bounty possible. His nostalgia also came out when he talked about an old man who was asked, "What's the biggest change you've seen over the years?" His reply was, "Honesty in the people." Mr. Glasgow went on, "Years ago when a man told you he'd be there tomorrow and help you, [or that] he'd be there Saturday and pay you, it was that way. . . . Nowadays a person tells you anything, and—" he snapped his fingers.

In Mr. Glasgow's view the modern world has lost important values such as honesty and reliability. In his opinion, even the process of passing on traditions has been lost.

As he showed me the house he commented, "Now they tore out the door frames, and these door frames was put in in 1901. Put in in the fall, and I was born in January. I knew that by folklore, that's why. Remembered." He laughed.

"How do you know it?" I asked.

"By folklore."

"Yeah, what do you mean?"

"The way it was done."

"Oh, it was passed on to you. Yeah. How do you know about folklore? Have you read any of the books on folklore?" I paused. "Just your own family folklore?"

"Unh,uhh."

"Do other people call it folklore?"

"Oh—"

"Cause I haven't heard too many people—"

"It isn't, it isn't called anything. People don't—all they want is a jazz box and a radio. Now this boy that bought this farm here, he went down there to fix fence the other day. He went down there, wasn't down there fifteen minutes, he came back, and went to work and took his radio out of his car, and a battery down there."

"So he'd have it."

"Set there listened to the darn thing while he was fixing fence. Why, I wouldn't have the durn noise around for a fart. That's just the difference."

I had not used the term "folklore" in talking with him, and most people I interview do not call their own traditions "folklore." Thus I was curious about his use of the word. His response indicates his preference for the old days when people were more concerned with folk traditions and did not have the distractions of modern electronic entertainment. The specific knowledge he refers to was the remodeling of the house before he was born, but he knows about the remodeling and original building because of "folklore remembered." He also expressed his admiration for Ometa McIntyre's remembering the folklore passed on by his great-grandmother. My interest in the same kinds of things was enough to keep him talking for hours. In talking about his youth and the time of his parents and grandparents, he leaves out the bad things and emphasizes the good. In his life review, he has idealized the past so that it has come to represent all the possibilities of life.

This does not mean that as he engages in life review he has neglected the hardships of his life. As Butler points out, the life review often concentrates on "unresolved conflicts" (1964, 266), and Mr. Glasgow's feelings about his handicap have never been completely resolved. There were other hardships in his life; he said at various points, "But we've had rough sledding," and "I've seen the rough end of it." The accident in which he lost the fingers of one hand was one of several misfortunes.

Pointing at the hand with missing fingers, he said, "That's been off forty-nine years."

"How did that happen?"

"Oh, rusty lever on a corn shredder. Safety lever broke, and I got caught."

"Yeah. From what Steve Kelley [Adams County historian who led me to Mr. Glasgow] tells me, you get around, still do a lot. Says you build furniture, and—"

"Yes. I took that up. I had to be, stay there in the house, and I just took that up in the last year as a hobby. But I had, did, well, I ran a threshing machine for twenty-seven years. I have run machinery and everything, and I've seen, I've seen the rough end of it. I had phantom pains the year after I lost that. You know what I'm talking about?"

"What?"

"Phantom pains."

"Oh yeah. Where you thought you had pains in your hand."

"People have a toothache after their teeth're pulled. Well, mine's just the same as you rubbed the fingernails back and forth quick. Went to the doctor, told him I wanted something to kill that pain. Said, 'I can't give you anything.' Said, 'If I give you anything to kill that pain now, next year you'd have to double it, next year you'd be a drug addict.'"

Mr. Glasgow then told a joke, which I took to be a way of changing the subject from such a painful topic. Later he tried to describe the accident, but got so emotional that he could not continue, and I changed the subject.

Even before this accident, the family had experienced a series of financial disasters. His father invested in cattle and signed Mr. Glasgow's name to the note; they lost their investment and never fully recovered. His father died within a year, and Mr. Glasgow was left with the debts. His two best horses died from lockjaw, he could not afford to replace them, and he was left with two "old plugs" to farm with.

"So I only got out twenty acres of corn that year. And it come up nice, and oh, but it was pretty, and I went over it with the cultipactor and the rotary hoe, and went back one day, and it was about, oh knee high or a little better, and oh it was pretty. Started up across and it was a peculiar odor, and the horses commenced to snorting, and they didn't act very nice. Well, I had to pull out, and I noticed here and there a stalk wilting. Went back the next day, and it was wilting something awful. Called the county agent, and he come out and looked at it, dug up a root and here was chinch bug. In a week's time there was about nineteen acres of that, that you couldn't, it was disintegrated till there wasn't a thing there but just bare ground. Well that hit us hard. Interest day came due, and there was an attorney wanted the farm, and he went and bought the note, paid $300 more than its face value. And I was just about to go up Salt Creek. Well that little of corn I had, and I was there in the barn one night, it was pretty near ten o'clock, and I was husking. And in drove a machine, and an old Dutchman, John Schupert." There was a huskiness in Mr. Glasgow's voice, and he had to pause to get control of himself.

"And then, 'What's the matter, Bob?' 'Oh, getting along okay.' 'No, you're in bad shape financially, ain't you?' Well, I said, I thought it'd pay out maybe. He said, 'How bad are you?' Well, he brought a flashlight. He stayed for about three hours. When he left, he knew how many buttons I had on my underwear. Well, he says, 'I've never seen a fella was honest and would work, had a chance, but what he would come out of it.' He said, 'Here's a check for a thousand dollars. You go get them hounds off your back in the morning.' He says, 'If you need more, I've got more.' Well, I had at that time a little over a hundred and fifty head of hogs, and I was out of feed. Well, I went and bought feed, and he let me have some more, and fed those hogs out, and hogs at that time was hardly five cents a pound. The next spring they was eight and a half, and that put me over the riffle, and we've just had pretty good ever since. But we've seen rough sledding."

Later as we walked around the farm, I commented, "It's a real nice place."

"I'd a lost it if that old Dutchman hadn't come along."

"Yeah, he saved you."

"When he left that night, he knew how many buttons I had on my underwear."

"How well did you know him? Was he an old friend?"

"Well, acquaintance. He lived about five miles away. We'd never neighbored any. We'd never been in any contact, any social. But he was just one of those old Dutchmen that hated, what riled him was that lawyer a buying the note. See? See what I mean?"

"Yeah."

"He just hated to see that kind of injustice going on."

Besides financial problems, there have also been health problems for Mrs. Glasgow.

"Wife had a heart attack, and well she hasn't been well since. Forty-nine she had a major operation, and fifty she was having some difficulties and went to the doctor. Well, he said, 'Think it's adhesions from that operation she had last year.' 'Well,' I said, 'suffering and everything, gonna have to do something.' Then said, 'She's got gall stones.' Well, I said, 'Send her away, have it operated.' Well, he said, 'Next week.' Just kept on, 'Next week, next week.' Did that for about three weeks. And one Friday evening she had a spell of a different kind, and it was the hives. Well, got better, and took her over there." They called the doctor, but he did not come on time, and she got worse, and finally had an appendicitis attack. "But she's been an invalid all these years. She's had four bad heart attacks. How she keeps going, I don't know. She's only eighty-one."

Her illness has been difficult for him. "I started that [woodworking] three years ago. My wife was sick. And you take and set by a sick person twenty-four hours a day, it'll get the best of you. And I fixed that [woodworking shop in his basement], and I just go back and forth. The last four years, I've never been away but four times over two hours."

By talking about these difficulties as part of his life review, Bob Glasgow faces them directly and emphasizes his survival. He does not engage in self-pity; rather, he indicates that accidents, financial hardships, and illnesses can be overcome. He is here in the present, talking, showing his farm to visitors, doing woodwork, staying active, staying alive, living proof of his survival. Despite all of the hardships, Mr. Glasgow maintains a positive outlook on life. He has the perseverance of a Sam Laird, taking up woodwork in his seventies and with the use of only one hand. I think one reason his ancestors and the house and barn are so important to him is that, in some way, they make up for the misfortunes of his life. In his life review, the house and barn symbolically balance the negative aspects of his life. His grandfather was a successful man with whom Mr. Glasgow can identify; the house and barn are symbols of his grandfather's success and tangible evidence of the status of the Glasgows in the community. Taking visitors on tours of them, describing the construction details, and telling stories about his grandfather and Sam Laird are means of sharing in their achievement and showing that Bob Glasgow values the same things they did. His grandfather, whom he never knew, ends up being a more.important figure in his personal myth than his father. Several times he said "father" when he meant "grandfather," and he shares his name with his grandfather. He said of his father concerning the bad cattle investment, "That was one time Dad let me down." Since he does not perceive his father as being as successful as his grandfather, he skips a generation in terms of his identification and family storytelling.

Individual success and achievement orientation through competition are important themes in Bob Glasgow's life story, but they are balanced by a countertheme, cooperation. First of all, his stories of striving for achievement are not always positive.

"There was one outfit [group of farmers in one community] that was the hardest to work with. And they was always a sparring, 'I had the best grain, I had the most.' And one would say he had a twenty-acre field, well, and he [the other] would say, 'Only twelve acres in that field.' Have a big yield, you know. And they just sparring back and forth, and wanted to be the biggest, best. And Wes Jefferson and Orville, his boy, they were about the worst at it. And one fall their corn just didn't amount to anything, and [I] went there shredding in the community, and hadn't got to them yet, and their's wasn't going to turn out. And I gollys if they didn't both of them hang themselves."

"What?"

"They just couldn't face it to have the other people beat them."

"And they hung themselves, both of them?"

"Both of them. Wes hung himself. About the day after the funeral, why Orville hung himself."

"That sounds crazy to me."

"Yes, it's a form of insanity."

This story shows Mr. Glasgow's ambivalence toward achievement orientation and competition; it can lead to the kind of success his grandfather enjoyed, but if overemphasized it can lead to self-destruction, as it did for the Jeffersons, or it can be undermined by misfortune, as in Mr. Glasgow's own life.

Competitive achievement must be leavened with cooperation in order to succeed; the narratives of Bob Glasgow illustrate this over and over. The story of the barn building emphasizes the theme of cooperation—"everybody had to work together, cooperation"—and this is underscored in the story by his use of the metaphor of the folk dance as a cooperative activity. The threshing ring is another agrarian pursuit that requires cooperation, although each farmer benefits as an individual (Rikoon 1988; McMillen 1974, 87–100). I asked him, "Did you ever hear of the threshing rings?"

"That was just your gang to—that went with the thresher."

"Okay, so you—"

"The neighbors, just the neighbors come in all together. You take a, say now here's this here road on Moore's road, there was six farmers there. Well then they hired the, they furnished the team to haul the grain, and then they hired the fellas to pitch in the fields, and take care of that part of the work, and that was called that ring. And then I'd go, they had a ring here above town, and, Buck Run ring, and the next ring that I threshed was in around Calvary. You see, there was eight men in that group, and they didn't have to hire as many in the field.

"Well you'd go in and the first thing, you know, the man would tell you where he wanted his stack, straw stack. Well then you set the most advantageous place that you could for the wind to take the dust, the straw to the right place and the dust away from the men at the work. And then you'd set the machine level, and get your blow route and your blow belt rolled out and your tractor hooked on, and by that time there was usually a wagon there with grain. And they pitched, we'd get that job done, we'd go to the next place and the same thing."

"How many men would be working there?"

"Oh, usually about four in the field and six wagons, ten, and there was usually two to haul grain and two on the stack."

"Now those would be men in the vicinity, other farmers that had agreed to help each other out?"

"The teams were always neighbors, and the help was either hired from the neighbor boys or from wherever they could get it."

"You said there were eight men in a ring or so many men. The ones in the ring, what did you mean by that?"

"Well now, you take here, there was Ralph Joplin, Ray Seaman, Andy Easter, Morris Young, Leonard Young, John Moore, and Harvey Rucker, and Sam Hatler. Now that made up that ring, and that was, I would say, an average ring."

"What did that mean exactly?"

"That many farms. These men each operated their own farms."

"They helped each other."

"They helped, each one of them come, and each one of them of course returned back. Then whatever extra help they needed outside of that, why they had to hire."

A few minutes later, I asked him, "I was really wondering about the customs that went along with the threshing more than anything else."

"Neighbors. Having neighbors, had neighbors. You take a woman was gonna be, put a big canning on, why one or two of the neighbors would go in and help her, and then they'd change back and forth. That was part of their social life. Build up a friendship in a community that you couldn't tear down."

Neighbors, friendship, cooperation, community—these are central values in Bob Glasgow's life; they provide the appropriate and necessary context for the control of individual achievement orientation. His values about community and cooperation, like his general view of the agrarian past, are an idealization that does not always fit the historical reality; his view, in fact, is part of a cultural agrarian "myth." Historians such as Richard Hofstadter have pointed out that farmers in the eighteenth and nineteenth centuries did not practice communal action or have much sense of community (1961, 43). By the end of the nineteenth century and into the twentieth, changing economic conditions caused farmers to become involved in more cooperative ventures (Hofstadter 1961, 112–13), and this period may conform more closely to Mr. Glasgow's ideal. He sees the ideal of cooperation going back at least to 1858 when the barn was built. Mr. Glasgow's view of Sam Laird was as a commander, but one who needed the cooperation of his men to build a barn, and when the cooperative effort broke down, he lost his thumb. Mr. Glasgow's grandfather was a strong individualist bent on having the biggest and best farm in the county, but he had to have the cooperation of the community in order to get his house and barn built. Bob Glasgow worked by himself to make his farm a success, but he needed his neighbor, the Old Dutchman, to save him from losing the farm. Mr. Glasgow's life history is an American story: as in American cultural history the dominant values of individualism and achievement orientation are not without conflict. They can lead to stress and suicide; they can be thwarted by misfortunes out of the control of the individual. Finally, for Bob Glasgow, cooperation with neighbors is seen as equally important: individual goals must be balanced by community concerns. Here again, we see the significance of interconnectedness in the life of an old person.

The stories about the barn and the house contain themes analogous to patterns in other descriptions and stories he tells and in society itself; his life review incorporates symbols from several different dimensions. Mr. Glasgow makes this clear when he compares the barn raising to a folk dance; both depend on a strong leader and cooperation, as does the threshing ring. The house represents the stability of its owner, signifying his ability to support a wife and family, his dominant relationship with his wife, who is seen as another kind of property, and his standing in the community; these points are made every time Mr. Glasgow tells the story about the house. The values exist abstractly as part of the culture and find expression in traditional activities, in oral narratives, and in physical artifacts. Roland Barthes' comment on food and food behavior has application here: "the fact that there is communication is proven, not by the more or less vague consciousness that its users may have of it, but by the ease with which all the facts concerning food form a structure analogous to other systems of communication" (1979, 168). Certainly in this case, all of the facts concerning the Glasgow house and barn do form structures that are analogous to other systems of communication—narratives, folk dances, barn raisings, threshing rings, courtship customs, and social behavior. The barn and the house stand on the landscape as material reminders to Bob Glasgow and his listeners of the other kinds of communication, and each aspect of the tradition must be viewed as it relates to the others, because all of them are a part of his life review.

The rhetoric of Bob Glasgow's discourse supports and enhances the values he is pointing out. His use of the barn as a reference for narratives is similar to the artificial memory systems of the Middle Ages and Renaissance in which certain objects produced images used as a basis for rhetorical discourse (Yates 1966, 63–64, 129–39). The physical artifact is important in his storytelling; the barn, the house, and other objects become part of the story. He tells many of the stories with the object at hand, and when the object is missing, the storytelling is altered. When he told the barn-raising story in his house he referred to the barn in a distant way, "that side of the barn was all framed." When he tells the same story inside the barn, the reference is direct: "You see that frame?" He prefers to be on the site to tell the story. This was indicated when he said at the beginning of the interview, "Well, what'd you want to know about? I could tell you a lot more good if I just took you around town and showed you. There was a, in the first part there was the mills, the two mills that served the community." He went on to mention the cowhide belt from one mill that he owned and just sold last year. He would prefer to take me around town and show me in order to "tell me a lot more good." Showing and telling are part of the same process for him; one depends on the other. If he still had the cowhide belt from the mill, he could use it as a starting point for a description or a story. When he was telling me about his grandfather's gun, he said, "Back in these woods, well there's two places yet I could show you, where there was bear wallows." He showed me the gun, and if I had had time, he would have showed me the bear wallows.

He uses the artifact to structure the narrative. He takes the listener, who is also an observer, inside the barn, shows him or her the frame, and then begins the story of lifting the frame in which Sam Laird lost his thumb. He points to the beams in order to describe the size of the axe used to hew them. He tells the courtship story of building the house as he approaches it. Some of the stories he tells without artifacts are not as well structured as those with. For instance, his narrating of family history is not always clear; I had to use two print sources in order to get all of the events and characters straight. He was impatient with my lack of understanding and discouraged further questions. This was never a problem with the stories that involved physical artifacts; they provided a starting point and often a sequence of events.

The stories that depend on buildings and objects are set perform-ance pieces. On my second visit to the farm, several months after the first, he told the same stories in much the same way, standing in the same place, and pointing to the same features. He used the folk dance metaphor both times he told the Sam Laird barn-raising story, and he pointed to the beams and mortices on both occasions. The same phrases were used to direct the attention of the observer to features of the house and barn. First visit: "Look here at this piece." "Look at them heavy timbers up, way up yonder." "Now just look how smooth that is from here." "Here's something here. Several places you can see it." "Look here how this dove-tail cornered." "Oh, that door there was hand-carved and in panels and handmade in walnut, and it was a honey. And this door here, the closet here, and that door was a honey too." "Now here's the original fastener of the door. See. See that." "Look there, you see it?" Second visit: "Note how them braces fit up there." "Look how them mortices fit." "You see that frame?" "Look how the mortices fit, how the braces fit. Did you notice that?" "Now over there on that far side." These phrases function to link narrative and object together, not merely to illustrate the story, but to place the listener/observer within the story, to make it immediate. Bob Glasgow uses the pronoun "you" not only to make the *listener* aware of the performance but also to make the *observer* aware that it is a special kind of performance, one with a visual component. He does this with other objects besides the house and barn.

As we walked through the barn, he said, "Here's something I don't expect you see very many of," and he directed me to a large stone object on the floor of the barn.

"Now what is this?"

"That's your old-fashioned stone burr grist mill. It made the finest corn meal and buckwheat flour and wheat grits that a person ever got a hold of. Stone burrs. It's built light. A man bought it; I had a sale last year, and he bought it. Just pick up that corner."

I tried, and of course could not lift it.

He laughed as I grunted, "Oh, that's solid. That's really heavy. How old is that?"

"Oh, I don't know. Is there a date on it or not?"

"It looks pretty old. How long have you had it?"

"Oh, I've only had it for about fifty years."

"Oh, it was old when you got it."

"Oh yes, oh yes."

"Is it still usable?"

"Oh my, yes."

"When was the last time you used it?"

"Oh, about twelve months ago."

"Oh, to grind some corn?"

"Corn meal."

Notice how he pulls me into asking about the grist mill. He causes me to engage directly, physically with the object and then waits for me to ask questions about it. He used a similar verbal strategy in the house when he showed me the chimney.

"Now down in the basement in that first floor, across the top of the fireplace, there was a six by eight [beam]. Why [from] 1842 to 1909, and that fire, that old fire was in there all the time, right up there on that piece of timber. It never even showed a bit of smoke or char or nothing. Why?" He paused.

"I don't know."

"Anything that way, that they was gonna put anyplace that way so close to the fire, they boiled it in alum water, and you can't burn it. Them old fellas knew."

Rather than tell me directly about this piece of folk knowledge, he drew my attention to the chimney, pointed out the unique quality of the beam and asked me how it came to be. The artifact draws the listener into the description and helps to make the point about the wisdom and knowledge of the old days. Mr. Glasgow used similar rhetorical devices when he showed me old tools, harnesses, kitchen utensils, and other antiques.

Bob Glasgow has taken on a role as "old farmer" and family historian. He is an authority on a time that his audience is not familiar with because they are too young. He uses his age as part of his identity to attract attention to himself and to give him a reason to perform. The abundance of physical artifacts available to Mr. Glasgow gives him the opportunity to be an informal guide to a "living museum." In this he is like many elderly people who turn their homes into small museums: "All of the artifacts become ways to teach visitors who are too young to have known this world, or who grew up outside of it. The place and its past are distilled—freeze dried, actually—to be fully comprehended when narrative is added" (Hufford, Hunt, Zeitlin 1987, 67). Mr. Glasgow is the ideal guide because of his age— he knows firsthand about many of the objects and times he describes— and his family connection: he hasn't just read about the house and barn, he knows their stories because they were built by his grandfather. His guided tours of the farm become ritualized events in which he asserts his own identity and continuity.

> Ritual is an assertion of continuity. Even when dealing with change, ritual connects new events and elements with preceding ones, incorporating them into a stream of precedents so that they are recognized as growing out of tradition and experience. Ritual states enduring and even timeless patterns, thus connects past, present, and future, abrogating history, time, and disruption (Myerhoff 1978, 164–65).

When he repeatedly tells the same stories in the same place, he connects with his own past and the past of his ancestors. Although the house has decayed, the stories about it have kept it new, kept it forever the showplace it once was in reality. Talking in the present about the house, the barn, and the other artifacts from the past ensures that the values and patterns associated with them will be carried into the future by the person hearing the stories. These timeless patterns for Bob Glasgow have to do with family, achievement, community, and cooperation, concepts he believes will always be important.

NOTES

1. Adams County historian Stephen Kelley first led me to Bob Glasgow.

2. This summary was compiled from Mr. Glasgow's testimony in addition to information from a county history book (Evans and Stivers 1900).

3. See Csikszentimihalyi and Rochberg-Halton 1981, 1; Glassie 1985, 48; Gowans 1986, 377; Meining 1979, 6; and Rapaport 1969, 16.

4. For more on family folklore, see Zeitlin, Kotkin, and Baker 1982.

5. The buildings, as symbols of the past, are related to what Mikhail Bakhtin calls chronotopes, "points in the geography of a community where time and space intersect and fuse. Time takes on flesh and becomes visible for human contemplation; likewise, space becomes charged and responsive to the movements of time and history and the enduring character of a people. . . . Chronotopes thus stand as monuments to the community itself, as symbols of it, as forces operating to shape its members' images of themselves" (1981, 7).

5

Alva Snell
Occupational Identity after Retirement

"My father was a commercial fisherman, my grandfather was a commercial fisherman, my great-grandfather was a commercial fisherman, so it's just natural that I do it, of course. My father was running a boat, and I went with him on a boat. Those days there was lots of herring in the lake. That was the first job a boy would get going out in the lake. They would cut the herring down the middle, scrape the insides out. . . . And, so I worked that year and every other summer till I got through high school, and as soon as I got through high school—you know how it is—a boy wants to leave home, and they called from here, Kishman's, a fishery in Grand River, and wanted to know if there was any boys down there that wanted to go out in the lake and clean fish, and of course, that was me. 'Yes, I'll take it.' So I came and went to work on one of the boats. Well, then the next year, the captain of the boat called me and wanted me to work on the boat. So, I've been here ever since. Not cleaning fish, but he wanted me as a crew member, you know. And so there's been a lot of changes."

Alva Snell was telling about how he got started in the commercial fishing business. At seventy-five, he has been retired from his occupation for many years, but he maintains contact with the fishing industry, and his self-image is still that of a commercial fisherman. He lives in Vermilion, Ohio, on western Lake Erie, which is where he lived and fished all of his adult life. After his retirement from fishing, he went into the business of cleaning fish for sport fishermen, and he was still doing this in 1983 when another folklorist, Tim Lloyd, and I interviewed him at his home and later at his business. Even before he went out on boats to clean fish, he was working in the fishing industry.

"Well, anyway, I was a young boy in World War I, and I remember the principal of the school and the people that ran the fisheries coming up to the school and asked all the seventh- and eighth-grade boys to stand up. When they all stood up, they said you, you, you to such and such a fish house, and you, you, you. They had to put up ice because so many young men had gone to war, and they had to get the ice up. In those days they took it out of the lake or river, and they had to get it. Otherwise, there would be no fish the next year. They didn't have ice machines like they have today, so they didn't have enough help, so they got seventh- and eighth-grade boys, and even women were putting up ice. I worked in a fish house when I was thirteen years old after school and in the summertime, and started out in the lake when I was fourteen years old. That's 1918. The boys hadn't all got home, you know. And anybody who would go out in the lake, they would take them. Took me out in the lake in 1918."

Starting in commercial fishing at the age of thirteen and working in it for over fifty years has given Alva Snell a strong occupational identity that has persisted into his retirement years. His life review is largely a reminiscence of his years as a fisherman. Just as Leonard Bryan's identity goes back before he was born to his father, and Bob Glasgow's to his grandfather, so too does Alva Snell's extend back to his father, grandfather, and great-grandfather, since all of them were commercial fishermen. In his case, occupational and family identity reinforce each other: family stories are also occupational stories giving them added meaning in Mr. Snell's life. His grandmother was his source of information about his grandfather and great-grandfather as fishermen.

Tim asked him, "Do you have any idea about when it was that your grandfather started fishing?"

"Oh, close to it. I've got a picture of it here when he was born. I can tell you. Let's see. I can't find it right now, but I think he was born in 1840. I know my grandmother was quite a bit younger than he was, and she said she was a big enough girl during the Civil War so she remembered some of the Civil War. When she married my grandfather, he was running a schooner here on the lake. She went on the boat as cook. And then he got the job running the fishery up there in Fairport Harbor. So he died when I was real young. Just how many years he fished I couldn't tell you. He died when I was about three. Great-grandfather, that would be my grandmother's father. They lived on the lake bank just this side of Fairport. She says she can remember him—my grandmother was telling me this, the one that lived to be ninety-three—said she can remember him working all winter long making nets ready for spring. They would fish in the spring until the weather got so he could do the farming, and then he would farm, and then fish again in the fall."

Commercial fishing was a rough life; the work was hard and fishermen had to face many hazards such as storms in the lake, huge freighters in thick fog, and ice early and late in the season. The hardships of being a fisherman is one of the themes in his life review.

I asked him, "When you were talking about the weather, you talked about the freezing weather. What about in the summer or other times when just storms would come up?"

"See that scar right there? Can you see it? Well, I've had nine of them, and they are skin cancers from working out in the sun."

"That's an occupational hazard then."

"There's one right there, and one on that arm, behind my ears, and all over."

He shows off his scars almost as if they were badges of honor, emblematic of his occupational identity, indicators of the hard job fishing was. As an elderly man, he displays the scars as a connection to his former active life as a fisherman. When Mr. Snell talks about commercial fishing in the past, he often implicitly or explicitly contrasts it with fishing today, and he feels that his time of active fishing was superior in several ways. For one thing, he thinks that men worked harder in his day.

"Now like, well I stopped around there at the barber shop, you know. . . . I was in there one day, and one fella was complaining about, you know, working so damn hard. Eight hours a day and five days a week. I said, 'Well God, I've got the record where I can

12. Alva Snell. (Photograph by the author.)

show you where I would work from Labor Day to Thanksgiving and not have a day off, which [is] seven days a week when you was fishing, you worked seven days a week.' And I can remember getting home for Thanksgiving dinner one time at ten. That's the way you worked then, you know. If you were fishing, you had to make it while the fish were around. We didn't take any days off. We was there."

Later he told a similar story. "Tell you another funny thing that happened, you know. Years ago, as I told you, you worked seven days a week, and there was no eight-hour day like there is now. In fact, I joined what they called the trap-netters' union at one time. There was lots of fishermen at that time, and the contract called for ten-hour days, eleven hours in the spring and fall when you was setting and pulling the nets, to get them out of the lake or something. But you worked ten-hour days and didn't think anything of it. Finally, got to a nine-hour day. Finally, down to eight. Well, I was out in the lake and just started with an eight-hour day, and looked at my watch, and said, 'Oh my gosh, the day is [over], we gotta get started for home. We're going to be working overtime.' And one of the fellas said, 'I've never seen anything like it.' He says, 'I can stand on my head eight hours.' Other fella in the boat says, 'Why, I can hold my breath for that long.' It seemed so short after working for ten hours to work for eight."

Other retired fishermen we interviewed expressed the same opinion: work was harder and men were better back in their day. When retired fishermen get together, they reinforce these attitudes in each other. Alva Snell told us that he still sees one of the men he used to work with.

"Do you get much of a chance to talk to him?" I asked.

"Oh yes."

"When you get together and talk, do you talk about your days as commercial fishermen?"

"Of course, not so much now. We've talked it all over a number of times, but we will, when something will come up, we will say, you know, well, so-and-so, if they would have done it a little different, they would have made out a little better or something. They were half trying or they don't know what they're doing. That outfit down at Kishman's now, we talk about it all the time. Hell, if we were there, we'd be catching some fish. They got a job, and that's all they care about."

"Did you ever tell some of these experiences like, well, recall the time that such-and-such happened?"

"Oh, yes. It comes up, you know. If that's been your life, well, things come up that's happened during your lifetime, that [was] either was funny or sad."

Retired fishermen define themselves at least partially, then, in opposition to other groups (Spicer 1971; Bauman 1971; Dundes 1983), in this case younger fishermen. By contrasting themselves to still active fishermen, retired fishermen can maintain a positive identity: they worked harder and were better fishermen than those operating today. Retired workers have an even greater need for a positive identity because they no longer have the day-to-day activity to define themselves occupationally; they have passed from instrumental to largely expressive roles. In retirement, workers use the telling of occupational personal experience narratives as a means of maintaining identity (Santino 1989; Lloyd and Mullen 1990). Mr. Snell suggests that his positive identity is a question of values: the young fishermen are only passing time in the job; they do not care about doing a quality job the way he and his friend did. It is as if work itself had more value in the old days.

Not only were the fishermen better in the past, the environment in which they worked was also better. Mr. Snell complained about the pollution of the lake, as did many active fishermen, but he brought the perspective of fifty years' experience to his judgment, contrasting the present with the past.

"Now that's another thing, when I started fishing, if you wanted a drink of water, you had a coffee can with a string on it, and just throw it overboard and had a drink. That's all there was to it. We drank right out of the lake, and didn't think anything of it. Then World War II, and then you didn't want to get it splashed in your eyes, 'cause it would make your eyes sore. You know, it got that bad."

He and other retired fishermen also talked about the former abundance of fish in the lake in contrast to the paucity today. This points to a theme noted in occupational folklore scholarship that has implications for old-age research: "Every industry's workers seem to have a conception of a golden age, a time before the present when things were different or somehow better " (Santino 1978, 204). Mr. Snell and his few surviving fishermen friends form an age cohort equally bound by age and occupation. One reason Alva Snell and his cohorts have constructed an idealized past is that they have a need for a positive occupational identity. If the past was better, then they were better. Since they are no longer actively involved in the occupation, they have a special need to be superior to those who are. The "golden age" and "golden men" images give them an identity that the work itself provided in the past.

Ed Lampe, one of the men whom Mr. Snell and other local fishermen remembered from the old days, takes on heroic proportions in the stories told about him. Mr. Snell gave his version of an often-repeated story.

"They tell me he used to get leads for gill nets, you know, about that long and big around as your thumb, you know, weighed about a pound, pound and a quarter, two pounds or something like that, depending on what you want. Well, anyway, they would come in boxes when they would buy them, you know. They said he was going up the street here one day with a box under his arm. He stopped to talk to somebody. He stood there about five minutes talking with them, and finally said, 'Well, I guess I better go along. This thing is getting kind of heavy.' Weighed two hundred fifty pounds. That's what the box weighed. He was standing there with it under his arm talking."

There is a tradition of strongman heroes in American occupational folklore such as Maine fisherman Barney Beal. Richard Dorson collected an entire cycle of stories about Barney Beal, and many of them focus on his casual displays of great physical strength (1964, 40–54). The strongman seems to have special meaning for retired fishermen because he represents the golden age: for Alva Snell and others Ed Lampe is symbolic of the greater capacities of working men in the past.

"Time they tell he was either going or coming from down the other end of the lake someplace. Years ago, trains, you know, didn't run as fast as they do today. It was no trouble to hop a train to go someplace. Back when I was a kid, I would hop a train to town.

That was nothing. They went slow and you would jump off. Well, anyway, he was going someplace and hopped on this boxcar that was open. When it lightened up in the morning, well, here's three or four fellas on the other end all asleep. Of course, he was all alone. They made out they was going to rob him. They started talking pretty rough. He went back in one end. They kept getting closer to him, and finally he started to run for the other end, and as he went past the open door, he run and grabbed one of them and throwed him out the door, and run to the other end of the boxcar. And he run for the other end, and going past, he knocked one out of the door. When he got them down to about two, they decided to leave him alone. Oh, yes, he was a tough one."

"He was a tough one," and from this story it is clear that he was also a smart one. The hero in legends represents the qualities of an ideal man to the group telling the legends; in this case retired fishermen admire both strength and intelligence in their work. When Ed Lampe defeats the men who are going to rob him, he represents the ideal fisherman confronting outsiders, thereby reinforcing group identity. Mr. Snell's telling of these stories clearly shows that he admires Ed Lampe, but in two other stories a certain ambivalence can be seen. Lampe had a reputation as an experimenter with boats and engines: he put a car engine in a boat once and rigged up belts to it to drive the boat.

"Well, he was out in the lake one time, and it got pretty rough. And got a little water in the boat, and he didn't stop to bail it out, and of course, a little oil always in the bottom of fish boats, you know. Got splashing up on his belts and first thing you know, the belts get slippery and he couldn't run. That's one of the things they tell about him trying his new tricks. And then he had this one boat . . . he was fishing down the lake quite a ways, and got ready to go home. . . . And he run a little ways, and he says, it was blowing strong from the west, and he says, 'Guess we better anchor here,' he says, 'so it dries out.' So they throwed over the anchor and laid there, and they said the boat was made out of sheet metal of some sort, kind of thin. He didn't make it too sturdy, you know, and everything they would go up on the seal, boy, they said they would come down and it would shake, you know. Finally, he says, kept blowing harder, and he says, 'I guess we're going to have to go home anyway. Better pull the anchor.' So they said they pulled the anchor, run all the rest of the night, and when it lightened up in the morning, they was right in the same place they was the night before. He was running all night long, but he wasn't going ahead any."

He was admired as a strongman as well as an intelligent man, but his intelligence got him into trouble when he tried experiments on the boat. Alva Snell and the other retired fishermen are essentially conservative in their views of their shared occupation: they believed in following traditional methods of fishing. The lesson of this story seems to be stick to the tested methods of operating a boat. This fits with their attitude toward new methods of fishing adopted after their retirement. As Mr. Snell said, "They don't know what they're doing." The hero legend has an important place in the life review since it projects qualities of the ideal man from the past that the storyteller identifies with in the present. Alva Snell uses stories about Ed Lampe to indicate that despite his own age and weakened physical condition, he was once strong enough to do the kind of work the hero does.

Not all of the old fishermen were heroes; there were also local characters, eccentrics who fulfilled the commonly held stereotype of commercial fishermen as filthy alcoholics (Gilmore 1983; Mullen 1978, 113–29). Alva Snell and the other retired fishermen in Vermilion tell stories about one of these characters, Jib Snyder. One fisherman said of Jib Snyder, "But he was dirty. Oh, stink. You could smell him a block away." Mr. Snell said that Jib only got a bath once a year when Dr. Dickson took him to the hospital to get cleaned up by the nurses, and Jib would say, "Gee, those nurses' hands were so soft." Mr. Snell told a couple of stories about him.

"Now, let me see, was it Jib who was fishing for catfish, and he had it on the bottom of the boat, and he was rowing and one of the oars came out, and he fell over back, and he had an oar right in the middle of his back, and he couldn't get it out, you know. Couldn't reach it. Darn, had to come on in. He was fishing, and he just had this little boat, you know, and he was fishing all alone in it. He would fish for whatever was the best fish at the time, you know. Catfish or he would fish for herring or whatever happened to be around. And laughing one day, he says he was getting two cents a pound for herring at the time, and old Henry Kishman, the old fish company there years ago, says, tells the house foreman there, he says, 'Tell so-and-so can't take his fish for awhile. The son of a bitch is gonna get rich.' Two cents a pound. I had a grandmother that lived on the lake bank down here beside of Fairport, and he used to go in no more than a rowboat. He'd go from here and row down there to Fairport, sixty or seventy miles. Fish down there for awhile and then come back."

For a retired fisherman such as Alva Snell, telling these stories is a means of dealing with the negative stereotype that the general public has of commercial fishermen. Rather than ignore it, he confronts it directly, laughs at it, but makes sure that the listener knows that he and other responsible fishermen are not like this. Jib Snyder stories often mention his heavy drinking, a trait commonly associated with fishermen, but Mr. Snell disassociates himself from this image.

At another point in the interview, Tim asked him, "What do fishermen do for recreation?"

"Well, the natural thought when you speak of a fisherman is he's going to spend his spare time in a bar."

"Is that true though?" Tim asked.

"Well, I didn't drink," Mr. Snell replied, "and I didn't smoke. But I spent a lot of my spare time just traveling."

I asked him, "So this stereotype of the fishermen drinking is just that, a stereotype? Some of them drink, but not all of them."

"But not all of them, no. I know another man here in town that I fished with. Took him out when he was young. I always took him on the boat when he was young, and I ended up fishing on a boat he was running down there fishing. He don't drink. Oh, he might take a drink, I don't mean that. But he's a hard worker, took care of his mother, and done all right. He owns about a dozen houses around town."

This is another good example of a concept I mentioned earlier: in "oppositional identity" one group forms its identity partially on the basis of differences from other groups, not just on shared values within the group (Spicer 1971, 797). Without us mentioning drinking, Mr. Snell brings up the stereotype of the drunken fisherman, an outsider's view that he contrasts with his own identity as a non-drinker and that of another responsible fisherman who comes close to a positive stereotype himself—a hardworking property owner who loves his mother. Every time Alva Snell tells a Jib Snyder story he is implicitly making the contrast between himself and the negative stereotype.

Alva Snell, like most commercial fishermen on Lake Erie, sees himself in conflict with several different groups—game wardens, sport fishermen, pleasure boaters, and poachers—and he told stories about confrontations with these groups. Game wardens were considered adversaries even back in his great-grandfather's day.

"Yes, there's always been some law as far as I can remember. Then I've heard stories, 'cause I said my father and grandfather and great-grandfather were fishermen. They tell a story about my grandfather who was running a gill-net boat down there at Fairport Harbor, and the game warden was on the boat. They were into the dock, you know, working. Been out fishing. The game warden was on the dock giving them a hard time. What it was about I don't know. All I know is the story they tell, and finally one of the fellas throwed the lines off the stern of the boat, and somebody else on the front of the boat pushed the boat out, and they started down the river. The warden says, 'Where we going?' My grandfather said, 'We're going out in the lake and drown you.' You see, there was laws back, that was a long time ago."

His grandfather's comic threat against the game warden probably represents a suppressed desire on the part of many commercial fishermen. Mr. Snell complains about the unfairness and uneven application of the laws.

"Did the boat you were on ever have any conflicts with game wardens?" I asked him.

"Oh, yes, I got arrested many times. A place down here, that fish market, a fella come along and wanted to know if he could go out on the lake with us. I said, 'Sure.' After we got out there, he wanted to help, you know. He was real interested and wanted to help, and he was sorting fish. You know, you get small fish in the dip nets. You know, you see how they done it up there. You got to get the big ones out and throw the little ones overboard. Well, he wanted to help, and he was sorting fish. We was clear out by the line by the Canadian border a ways away. And we came in and went to unload our fish, and there was the game warden on the dock. He looked the fish over, and had too many small ones. You're allowed a percentage for mistakes, but we had too many, and I had never had any trouble before, but I figured that fella that was sorting, he hated to throw them away. We're used to throwing them away, but he throwed too many in, and they took my whole catch. It was Thursday, and I wanted to fish for fish market for Friday. They took the whole catch, and I got arrested, of course. Same time I went over to one of the other fish markets. The fella that was buying it was from Canada. Hell, he had smaller fish than I did. They let him get away with it. I couldn't."

The warden did not always win, though, as Mr. Snell illustrated when I asked him, "Generally, were they fair to deal with or were there some problems down through the years?"

"After all, that was their job. Once in a while, you would kind of think maybe they came on a little too hard, but after all it was their job. I remember some of the last fishing I had done, I was on a gill-net boat down here at Kishman's, and we were fishing down almost to Lorain on the outside a ways. We were just getting a lot of fish that were just under the margin. Had to measure them all 'cause it was so close to it, and we was laying there anchored, and picking fish out of the nets, you know. And I said, 'Gee, those are nice fish to throw away. I think I'll take a nice mess of them home.' I started throwing them in a box, and somebody else said, 'Yes, save me a mess, too.' Next thing you know everybody in the boat thought they ought to have a mess, and so we throwed them all in a box so we could clean them on the way home, and get them in their dinner buckets when we got in, so nobody would see us, you know. Somebody looked up and there was a state boat coming right at us, and it was getting right close. Gee, I jumped up quick and put this box, had these small fish in it, and dumped them over the side of the boat on the opposite side, you know, so they couldn't see it. They was coming from the other end. Dumped them overboard, see. They pulled up and tied up and got on the boat, and I started measuring the nets and looking at the fish, and of course, these fish that I had throwed overboard, part of them were dead. Being out of the net, they are a little different, and they started to drift where we was anchored, drift up from behind the boat. And one of them fellas sees it, and oh boy. He jumped into the boat, you know, and he had a dip net and he started to bail them fish out of there. The other fella stayed on the boat. There was two of them. Well, the fella on the boat, he called in. Of course, they had the means to call Sandusky. Time we got into the dock out here at Kishman's, of course, there was four, and they took all our fish.

"Had to go down to Lorain for the hearing. Of course, we was fishing down off Lorain. That's where they took it, to court down there. Ray hired a lawyer down there, and he come and had a talk with us before we had the hearing, so we learned a few things, you know, that we didn't know about what was going on. So we had the hearing, of course, and this lawyer got up and he says, 'Any other boats in the vicinity?' 'Oh, yes, there were other boats around.' He says, 'How do they know those fish were yours? Maybe they was somebody else's that drifted there. Got a mark on them some way to tell they was yours?' 'Well, no.' Oh gee, the wardens got so mad. That lawyer was so smart. He could do things, and he knew how to. So, finally, the judge says, 'Where's the fish?' Do you know they had done something to those fish, either sold them or ate them or something, so they couldn't produce them, and the judge threw the thing out of court, and you know, when we went out in the hall, of course, there were a lot of people there because a lot of them knew us, you know, and they was all there to find out about it. The warden was there, and he said, 'I'm gonna show them goddamn fishermen every time I get a chance.' He was mad because he got beat. He knew, in a way, that we was at fault. You're not supposed to take small fish, but we was only taking enough for us for ourselves, you know. It wasn't like we was going to take a hundred pounds in and sell them, but nonetheless, when he seen them drifting by, he went wild."

Taking fish home in a lunch bucket was common practice for fishermen, but it was against the law, one of the laws most fishermen considered unfair. When he tells these stories, Mr. Snell is again expressing his own identity in opposition to someone else. His and others' stories about game wardens are similar to the "authority stories" collected by Tim Cochrane from commercial fishermen on Isle Royale in Lake Superior: "authority stories are built upon a conceptual polarization of two groups [by asserting that] rangers' and wardens' actions are wrong, thus fishermen's [actions] are right" (1983).

Opposition of the two groups is at the center of the formation of occupational identity in the personal stories of Alva Snell and others. Now that he is retired, he no longer has confrontations with game wardens, but the stories continue to be told because they are a significant means for him to maintain his occupational identity.

Sport fishermen are also seen by Mr. Snell as an opposing force because they are in league with tackle manufacturers to lobby for more regulation of commercial fishing and even for outlawing it altogether. He tells of several encounters that characterize sport or "hook and line" fishermen.

"I'm in arguments all the time down there cleaning fish for the hook and line fishermen. You can't believe the foolish things that they will come in and say. They complain about commercial fishermen, and they don't know what they are talking about or not. And what gets me, being a commercial fisherman all my life, they will come in with perch that long," he demonstrated by holding his fingers a few inches apart, "and curse the commercial fisherman for catching all the big ones and just leaving in the small ones. And here they are, they are killing off the little fish that never spawned. . . .

"They will catch them little things that never spawned. And I've taken sometimes some of them and thrown them on the scale where you can't believe. Little three-inch perch, three-ounce fish. It would take six of them to weigh a pound, and still they are cursing the commercial fisherman for ruining the fishing. Well, gee, now I would have to estimate how many small fish we clean a year. I know how many fish we clean, but I can't take time to measure them all, but I know that there are some here that we have cleaned a number of times of little fish like that. It's all right; they got hooked. And what are they going to do with them? They throw them back, and they're dead. But they don't think they are hurting the fishing any, you know. Oh, no, it's all right; it's the goddamn commercial fisherman who's got all them big ones. And it burns me up. I mean fair is fair, but they can't see it. They think they should have all the lake. I think the commercial fisherman has been hurt by the hook and line fisherman that follow fishing. You would be surprised how many people come into my place wanting to buy fish. I say, 'No, we don't have any to sell.' 'What do you mean, you can't buy fish? Oh my goodness.' It isn't everybody's got a boat that can go and catch a fish. They want to go and get some. They will come from way back south to the back of the lake and get some fish and can't believe. It's a bad situation. I feel awful bad about it. Not that it makes a difference to me. I'm too old, but I do see both sides of it. I see where catching fish that long, certainly by the tons, isn't helping things."

Later he added, "We always had fish of some kind. Now suddenly there isn't any fish. Commercial fisherman's fault; he caught them all. How about these thousands of boats that are catching them? Here's another thing, you can't believe, you know, you talk about the goddamn commercial fisherman, but how about these hook and liners? Now this is God's honest truth; I cleaned eight pounds of blue pickerel that long," he indicated a length underneath the legal size, "for a fellow one day this last week. The limit is six pickerel. Now, it isn't my business to turn him in. But if he had eight pounds, and I imagine he had twenty-five little fish. Well, you know, he hooked them, and they was going to die. . . . He ain't supposed to catch them, but that's the way they get away with it. Now what am I supposed to do? Turn them in? And then somebody set fire to my building, see, so I gotta keep my mouth shut. But I know what's going on, and oh, that's all right. You can't quit when they are biting that good, so they go on fishing. But the commercial fisherman, oh boy, they blast him for ruining the fishing."

He seems much more passionate in his attack on sport fishermen than you would imagine for someone who is no longer a commercial fisherman and who depends on sport fishermen in his present business. "Not that it makes a difference to me," he says, "I'm too old, but I do see both sides of it." Clearly it does still make a difference to him; his age supposedly removes him from concern for the issue, but it also gives him what he considers a clearer perspective on the situation. His involvement in the issue springs from his deeply ingrained occupational identity, and one source of the depth of identity is the opposition to other groups. Sport fishermen became his enemy because their numbers proliferated and they began to criticize commercial fishermen; he cannot forget the criticism because as he sees it, sport fishermen are trying to destroy the occupation that is the basis of his identity.

Mr. Snell has a negative attitude toward pleasure boaters as well. He told a story that explains why.

"Well, sometimes you get kind of like a yacht broke down out there, and I went out to it, and I told the fellas I was fishing out of Lorain. I was going back to Lorain. . . . I said, 'I'll take you to Lorain if you want to go.' 'Well, okay'. . . . Well, I knew they had been drinking. I could tell by the way they was acting. One fella got up on the nose of the yacht, you know, and they fastened a line there and made everything look good. So we got all ready to go. I said, 'Go on, get back down in the boat.' 'I'm all right; go ahead, go ahead,' he says. Well, I started ahead real easy. I figured, sure enough, just as soon as that line tightened up, overboard he went. Had to go back. He had a great big paunch on him. He was drunk. Tried to get him into the boat, and we could not get him. That boat's got what you call a fender streak. You know, it runs all the way around the edge of the boat to keep them away from the dock and one thing or another. So, we tried and tried. Finally, I said to the other fellas in the boat, 'You pull up on his arms, and I'll reach overboard and get one of his legs. Maybe we can roll him in like we would a pig.' And all the time the fella was saying, 'I'm done for, I'm done for, I'm done for.' And finally, we rolled him down into the bottom of the fish motor, and he laid there and rolled around like a big pig, down dirty in the fish and tar and dust and everything on the bottom of a fish boat. He said, 'I'm done for, I'm done for.' 'You're all right. Shut up.' So we got into the dock. I think we put him back in his own boat, if I remember right. Pulled him into the fish dock, got in. He come over with a bottle of booze and wanted to give it to us for pay for helping him. I says, 'Hey, buddy, you had no business out in the boat, and you see what happened. It's your damn fault. Just take your booze and go on.' I felt a little bit disgusted by it. We had worked overtime to get him in there, and then give us a bottle of booze. Here he pert near drowned."

The story contrasts the sober hardworking fisherman with the drunken wealthy yachtsman, and by contrast reinforces the positive identity of the commercial fisherman. Alva Snell's perceptions of class distinctions also underlie the story: the rich man who does not have to do manual labor is fat as a pig and has time to get drunk on his pleasure boat. In the context of the public stereotype of drunken, filthy fishermen, this story rejects that image of fishermen and places it on the yachtsman who "laid there and rolled around like a big pig, down dirty in the fish and tar and dust and everything in the bottom of the boat." A satisfying reversal is affected from the point of view of the fisherman so that the story still pleases him years after his retirement.

Alva Snell's occupational identity as a retired fisherman is also based on his own values; he strongly believes in the work ethic. When I asked him, "What makes a good fisherman?" his reply indicated the centrality of the work ethic to his self-image.

"Well, Chester Jackson and I were both saying the same thing: you gotta be hungry. He was and I was, see. And we talked about it a lot of times. Says you gotta be hungry, gotta want to make some money. Figure that's a way of doing it; well, you put in a few more hours, and work a little harder. Now, Chester, he started out, he was as poor as they could be. Didn't have anything, but he was a hard worker, and he worked hard and got to be a good fisherman. Saved his money, and—" The tape ran out here; after a new one was started, Mr. Snell continued. "That's right. You had to produce more than the other fella. Then you was the one that was making the money. I know when I went to Lorain to fish, after I got off the boat you took the picture of, you know, they had four trap-net boats there at that time. And I didn't have unemployment those days, and for trap-netters, you worked in the wintertime. They fixed up their nets for spring, you know, and I needed the work. I couldn't be laid off all winter, so I went trap-netting.

"Well, I only trap-netted there not over a couple years, and I was on the outfit, and he came to me one winter when we got through, and he says, 'You're to run a boat in the spring.' Well, land, I was only a young fella, and I said, 'I don't think that's gonna work. You got men that's been here for years. What are they gonna think, seeing a young fella like me running the boat?' He says, 'That's the trouble with them.' He says, 'They don't know any more now than they did twenty years ago. I want you to run the boat.' 'Well, okay.' Well, right away I was high boat. I mean I caught more fish than the rest of them. Every Saturday night, payday, you know, they come to me. 'Well, you want to work tomorrow?' 'Cause everything that needs to be done, they'd ask me. And if I says yes, we should do so-and-so. 'Okay, take the whole day, and we'll work tomorrow.' Well, I wanted to work. I was hungry. I needed the money. And it used to kind of get some of the other fellas. They would say, 'My God, his outfit and he asked him,' young fella like me, 'if we ought to work tomorrow.' But I was hungry. I was like Jackson, you know. He wanted to work, so that's the way it is."

I remarked, "He said that even some people called him 'Slave Driver' Jackson."

"Well, that's right. He was hungry, and I was too. Yes, when he was fishing. You know, when you always find out what the other fella has got, how many fish, no matter whether he's at the same fish house you are or another one, you say, well, what did so-and-so do today? Oh, he had so many. Jackson says he never tried to beat anybody else. It was always me [he was] trying to beat 'cause he knew I was the one catching the fish, and I was the same way. I would find out how many he was getting. I wanted to beat him."

An American success story: his achievement orientation pays off in bigger catches, promotion, and the envy and respect of others. This event took place when Mr. Snell was a young man, just starting out in the business, but he recalls it with pride during his retirement years. This is one of those central stories in the life review, a turning point in his life after which he went on to great success. Occupational identity for him depends not just on being a fisherman but being one of the best fishermen, one who was hungry and worked harder than the others. He maintained his desire to catch more fish throughout his career, even getting involved in a friendly competition with Chester Jackson. Their competition is a model for the American system: initiative and self-reliance led to success for both. Mr. Snell is similar to Bob Glasgow in emphasizing achievement orientation in his life review.

Alva Snell's identification with his job runs so deep that it seems to be the central identity feature in his life review.

Tim asked him, "Everyone says it's hard work, but everyone says they wouldn't have it any other way. Why do you think that is? Why do people like it?"

"Well, I don't know. One of them things. I was just reading an article in the paper, magazine tells what percentage of people don't like their jobs. A big percentage of them didn't like their jobs. They had to work out somewhere, and they wanted to get away, retire. I never felt that way. Of course, on the other hand, I didn't have too much as a kid. I was brought up poor. My father was a fisherman, and he drank, you know, like most fishermen, so we didn't have too much. If I wanted anything, I had to get up and get it. A fella older than I was, I knew real well, used to have a saying. He says, 'A poor man should get his pleasure from his work.' You know, that's true. If you like your job, like me, I don't play golf, I don't play bingo, nor anything. I do like to travel."

"A poor man should get his pleasure from his work." Significantly, this proverbial expression comes from a man older than Mr. Snell, thus showing the wisdom of the elderly. The saying has direct application to his life. He comes from a poor background, and he invested time and effort in his work, which paid off for him. Since he did not have much leisure time, he never developed an interest in hobbies. His job was his life, and he enjoyed it. What does a man who was totally involved in his job do after retirement? Anthropologists identify retirement from life-long occupations as a major cause of discontinuity for the elderly (Manney 1975, 19; Moore 1978). How did Mr. Snell manage to maintain his sense of continuity? Running a fish cleaning operation for sport fishermen was one means by which he maintained this continuity. Although he no longer goes out on the water, he is close to it. His only leisure time activity is traveling.

"I spend a lot of my spare time just traveling. I wanted to see how a young fella catches his fish. I have been three or four times to Nova Scotia, and I've been to the mouth of the St. Lawrence River all the way down the coast and around, been to Gloucester, Massachusetts, Cheasapeake Bay, out on shark fishing boats out of Florida, all along the Texas coast. I've been up and down the Pacific Coast, went into salmon cannery out there in Seattle, boat just coming in from Alaska. Bought a case of salmon. I've been to all [the places] where other people has fished. I get there and see it. And I've enjoyed myself that way. It's interesting. To me it was interesting. And so, I've liked it."

His occupational identity even sustains him on vacation and continues to give meaning throughout his retirement. This does not hold true for all retired people. In Kaufman's research, work was just something to do and was not a source of satisfaction for half the group being studied. "For others, especially those with professions, the work role has been a primary source of identity, and occupational achievements have been the main source of gratification and positive self-esteem" (1986, 102). Alva Snell's case shows that a working-class person can also achieve self-esteem from occupation.

A rhetorical analysis of his speech and storytelling indicates that his occupational identity in retirement affects the way he presents himself verbally. He sees himself as a spokesman for the fishing industry, and he is known locally as a good speaker for yacht clubs and civic organizations.

"I used to have pictures taken with an eight-millimeter camera, motion pictures you might call them. And one time the Sandusky Yacht Club asked if I would come up there and give a talk about fishing, and I said, yes I would. I said, 'I've got some pictures I could show you.' 'Fine.' So I went up there and showed them pictures. . . . 'Say, could you come back?' My God, I pert near wore the pictures out. Finally had to quit. Finally had to quit. They had me on the go all the time around the country, Lorain and all the places, all back south here."

"Showing the films?" I asked.

"Showing the film and giving a talk. You know, people would come up to me after I got through, and say, 'You know, I wasn't going to come tonight. I thought I didn't want to hear about fishing,' but says, 'this has been the most interesting thing I've ever had, you know.'"

His reputation attracts reporters, folklore students, and others interested in his stories about the old days of fishing. "Reporters coming around all the time. . . . Fishing was kind of something different, and they wanted to take your picture and ask you questions." A folklore class from a nearby college videotaped him during an interview. "They ask a question and want me to go ahead and talk. Of course, I'm a good talker. You can see that." Mr. Snell has self-awareness about his role as performer: he is a good talker, and he knows it. Specifically, he has worked out a role as "old fisherman" for these interviews and talks at local civic clubs. "I'm about the oldest one left around. It seems that way. Everybody I ever fished with is pert near dead." The passage of time has left him the major representative of the "old days." Like Bob Glasgow, one of his major roles in old age is as an authority on the past.

Several interesting rhetorical devices reinforce his role as old fisherman. The most prominent device is the use of phrases that frame his stories as talk about the old days. He often starts a story with "I can remember," "In those days," "At that time," and "Years ago," and then repeats these phrases throughout the story. He uses contrasts between the past and the present that emphasize the frame: "they didn't have ice machines like they have today," "so there's been a lot of changes," and "they don't make them as long today as they did years ago." He often ends a story with a phrase such as "So I've seen a lot of it." These reflexive devices remind the listener that the story is set in the past and that the storyteller knows about it firsthand in a way the listener does not. You might think any person talking about the past would use these devices, but as a matter of fact the other retired fishermen we interviewed did not use them as frequently, and neither did all the elderly people interviewed for this book. Not every old person sets himself or herself up in such a self-conscious way as a performer talking about the past.

As a self-conscious storyteller, Alva Snell has a strong sense of the "ownership" of stories. This comes out in his reluctance to tell what he considers other people's narratives. Near the end of my second interview with him, I tried to elicit a particular story I had already heard from someone else about Ed Lampe and Jib Snyder.

"Well, let's see, somebody told me one time that about Ed Lampe coming back and Jib being in the jail."

"Well, that's been told and retold so many times I don't know whether I can get it right. The jail was right up the top of the hill down there around by Kishman's. Poor Jib was in there locked up hollering his head off. Well, I don't know if I can tell that any better, or not as good as you've heard it before."

"Well, it doesn't make any difference. Just what did you hear that happened?"

"Well, all I know is something—he was in the jail hollering his head off in there, and Ed got up and got him out, didn't he?"

"Well, that's what I heard. He just let him out."

"Yes."

I then went on to tell the story as I had heard it. This is a frustrating experience for an interviewer and a problem all fieldworkers will recognize: eliciting a story rather than having it occur spontaneously often results in the kind of fragmented story Mr. Snell gives here. His disclaimer, "I don't know if I can tell that any better," and his appeal to me, "didn't he?" indicate that it is not his story, he does not feel entitled to tell it (Shuman 1986). He considers himself entitled, however, to tell some stories heard from others. Earlier in the interview, Mr. Snell narrated several Ed Lampe and Jib Snyder stories that other people told him: he had made these his own through repeated telling, and he told them confidently and well. It was only when I asked for one that he knew I had already heard elsewhere that he became diffident. He will not tell stories he does not feel entitled to because he has a strong sense of which ones are his own. He makes a further distinction when he tells a "borrowed" story by introducing it with such phrases as "They tell me," "They tell a story," and "Time they tell." In contrast, he introduces stories based on personal experience with "I remember" and "Years ago I." He tells more personal experience than secondhand stories, and the personal ones are clearly his favorites. This is in keeping with his role as performer: direct identification with the event being narrated enhances his position of authority and puts more emphasis on himself.

His self-image as the "old fisherman" storyteller is a means of establishing continuity with his own occupational past, of maintaining occupational identity after retirement. He recognizes the potential for an old-age problem when he talks about starting a fish cleaning business after he retired.

"Oh, you got to have something to do. I'd die if I just had to sit around."

Tim said, "Still, you're still working with the fish."

"Yes, something to talk. People coming in all the time. Of course, I tell them what they do wrong, and people coming in all the time and talking and you get to know them. It's something to do."

The fish cleaning business is important not just as a financial investment, then, but also as a place for talking, a place to meet new people to tell about the old days of fishing on Lake Erie. Mr. Snell fits the pattern of activity theory more than disengagement theory: he has resisted the shrinkage of his social world by finding substitutes for the work he gave up. Alva Snell has found a way to keep vital in retirement by linking up with his own occupational past. He tells stories about a hero of the "golden age" of fishing on Lake Erie, thereby associating himself with those days. He tells stories about one of the old local characters, almost as if to say that even eccentrics are not what they used to be. Finally, and most important, he tells personal experience narratives about his fishing experiences, which keep occupational memories fresh in his mind. He has enhanced his identity as a commercial fisherman by making himself the "old fisherman," the voice of the way things used to be.

6

Quincy Higgins
The Performing Personality
in Old Age

Quincy Higgins had been gently pulling my leg throughout the interview. "Well, they's a fella right down here one time had a, had a, a cow, had a hillside mouth. She had a short side and a long one. She'd go round this-a-way and eat grass, you know, and she'd run in it, then go back down and start again."

My coworker, Geraldine Johnson, and I laughed at this.

"There, one side of her mouth just fit that hillside . . . and pick up the grass, she cut it. She cut around side the hill, then pick up, run empty and come back."

"No kidding."

"That's right."

"You're pulling my leg."

"No, that's right."

Mrs. Higgins interjected, "That's not true, you know."

But he continued, "That's right, she made a nice red cow. Yeah, yeah."

"He's pulling my leg, isn't he?"

Mrs. Higgin's sister said, "He sure is."

"No, it's a fact. This fella Carpenter raised her. Yeah, Brady Carpenter raised her. And he's jimper-jawed, and the cow was, too."

I laughed.

"Said the cow got it—cow's mamma got scared by him, calf was jimper-jawed."

"You got me again."

Gerri Johnson said, "He couldn't get you."

"Yeah, he can, time after time. You don't expect me to believe all this, do you?"

"You can sort it out, believe what you want to," he laughed.

"I'll, I'll have to listen to this tape, sort it all out. I can't figure it all out now. You got my head spinning."

I self-consciously played the role of greenhorn from the city to his of country prankster, but Quincy Higgins was right: I needed to sort it all out later in order to entirely understand the meaning of our interaction and what it revealed about him as a performing personality in his old age. There were many hours of tape transcriptions to analyze since the tape recorder was going most of the day Gerri Johnson and I spent with Quincy Higgins. We were working on the Blue Ridge Folklife Project for the American Folklife Center at the Library of Congress; Gerri had contacted him first, and we had decided to go back so that we could interview both him and his wife. On September 9, 1978, we went to his farm in Allegheny County, North Carolina. Quincy Higgins was born in 1900 and has been a farmer all his adult life and a lay preacher in the Regular Baptist Church for forty-eight years.

We first recorded him standing next to his pickup truck in his front yard; on the tape you can hear the chickens clucking in the background. He was chewing tobacco and wearing his farm work clothes. As with many men who chew tobacco on the Blue Ridge, he had tobacco stains on the front of his shirt, a sign of membership in the local masculine culture. After we talked in the front yard for awhile, he took us in the truck to the highest point of land on his farm, and we recorded our conversation the entire time. After Gerri and I went to lunch in town, we came back and recorded him, his wife, and her sister in the kitchen of their farmhouse for the rest of the afternoon. The opening interchange of this chapter is typical of the session: Mr. Higgins interspersed pranks and tall tales with his telling of historical legends, family stories, witch and ghost tales, jokes, and personal experience narratives.

He has a self-consciousness and a strong identity as a performer, which has been with him all his life and has become even more important in his old age. One way this comes out is in his awareness of storytelling technique.

13. Quincy Higgins. (Photograph by the author, BR8-2-20398 / 26A.)

At one point I asked him to repeat a story that we did not get on tape, and he said, "Guess I oughta shorten it."

"No, tell it the same way you were telling it before."

"Oh. I mean, you want some season in it?"

As with most good storytellers, he knows that a good story depends on the "seasoning," what folklorists call the "texture" of the performance (Dundes 1964; Ben-Amos 1971). He seasons his performance with various spices, one of which is switching modes from serious to comic without any warning. While talking about a serious topic, Mr. Higgins would work a joke or prank into the conversation. Here again, he is aware of and comments on his role as prankster. He told about pulling a prank on some tourists from Ohio and added, "And they giggled, you know. Yeah. I wanted to put the show on, you know." He puts on the show whenever he encounters people who are not part of his family or his immediate circle of friends.

I commented on his verbal encounters with others, "You sound like you always get the best of them."

"Well, I don't intend to do that, but, uh—"

"You do it anyway."

"But, uh, uh—"

"You got a quick tongue."

"Well, you got to have a quick mind."

"Yeah."

"To control that quick tongue."

His quickness of tongue is obvious to anyone who is around him for any length of time, but he is aware that success as a performer depends on more complex social and performing abilities. A story must have the right seasoning, and a prank or joke must be pulled at the right time and with the right audience. He gave us several examples of his pranks, and as is obvious from the transcription that opens this chapter, he also pulled several on us.

I was taking a photograph of Mr. Higgins and said, "Well, I wanted to save this moment for posterity. Go down in history."

"Yeah, yeah," Mr. Higgins agreed.

"Isn't that a good idea?"

"Yeah. Save ourselves first, then our posterity."

We laughed here and often during the day as his quick wit kept us alert for his jokes. I think he had two meanings in this instance: save ourselves in a religious sense and, punning on posterity, save our posteriors. He often mixed religious and secular language and images. For instance, in the afternoon he referred to our trip to the top of the mountain that morning.

"Did you record what she sung as I come off the mountain over there this morning?"

"No."

Mr. Higgins sang, "Lord, I'm a-comin' home," and he laughed.

"Is that what she sang?"

"That's what she's singing as she come off of that mountain."

"I heard her praying when we were going up."

Gerri said, "Boy, you heard me praying even louder when we were coming down."

Mr. Higgins got in the last word, "You was singing 'Open wide thine arms, Lord, I'm a-comin' home.'"

One of his favorite seasonings is to sing as part of storytelling or joking, and usually the songs are hymns, even when he is telling a secular story.

Besides the joking one-liners, he also told several narrative jokes. These he could work into a conversation no matter what the topic was. Because the next county over was legendary for its moonshine activities, I asked him if he knew about it, and he responded with a story.

"Well, back in, whenever them, bootlegging crowd was going on, you know? Some old fella on Roaring River, he's always bootlegging, and some of his neighbors wanted to report him up. They report him up, and, and Bud Boggers and Mr. Barry, Mr. Dancy, come over and hunted all day. Didn't find nothing. And they got back to Wilkesboro, and a few days later they got another report. And they come back, and they hunted all day, and they didn't find nothing. Come on up through the barn lot there, and some lady come out on the porch. Throwed the dish water out, where she'd been washing dishes. 'Hey, lady!' Mr. Bogger says. 'Hey, wait a minute.' He walked on up, and she stood there, washing the dishpan out. Said, 'We've had a report about a still over in here.' Said, 'We've hunted for two solid days and can't find it. So I'll just give you ten dollars if you can give us any evidence leading to the still.' He's walking awful close to the porch, you know. And she took the ten dollars. She lifted up her apron, says, 'There's the still.' Says, 'The old man's got the worm.' Said, 'If you wait till he comes, we'll make a run.'"

For those who don't know, a "worm" is part of the equipment on a whiskey still. Mr. Higgins claimed that this was a true story, and he used actual names in it, but since it turns out to be a joke, he has misled the listener, and the interchange is a prank or hoax. He hesitated telling the story because it was "a little bit rough." "Not too rough, but might not want it on tape." I encouraged him to tell it; his wife and her sister had heard it before, and he did not seem to mind telling it in front of them or Gerri. He considers it an acceptable joke in mixed company because the sexual references are not direct but rather depend on puns. Still, this might be considered a surprising story for a lay preacher to tell, but Mr. Higgins's stories and conversation reveal a blend of sacred and secular interests. He freely mixed spiritual references in with material ones. In fact, one of the central themes of his life story is the interaction of material and spiritual values.

Also important in this story is the basic situation in which the country woman gets the best of the supposedly more educated authorities. Throughout his personal experience narratives, which he tells as part of his life review, Quincy Higgins depicted himself as an uneducated country man who verbally defeats or impresses an educated city person. This is analogous to the situation of the interview: two educated folklorists interviewing the country man who plays the role of the naive bumpkin and then uses his quick wit to show that an uneducated man can be their superior. We were his foils just as the tourists and other outsiders he hoaxed were.

At one point in the interview we were talking about planting by the signs, which he and his wife both believe in, when he said, "That one feller out here, planted, planted onions and taters right along side to side. And he said them onions growed so strong, that them taters right by them watered in the eyes."

In the middle of a serious conversation, he uses a tall-tale device, the ludicrous image (Boatright 1961), to hoax his listeners. The effect is heightened by the juxtaposition of the lying image with a belief topic, planting by the signs. He lulls the listener into thinking that what he is about to say is serious, and then reverses direction with the punning ludicrous image.

He uses tall tales and tall tale imagery to pull hoaxes on tourists he happens to meet.

"See, be down there and see [the moon] shining. I had some feller up here from Raleigh and told him, I said, 'When it's a full moon, you can see both sides of the moon at once when you're up here.' He says, 'I want to come back when that moon's full.'" We laughed, and Mr. Higgins continued, "I didn't believe in that stuff, you know."

"Yeah. Do you, do you pull things like that on people that come in here from the outside?"

"Oh yeah, that's, that's them greenhorns, is the ones I want to pull."

"What have you pulled on them before?"

"Everything."

Later I asked him about a prank he mentioned off the tape, "What about that thing you pulled on the people from Ohio?"

"Oh. Up here on the mountain? Up on the [Blue Ridge] Parkway? Yeah, they drove in there; my son-in-law and me, I's looking around, about, and three cars pulled in there that had Ohio tags on them. One of them was sorta inquisitive, says, 'How in the world folks live around here? How long do they live?' I says, 'Lord mercy!' I say, 'Some of them lives to be ninety-eight, some a hundred, some a hundred and three.' I says, 'Never wear no hearing aids, nor have no glasses, nor nothing.' I said, 'One day they's two of them walking around that path out yonder, where you see over Wilkes County, twenty-five miles over into another county. One of them, that one that sees good, he says, 'Can you see that fly on top that barn over there in Wilkes?' Said, 'No, but I can hear the shingles rattle as he walks'" (AT1920E, "Lie: Seeing (Hearing) Enormous Distances," Aarne 1964; also see Halpert 1985).

Significantly, the tall tale projects a positive image of old age in the Blue Ridge Mountains. Even though the story is a hoax, it still makes a point about the longevity and acute physical abilities of elderly people in this region as opposed to outsiders. Mr. Higgins is proud of his own physical strength and agility at the age of seventy-eight, and his pranks and hoaxes prove his mental abilities are still sharp. He gets the best not only of outsiders but of younger people in many of his encounters. Performance itself is a relevant feature of old age: Quincy Higgins uses the performance of pranks, hoaxes, and tall tales to attract attention to himself, to keep younger generations from disengaging him. His pranks show him intruding into other people's lives whether they want him to or not.

He also pulls pranks on local people if they are appropriate targets.

Gerri requested of him, "Tell him about that telephone one, where you were testing out your new telephone."

"Yeah, that, that, calling a high school professor. And his wife answered. I said, 'Can I speak to Fessor?' She says, 'Somebody wants you on the phone.' He says, 'Hello?' I says, 'Fessor, can you, tell me something? I wanted to ask you a question.' 'Well, I will if I can.' I said, 'Do you know how to make Budweiser?' I knowed they could drink lots of it, I thought maybe knowed how to make it. 'You know how to make Budweiser?' He said, 'I couldn't tell you a thing about it.' I said, 'Send him to school.'"

We laughed.

"He says, '*Con*found you!'"

Quincy Higgins's practical jokes are similar to his tall tales and other hoaxes; they all use playful deceit to cause confusion or embarassment in the victim (Bauman 1986, 36). In the previous example, Mr. Higgins tells a traditional tall tale within the context of an encounter with tourists, and then tells the story of that encounter in another performance context to folklorists from the outside who are analogous to the tourists. In both contexts, he is in control, giving out or withholding information in order to manipulate the listener (Bauman 1986, 38). This is a playful exercise, but the practical joker / tall-tale teller is still being competitive and demonstrating his dominance and control (Bauman 1986, 36; Brandes 1980, 116–28). Significantly, Mr. Higgins is establishing control over outsiders who consider themselves superior to Blue Ridge residents, or he is controlling local people who have a higher social status than he. The professor is an appropriate target because he drinks beer—the implication is that this is immoral behavior for a high school teacher—and because he is educated. In Quincy Higgins's mind the teacher's education has given him an inflated reputation—he thinks he is better than those without his degrees. Mr. Higgins's stories present tourists in the same light: they act superior to the "ignorant hillbillies" they encounter along the Blue Ridge Parkway. His practical jokes, tall tales, and pranks function to reverse the roles: the hillbilly becomes superior to the tourist, the uneducated country man fools the educated professor, the old man gets the best of the young man.

This is an especially important function for the elderly: as a person gets older, he or she loses some of the control acquired in life (Myerhoff 1978, 261–62), and pranks and hoaxes can function to symbolically maintain control in at least one area of interaction with others. The passivity associated with old age (Gutmann 1977, 306) is countered by the active role of performer of jokes, tall tales, and pranks. In a way, the game continues with this book; the folklore professor may momentarily have the upper hand by analyzing the country farmer, but I imagine Quincy Higgins will have a few words to say about the "fessor" after he reads this chapter.

I may have more education than Mr. Higgins, but he has performing skills that I'll never have. These skills depend on self-awareness and perceptions about his audience and the way they perceive him. He knows that his pranks and jokes can cause a negative response; people might not like the fact that he always presents himself as the winner in these contacts with others. He might be projecting the same arrogant superiority he is trying to deflate. To avoid this, he sprinkles self-deprecatory remarks throughout his conversation. We were on top of the mountain, and he was pointing out features below through the haze. "When it's—ordinarily, I, I just sorrowed because it's hazy like it is, but ain't much we can do about it. Of course, as windy as I am, ought to be blowed away, oughtn't it?" He makes fun of himself in other ways.

"I seen them folks down to Galax a while back, and they wanted to know if I still lived where I used to. I says, 'Yeah.' I said, 'I'm quarantined.' 'Quarantined!' I said, 'When the neighbors found out they's fifteen younguns at my house they said, 'Don't you let him move in our community.'" "Yeah, I met Mr. Todd down there a while back—he used to live over at Glade Valley, he moved to Hill Creek, Virginia. And he helped tell about what I said to his wife one time. I's over here to Elk Creek to see them. And his wife says, 'Quincy,' says, 'How many children do you have now?' I says, 'I believe the last time I asked the old woman she said they's fifteen.'"

He may make fun of himself for having a large family, but he is also proud of them; several times he mentioned accomplishments of his offspring as adults. References to his children, then, are a positive part of his life review, reflecting his self-image as an effective parent. His ability to mix self-deprecation with pride in himself came out in other topics as well.

"See, when you, if you, when you's up in Washington, around the Archives Building [The Library of Congress], around, you never thought about ever meeting a fool like this. But you can go back through there now and say, 'Well sir, I'd sort of like to have that feller's presence around here. Reveal this to me, tell me that, and so on.'"

After he calls himself a fool, he then projects the image of a sage (with the implication of an old sage) whose words would be respected at the Library of Congress. This ambivalence toward himself runs throughout his speech; part of it is a device he uses as a performer, and part of it is a reflection of an inner conflict about himself. He is self-conscious about his lack of education, but he knows he is intelligent and witty. His presentation of self to others reflects both sides of his self-image. I think that his role as jokester and prankster comes out of his insecurities about his lack of education.

Presentation of self in order to achieve successful social interaction is important to Quincy Higgins; he talked a lot about getting along with people, and he seems to have consciously worked at developing a well-liked personality. This process goes back to his youth, and continues to the present. His performing self is part of his core identity that he has maintained throughout his life. As gerontologist James D. Manney, Jr., points out: "Developmental psychologists have found that personality types remain extremely stable over the life span, at least in terms of the way individuals adjust or fail to adjust to their social milieu. The face the older person presents to the world is very consistent" (1975, 20). Quincy Higgins has been a performing personality since his youth, and he told a story which illustrates this.

"Way back in—I was a-working this, five dollars a week, you know. I got to writing to a lady up Piney Creek. I hadn't seen her, been a-writing to her practically all the summer. And, I hadn't seen her, but I wrote and told her I's a coming up one Saturday. Well, I got me some officers' leggings, you know, and got me some riding pants, and got all fixed up, and got on a nice horse—belonged to the landlord—and rode up, seventeen miles, see this girl. She's sitting out on the lawn, you know, her and her sister-in-law. Hattie White was her name, from Piney Creek. . . .

"Anyhow, I stood there, I got introduced. Neighbor went along with me, you know, to give me a big introduction, you know, and start us off on the right foot. I stood there and talked with her so, several minutes. I says, 'Hattie, would there be any room in that car for me?' Said, 'Law, yeah, Mr. Higgins, get right on in here.' That little Model A, you know, didn't have that capacity we got now. And they's both pretty hefty, and I weighed a hundred and eighty-six, and so on. Went on in there. Sorta like sardines. Next thing she knew, my head was laying over on her shoulder. And she comb, was combing my hair, you know, just wavy and black. And says, 'Mr. Higgins,' says, 'You don't seem like no stranger.' Says, 'Seems like we just grew up together.'"

He later said that he had been "putting on a little show" for her indicating that all of his personable qualities were not innate; he self-consciously projected a likable personality. This story is part of his life review, taking him back to a time when he had dark wavy hair, reminding him in his old age of his youthful self and establishing continuity with his core personality. Sexuality is an important part of his self-image then and now: he flirted with Gerri during the time we spent with him, and his references to his fifteen children express his virility. His winning personality when he was young was an aid in courtship, and it also helped him with people in general. A friend told him when he was young, "Quincy, the expression you wear on your face will take you through this world." After he told us this, he commented, "Well, that's been just as, that prophecy has been just as perfect as could be. I ain't never met no bad enemies, I never met no strangers, and I've always got reckonization." One way he has gotten "reckonization" is through his joking.

"Well, I met a lady up here . . . in a store, back about a year ago. Up in from Florida. And I just tore into her like I have you-all, you know, and just letting my five cents, two cents, whatever you call it, explode. And that lady just hit me on the shoulder, says, 'Mr. Higgins, I've never met nobody with your sense of humor.' And the man says, 'You beat anything I've ever seen.' Well, I says, 'I don't want to lose nary a friend, I want to make some new ones.' Well, you can get acquainted with people, just the nicest kind, if you come in on the landing pad just right."

His metaphors are revealing here: "I just tore into her" and "just letting my five cents . . . explode." These suggest the aggressive nature of his personality, the way he asserts himself when interacting with others. Again, we see that he uses verbal interaction in order to control situations. Clearly, he is not one of those old people who voluntarily disengages; he continues in his old age to expand his social world.

By being a performer, he has developed a widespread reputation.

"My son-in-law was here [one] night; he wanted to know if I knowed Ben Calder down to Elkin. I said, 'Well, I don't know whether I do or not.' He said, 'He knows you.' Yeah, I's up in Maryland one time, shaking hands with some ladies and gentlemen, you know, says, 'I'm Quincy Higgins.' 'We've heard of you.'"

Gerri said, "Is that right?"

"Four hundred miles away they'd heard of [me]."

His personality and ability to joke with people have also been significant factors in his preaching.

"Well, I's down in Galax one time, I had a wonderful service, you know, and after that, everybody's feeling, great, you know, and elevated in spirit and mind and all. And I was just a running full blast, you know. Had all the tension, and that all was a flowing, so on. They's sitting up in the shade. And everybody was just tearing their sides, you know, at that philosophy, I said, 'Pour it out.' And, I said, 'Well, no fool's no fun.' Lady just busted, she says, 'If you hadn't a come, wouldn't had none.' She picked the fool out of the crowd instantly. Yeah, she picked the fool out of the crowd right certain. Well, just take everything good-natured, and all it means aside."

His self-deprecation and his sense of humor enable him to handle a situation when the joke is on him, even when he is the central performer, as in the case of preaching a sermon.

He is proud of his role as a performer, but there are other accomplishments in his life of which he is also proud; these achievements are the subject matter of many of the personal experience narratives in his life review. As he talks about his life, he reveals his basic values both symbolically in narratives and more directly in general statements. He told us about conducting funerals for his neighbors without charge.

"Well, that, that makes me feel elevated in spirit because the neighbors took in stock in what they thought I's trying to do. I tried to be honest, and be nice to everybody, and so on, and overstepped my bounds sometimes to help somebody. But, feller never lose nothing by that, and I, and I've baptized four hundred and never charged nobody a dime. See, there's eight hundred and twenty-three that I've went, helped. Never charged them a penny. But got along somehow. I's up here in town back yonder a year or two ago, and some feller says, 'Quincy,' says, 'how you make it? How you—' I says, 'Finest you've ever seen.' I said, 'I ain't got no deeds a trust hanging over me. I've got my taxes paid. If I've got a enemy in the world I don't know it.' Well, he says, 'You know, I haven't met nobody like that.' Well, if you could feel sure—you got the [advantage] on everybody else, if you just knowed it. You can be a friend to everybody, whether they're your friend or not. You ever thought about it like that?"

This statement indicates how Quincy Higgins's values are a mix of sacred and secular concerns, of spiritual and material ideas. He starts out talking about his accomplishments as a preacher, then shifts to his financial state, and ends up talking about the value of friendship. These values are all related in his overall world view; he sees his financial well-being as a result of his spirituality. He has baptized hundreds without charge, and his financial reward has come from other sources. His friendly attitude toward people is based on religious values, but it has also helped him financially. A few minutes later, he made another statement that related religious and secular matters together.

"They say, 'In God we trust.' I's awful glad that old pioneer had that put on our money. You know, for years, didn't have that. And some old feller wanted a little, evidence there. And he wrote in to Congress, and told them he wanted to have that put on the silver money. 'In God we trust.' Well, it'd been, minting and a-molding there for years afore they ever put that on. Law, yeah, it's, it's a miracle to think about that. How a feller can accomplish things if he's made up his mind he's going to do that. If he's made, if he's got his, zeal, and his intention set, and keep it a military secret and carry it out. You know, if Eisenhower and all them fellers over there'd a told the Germans what day they's a moving, they'd a lost every battle. Wouldn't they?"

He manages to work God, money, and the military together in one statement, but what unifies this declaration is the value of achievement orientation. He uses the military metaphor to make the point that in order to acquire money, one must not reveal his plans to others. Trust in God but not necessarily in your fellow humans. This statement is fairly general, but he later made direct references to his own achievements.

"Well, wonder if you start out here working five dollars a week, and wiring your shoes on your feet with fencing wire, and reach that elevation [owning property worth hundreds of thousands of dollars]. Now that's something to be wonderfully thought of. Ain't it? . . . I've wired my shoes on my feet with fencing wire. The soles come off. And I'd run out there to the fence and get me a wire and wrap it around there and, and hold that on it like I do that thing, that day's work. And next morning I's in to mend it, but didn't have time to wrap that wire back around, put in another day. Yeah, and then get out there, go see about the corn, find it ready, and, and go to cutting. Dinner time come on, two miles from home, and let, eat apples for dinner, and lay down, sleep a little, go right back and cut corn till dark. Without any dinner."

His personal achievements have come from hard work; he emphasized several times how he has risen from humble beginnings to his position of prosperity.

When we were at the highest elevation on his property, he said, "Well, you know now, Brother, it's a, it's a thrill of a lifetime to know you come in here a pauper, working for five dollars a week, and now could say, well, my [property] line goes around here." He pointed out over the landscape with a sweeping motion and said, "yonder, so-and-so."

This statement can be seen as a summary of his life review since it reveals the central achievement of his life and his pride in his individual accomplishment. His personal narratives about his accomplishments describe his rise from poverty in more detail. In his agrarian achievement orientation he is similar to Bob Glasgow and Alva Snell, but there are significant differences in their stories about achievement. Quincy Higgins tells in chronological order a series of narratives that trace his life from poverty to his status as a landowner today.

"I started out over here in a, a rented, little rented house, an old log house, rented. Then I built me a little house, twelve by twenty. Moved into it and that's where our first baby was born, right over here. Our two first ones. And went on and bought this place out down over here two years later, and moved into it. And they's more baby chickens. And I had to have some more room for a table. So the weather boards on the walls, building, I just took them off and set them out the edge of the porch, and made me a dining hall, you know. And some of them knots come out of that lumber. Now, I never did seal it, never had time. And wind come over that mountain in the nighttime, setting there, eating supper by a lamp, a kerosene lamp. And blow that lamp out. Setting on table. And I'd get up and get another broom straw, and, and relight the lamp, and finish eating, and go on to bed. Sleep like a log."

This story emphasizes details of pioneer life—log house, kerosene lamp, holes in the walls—that make Quincy Higgins into an Abraham Lincoln figure that fits into the upward mobility theme of this cycle of stories. As a narrative in the life review it takes him back to his humble beginnings, which provide a contrast to his prosperity in old age. Once this is established, he can go on to the next chronological step, buying the land.

"Well, I had my eye on this farm from the time I operated. But I never told a soul. Well, the first time I got a good chance to buy it, I had a thousand dollars of my own money, and it cost five thousand. And I had a thousand dollars. I went over to Independence, Virginia, and seen Dr. Moxley, and told him what I had in mind. And he says, 'I'll just try to help you out.' He wrote me a check for four thousand.

I come back and bought this. Well, I've been offered a hundred thousand for it.

"And I'm—I wouldn't live nowhere else. This is the only place for me; I've been right here for fifty-five years. And I'm well satisfied, and the neighbors is all fine people. We ain't never had no trouble. I've attended thirty-two funerals right here in a two-mile radius of home. Has made me feel wonderful. To think about thirty-two people dying here in two miles of here. They'd want me to come and say a few words at the funeral. Well, I've attended 423 funerals. Never charged nobody a dime. My nose was battered, but I'd stood and fought."

He shifts time frames in the middle of the story from the point when he first bought the farm to the present in order to emphasize the continuity of living on the same land and in the same community. The time shift also emphasizes his achievement: he has risen from having to borrow four thousand dollars to owning land worth a hundred thousand dollars. The comment about local funerals again shows how closely his identity as a preacher is related to his identity as a farmer and landowner; both roles are played out in the same community with the same people. His religious beliefs explain why funerals made him feel wonderful; those who died are going to their reward in heaven.

His rise in the world was not without adversity; he had to survive foreclosure on the farm during the Depression.

"I bought that mountain up here, sixth of August, 1923. And two years later, I wanted to buy an extra, an addition, a farm that adjoined me. And I asked the land bank for three thousand dollars. And they granted me twenty-five hundred. Said they loaned this money, as much on the man as they, as they did the property. They wanted to help me to own it. And so they loaned me the—actual three thousand, they loaned me twenty-five hundred. And eventually, I paid that all back. And in the, in the thirties, the Depression come on, and they's selling out farmers from everywhere. They told me they's selling out three farmers every day. And they wanted me to sign up—had the questionnaire all filled out and everything lined up for me to sign, and set me in the road. And I couldn't get him to agree with me on nothing. I said, 'Brother,' I said, 'Do you remember what Ben Franklin said?' Says, 'What did Ben say?' Said, 'Ben said, 'Your nose may be battered, and your jawbone nicked, and your visage may be a sight. . . . But remember, you ain't never whipped as long as you'll stand and fight.' Says, 'Mr. Higgins, you still want to fight this thing?' I says, 'I'll fight her till I die.' 'A man of your ambition ought to have some help.' Says, 'I'm going to recommend to the federal land bank to grant you a five years' extension on your loan.'

"He offered this recommendation, and the bank received it, sent me a statement showing that they had, set this hundred and sixty-two dollars, which I's a-paying annually, set it up on a five-year period. Pay up over ten dollars extra ever six months. And before the five years was up, I had my loan in current condition, and had three or four, five hundred dollars in the Northwestern Bank. And four or five years later, I come back and met the secretary of treasury in the courthouse at Sparta, and told him to count up and see how much I owed him. And they's twenty-two hundred and some dollars. And I says, 'Brother, write a check for it,' and I tossed him my checkbook. And he says, 'Quincy, you're making a mistake.' I said, 'I know it. I made a bad one yesterday and one the day before. I want to make one ever day this week.' And he wrote the check, I signed it. He went on back to Wilkesboro, deposited check, Northwestern Bank paid it off. And I become free."

He used the Ben Franklin quote in an earlier story in a similar context: it illustrates his determination to succeed in the face of adversity. He recognizes that he must have the help of others, but he still values his individuality. He finally achieves what is one of his goals, to be financially free. By telling this story in his old age, he can relive a triumph of an earlier stage of life, one that was instrumental in making him who he is today.

The land is more important to him than the money, though. He told one story that illustrates this.

"There's a company feller, real estate man, come here one time from Greensboro? And wanted to buy me out, wanted to buy this down in here. I's listening to this and that, you know, and I says, 'Brother,' I says, 'Ain't no use to go down looking at it.' 'Oh, yes, I've got the money.' I says, 'I'd like to have it in my hands. But isn't no use a going.' I said, '[When I] was a renter down there, I was cursed and ordered off a that property.' I said, 'When I come back, I come to stay.' I said, 'I've had to sweat blood to, to pay for it.' And

I says, 'When I come back, I come to stay. And that's the way I want to keep it, Brother.' I says, 'Don't bring me your business. Don't bring me business.' He got right in his Buick and left."

This series of stories about his achievements emphasize Quincy Higgins's rise from poverty to wealth; the land is worth a great deal of money, but this is only part of the symbolic value it holds for him. His continuous occupation of the same soil has made the land part of his identity. He came back to stay because this is where he is truly himself; he is a farmer on this land and a lay preacher to this community. If he were to be taken off this land, he would lose part of himself. At the age of seventy-eight he might think of retiring and moving to town to be near his children, but that would cause him to lose his continuity with his own past, which is such an important part of his identity in the present. His achievements in life are best represented not by money in the bank but by the land itself. He can take visitors to the highest elevation on his land and point out what is his and indicate that what they see is a part of him.

The last story also illustrates a recurring theme in his life review: the conflict between Mr. Higgins and those who consider themselves better than he. When he was a renter, the owner cursed him and ordered him off the property. By becoming owner of the same land, Mr. Higgins has proved his worth, that he is equal to or better than the person who evicted him. As long as he stays on his own land, his worth will be clearly expressed by his ownership. Bob Glasgow uses the buildings on his land as a source of identity in his old age; Quincy Higgins uses the land itself.

Throughout his life review stories, he describes situations in which he confronts persons with a higher social status: a United States senator, bank presidents, owners of companies, professors. He is acutely aware of his lack of education in comparison to these people. "I never got far in school books, never—I never went to school a full term in my life. . . . But I can figure with bankers and fellers like that." Mr. Higgins's language reveals his awareness of social distinctions: he referred to a "Sunday school professor and singing teacher" as being "up in the big bracket" with the implied comparison to his own status as a lay preacher. He is also cognizant of his behavior in regards to people "up in the big bracket."

When he was showing us around his property in the morning, he remarked, "The wife's having hemmorhages right now 'cause I'm out putting on a big front, you know."

Gerri asked him, "What do you mean, 'out putting on a big front'?"

"Well, just, showing dignitaries what the world looks like, you know."

We were the dignitaries, and he was putting on a big front for us. One of the ways he showed us "what the world looks like" was by telling historical legends to illustrate points he was making, stories about George Washington, Benjamin Franklin, Robert E. Lee, and Daniel Boone.

"You's talking about the victories and things like that, I thought about that old Dutch settler up there. On the Delaware River somewheres. He's out to feeding one morning, and he heard George Washington a praying. He seen his horse tied out there to a bush, you know. And he hurried to the house and told his wife, he says, 'Washington'll win the war.' Says, 'I heard him praying down here on the bank a the river while ago.' And put that great effort, and that guidance, gives you and me the liberty that we enjoy today. That right?"

Gerri and I agreed.

"The liberty and the, and the goodness we enjoy was won by the hand of George Washington. And he was guided. Some feller said that Washington wasn't a common man. Said he'd had thirteen shots fired at him. And never cut him off his horse. Well, he had three bullet holes through the crown of his hat, and one through the brim of it. You ever read that?"

"No, I haven't," I admitted.

"Good gracious! I need to be your teacher for about six months."

We laughed, and I said, "You sure do."

By telling us these historical legends, he had reversed roles on us; he became the professor, and we became his students. The dignitaries were no longer on a higher social scale. Like Mollie Ford and Jesse Hatcher, he is capable of assuming the role of teacher in his old age, although it is only one of several roles he plays: preacher, farmer, prankster, and joker. What he did with us is analogous to his role playing with dignitaries in several of his personal stories.

"Kerr Scott, our former governor, he got to be United States senator.

And up in Washington, he had a big office up there in the senatorial building. Well, I wanted to see Brother Scott, you know, and so I just got on the bus, went up to see him. Went up there and they's a nice lady, about his size [he pointed at me, six feet two inches tall], was answering the doorbell, and, and she wanted to know what my name was and so on. Told her. And I says, 'I want to see Senator Scott.' She commenced stuttering, you know, like he wasn't there. I says, 'Lady,' now I said now, 'You ain't a gonna send me back home.' I says, 'I'm from North Carolina.' I says, 'I've traveled four hundred miles to see Senator Scott,' and I says, 'You ain't gonna send me back home empty-handed and barefooted.' She says, 'Would you like to sign the guest book?' Had a great big book there—you know what a guest book is? And I signed that right on there, and she said, "Scuse me a minute.' She walks around the corner, then come back and beckoned me to chase her.

"Went around the corner, and I said, 'Brother Scott.' I said, 'Brother Scott,' I says, 'I'm Quincy Higgins from Sparta.' I says, 'I'm the one that worried you so much about good roads.' He come up out of that big leather chair, you know. Said, 'You didn't worry me about no roads.' He says, 'It's a pleasure to help you. A pleasure to help you.' And we embraced each other, you know, just like two school-boys, hadn't been together a long time. And we talked, and gabbed about these roads and things like that, and two great big fine-looking gentlemen come in, you know, dressed in broadcloth. And I's up ready to leave. And he says, 'Mr. Higgins,' says, 'sit back down. You got to rehearse every bit a this.' Oh, we—I'd been there hour and forty-five minutes. You know, that, that's my rehearsal. And lo and behold, I set right back down, and them fellers, setting over there behind the desk with their mouth open, and the, see the end of their tongue. I got through rehearsing, old Scott, he hit his desk with his fist, says, 'I told you fellers I get some recognization from North Carolina!' Yeah, just like they knowed that I was the next governor and runner-up, you know. Well, I thought that a man like Kerr Scott, one a the greatest governors the state ever had. If, if he'd recognize me like that, I, I, I was mighty well pleased. They, they—they's fellers round here in the county won't recognize me like Kerr Scott did. Law, law."

He repeats "big" and "great big" throughout the story to emphasize

University of Illinois Press URBANA-CHAMPAIGN AND CHICAGO

Listening to Old Voices: Folklore,
Life Stories, and the Elderly

by Patrick B. Mullen

Publication date: March 15, 1992

Price: $30.95

We would appreciate receiving two
copies of any published review or
mention.

For additional information contact:
Publicity Department
(217) 244-4689

54 E. GREGORY DRIVE, CHAMPAIGN, IL 61820   TELEPHONE: (217) 333-0950

the high status of Senator Scott (even his secretary is a big woman), but right at the beginning of the story, he puts himself and Scott on an equal level by referring to him as "Brother Scott." A similar leveling device is the image of Mr. Higgins and Senator Scott embracing "like two schoolboys, hadn't been together a long time." Quincy Higgins plays the role of the country bumpkin in the big city, but it is a pretended innocence that masks his wisdom. His language indicates his country origins—"send me home empty-handed and barefooted"— and at the same time makes fun of the proper manners of the sec- retary—she "beckoned me to chase her." His wisdom is apparent in the fact that the senator listens to his advice for an hour and forty- five minutes and then asks him to repeat it for two other "great big fine-looking gentlemen." Mr. Higgins ends up comparing himself to the next governor in order to get across how his status had increased because of this encounter. Despite all this, he gives a hint at the underlying problem of status in his life when he mentions that he does not get the same recognition from some people back home. As a life review story, this narrative allows him to relive one of the most prestigious events of his life, to project in his old age his successful image from an earlier stage of life. The story's polished telling indi- cates recurring performance; it is an important story in his overall life review.

The story is part of a tradition in American folklore in which the smart country bumpkin goes to the city and proves his meddle to the authorities (Dorson 1959, 40–41). (The tradition continues in modern America through such performers as Andy Griffith, who is originally from Mt. Airy, North Carolina, not far from Sparta, and whose early career used the country bumpkin image to comment on contemporary society.) Quincy Higgins's story reflects the clash of traditional values in a democratic society: achievement orientation suggests upward mobility and status, which is in conflict with dem- ocratic egalitarianism. Mr. Higgins's narrative cleverly juggles the conflicting values so that status is challenged but not destroyed. He recognizes status as a social fact, but he also indicates that even with his lesser education and rural background, he can achieve the respect of those who are perceived as being higher on the social scale. Status and egalitarianism continue to exist in a state of tension; the status quo has been maintained.

Shortly after Mr. Higgins told the story about Senator Scott, he told another one about an encounter with a local wealthy, educated man.

"Well, right there one time, Edwin Duncan—him and me was, I's a little older than him. And he had a college degree, and had a rich father. I didn't have no education, and I had a poor daddy, too. And I's in the bank here one day making a deposit, and he's in there, just him and me. And I started out, he got in the door first. Stopped right in front of the bank. And we got to talking, and he says, 'Quincy, I don't see how in the name of God that you've done what you have.' He says, 'They ain't another man in the state that woulda raised this family you've raised, and educated them. Not another man in the state.' When they covered out a hundred counties, you know, and brought me out in the midst of it, I told him that there elevated my spirit a sight. That a poor boy with just a free school education could run circles around a college graduate, with a twenty thousand dollar graduation check, you know. His daddy told me he give him a check for twenty thousand dollars the day he graduated. Well I never had that, five dollars, or more than that. And I don't guess had that much contributed to me."

Again, he makes the difference in education and privilege clear but indicates the educated man's respect and praise for him. Mr. Higgins told two stories about encounters with bankers who thought he was a poor farmer and treated him without respect until he let them know about his money and property. In one story he is trying to get a loan from the bank.

"And they's gonna let me deposit fifty dollars to pay the appraisers' expenses to come over there looking my farm over. I told them, I says, 'They ain't no use a that.' And I let on like I's a [pauper]; had three hundred-dollar bills in my pocket. And I, I knowed he wanted me to get out; he didn't say nothing, but he, I could tell the way he acted, you know, he wanted me to move. I just pulled out a hundred-dollar bill and handed it to him. I said, 'Brother, just keep the change.' He went up there among the clerks, you know, at the cash register, got the fifty dollars change, come back. And another man come in then. And, and we got to talking, and I says—wanting to send the appraiser—why, I says, 'I'll, I'll go out there, look in that glove pocket in that GMC.' I said, 'My deeds is right in there.' They went out there, looked in that glove pocket there, and got my deeds. And come back. And they kept my fifty dollars. And never sent no appraisers. But granted me the cash. They, they called me and told me."

"Money talks," as the old saying goes, and in this case Quincy Higgins's deeds also talked. Mr. Higgins derives pleasure from telling these stories in which he overcomes the superior attitude of bankers by letting them know his financial worth. Bankers who do not know him judge him incorrectly; business people in his own community who know him well see beneath his rustic appearance. He told a story which illustrated this.

"I's down," he named a local stockyard, "back here yonder, and they's some folks from over in here, had on gay clothing, I had on this old work garments. And they bought four hundred dollars worth of cattle. And they had a office checkbook, you know. And they's all, had—how do you call—Avon or something all over them. And had a wonderful perfume. I smelled like a barnyard, you know. And I didn't know about it till the week or two later. But they demanded some, registration cards, and driving license [from the perfumed strangers], and they come on up. Well, I bought eight hundred and thirty-five dollars worth. And I come in, just tossed them my check-book, you know, and they just took it and filled it out, and I signed it, and, 'Mr. Higgins, we'll be a-looking for you back next Wednesday.' And I come on home, and found this out.

"I went back down there next, what, two weeks later, I went back, and I bought thirteen or fourteen hundred dollars worth of cattle. And I tossed this lady my checkbook, and I just laughed right in her face, you know, ig-no-rant, you know. That's the first over the hill. She said, 'Mr. Higgins,' said, 'What are you tickled so about?' I said, 'I's a making fun of you.' 'Making fun of me?' I says, 'Yeah.' I says, 'A couple weeks ago,' I says, 'I had the neighbors in here, that had the office checkbook? All groomed up? And I didn't have on, reasonable work clothes.' I said, 'You had to have some registration cards and driver license and things.' I said, 'You never asked me a question. And I bought as many again cattle as he bought.' 'Oh,' she says, 'they ain't but one of you, I could find you easy, just find you easy.'"

He contrasts his barnyard smell and work clothes to the others' perfume and gay clothes (the tobacco stains on his shirt as he told the story became an implicit part of the narrative), but despite appearances, he was the one who had the respect of the stockyard owners. They know him as a financially stable landowner, and that is what commands respect. He also gets respect as a lay preacher, but here, too, he has to contend with people in a higher bracket, educated preachers and Sunday school teachers. We were talking about the importance of a sense of humor for a preacher when he told this story.

"I was called in a funeral down at Galax one time. And some hypodermic, you know, from over at Fries, Virginia, was called in with me. He was well qualified in his vocabulary, and I wasn't qualified at all. I asked Mr. Vaughan—Vaughan-Winn Chapel was where we were going to have the funeral. Well, I was acquainted with this lady [who had died], you know, been with her several services along, and been to her home and all. Well, they had this fellow from over there, you know, and come in, and Mr. Vaughan brought him around and introduced him to me, and we sat down and talked and he wanted to know how I wanted to arrange the funeral. I said, 'Brother, you've had a lot of experience and responsibility.' I says, 'You just arrange it to however you wish to, and,' I says, 'I'll just work with you.' Well, that thrilled him, you know, and he commenced spelling it out. He wanted to lead the way and lead the prayer and read the scripture and, and he wasn't acquainted like I was exactly, and he thought that me bring up the conclusion would fit right in. And went right on, he went, got along fine. I says, 'I've always got along with everybody.' I says, 'Never have had to take no crosses, no word.' Just got along with everybody, that's where your sense of humor comes in. There's a fellow in our country that is narrow contracted and, and they wouldn't offer themselves at all in a funeral service. And that's, that's in the ignorant class. You—it's hard to get along with.

"And so went on, and he said, 'I'll turn the service over to Brother Higgins.' I come up singing:

> Amazing Grace, how sweet the sound,
> That saved a wretch like me,
> I once was lost but now am found,
> Was blind but now I see.

They wasn't setting room in that chapel. They get it stretched up all around from every wall, wondering where that hillbilly come from. And I went on and sung:

Through many dangers, toils, and snares,
I have already come,
'Tis grace has brought me safe thus far,
And grace will lead me home.

And I started telling acquaintance with this sister, know how I'd been in her home, and how nice she was, and what a great Samaritan she was, and, and she'd shouted while I was a preaching, and so on and so forth. But I says, I'm expecting on catching up with her some of these days in the paradise with its eternal rest. And the first thing I know'd the big gate just swung open and I got out that, swimming in water, you know, and just swum away. Yeah.

"And when the funeral was over, the undertakers come on up, and he [the other preacher] says, 'Brother Higgins,' he says, 'how's you—you got a way out to the cemetery?' I says, 'Yeah. But I was gonna go with Mr. Vaughan.' I says, 'I got a truck sitting out here.' Ton and a half truck? Didn't look just right in a funeral procession. But it rode good. And I says, 'I'm gonna ride with Mr. Vaughan.' He says, 'I want you to ride with me.' I says, 'Well, you tell Mr. Vaughan that y—I'm riding with you and we'll just lead the funeral procession.'

"He went around and told Mr. Vaughan, and he said it'd be just fine with him. We got in his car. Nice car, you know, paid for by the members of the church. Now I never'd had a hat passed around for me. It was running on the rim. Rather have it like that.

"No, hadn't got out of Galax till he laid his hand on my knee, said, 'Brother Higgins, you really know the Lord, don't you?' Like he'd give everything he possessed if he could just lay them handbooks down, them prayer books and things, and depend on divine spirit. Well, I said, 'Brother, I hope I met Him somewhere back yonder. I hope I met Him. I hope I did.' He knew there was something there he didn't have. I wouldn't swap with him for the whole world. Couldn't afford to—that's all I got, brother. Yeah, that's all I got, and if I was to trade that off, of course, couldn't trade it off. But you know one feller sold his'n back yonder, for a mess of pottage, and he got in trouble over that. He wept and cried and looked for redemption but didn't find none. That was Esau, you know. He was a cunning hunter."

The recording of this story was included in a Library of Congress, American Folklife Center record album, *Children of the Heav'nly*

King: Religious Expression in the Central Blue Ridge. The editor of the album, Charles Wolfe, had this to say about it: "This story supports one of the strongest tenets of southern rural Protestantism: the value of inspiration or 'gift' over formal training or 'book learning.' The account has subtle class overtones and implications for the whole ethos of traditional versus modern" (1981). When seen in the context of Quincy Higgins's other narratives, Charles Wolfe's interpretation can be expanded. Divine inspiration has additional importance for Mr. Higgins because of his self-consciousness about his own lack of formal education. Therefore, his spiritual gift is related to the "subtle class overtones" of the story. He uses his inspiration to prove his worth in an implied competition with the other preacher, who is representative of the big bracket people mentioned throughout his life review stories. Quincy Higgins sees himself as a traditional person—he is linked to the past by his culture in general and by his religion specifically—and he clearly prefers traditionalism to the modernism of the other preacher. Because of his emphasis on tradition, Mr. Higgins has continuity with his own past, which reinforces his identity in the present, giving meaning to his old age. This story, like the Senator Scott story, is a major story in the life review, one that has been told many times.

He sets up the story in the beginning as a contrast between himself and the educated preacher—"He was well qualified in his vocabulary, and I wasn't qualified at all"—and Mr. Higgins seems to defer to the ordained minister's experience. As we have seen from his previous statements, he places great importance on getting along with everybody. After the other preacher has led most of the service, Quincy Higgins sings "Amazing Grace" in the traditional southern mountain style, high and nasal, what Mr. Higgins and the others there classify as "hillbilly." His shift into song in telling the story is extremely effective: the point about his "hillbilly" origins could not be made more forcefully than by actually singing in the mountain style. The class distinctions are made apparent: "hillbilly" suggests both traditional and uneducated, but Mr. Higgins has turned the meaning around from negative to positive by using it in this context. His singing and his preaching are inspired by God to such an extent that they lead to a transcendent experience: "And the first thing I know'd the big gate just swung open and I go out that, swimming in water, you know, and just swum away. Yeah."

He contrasts himself and the educated preacher by comparing their vehicles, the nice car paid for by church members and his own old pickup, which was running on tire rims. Mr. Higgins emphasizes elsewhere that he never took a dime for conducting baptisms and funerals. The educated preacher admits his inferiority to Quincy Higgins in terms of divine inspiration: "he'd give everything he possessed if he could just lay them handbooks down, them prayer books and things, and depend on divine spirit." This sacred story fits right in with the secular stories in proving that Mr. Higgins, despite his rural uneducated background, is equal to or better than people with higher social status.

He is proud of his understanding of the Bible and theology, which he has acquired on his own.

"[The Bible] says, 'And who shall'—there's where the question come in—'Who shall declare his generation?' I worked on that for years and years, wondered who'd tell it just like it oughta be. And it, sometime it, it dawned on me like this, visualizing again: that it'd take a poor sinner boy that'd been convicted by divine spirit, converted by the Holy Ghost, and made a new creature in Christ Jesus and called by the voice from heaven. When he come right there he'll declare that generation, just like the Baptist family has tried to. Law, I, I, I believe in that divine inspiration, and that alone." And a little later: "Law, yeah, I've read every—I've had folks try to tell me things, you know. I'd listen, you know, and I'd distinguish directly the difference between the Word and their philosophy. I'd just fall back there to straighten him out. I said, 'Now, Brother, if you're looking for the essence of the facts,' I said, 'here's the way it goes.' And they come right in, by him, you know, and him prepared, and me unprepared."

This statement is analogous to the "Amazing Grace" story in that the "poor sinner boy" through divine inspiration is able to teach "the essence of the facts" to someone who is "prepared," which must mean, in Mr. Higgins's terms, educated. Mr. Higgins tells other stories about getting the best of ordained preachers.

"I've, I've been in the presence of fellers that'd tell tales of today and so on. But I—they's too much referendum back yonder in the apostolic day. And one day this feller's preaching up here at a funeral, and he's talking about the soul of the man, you know? I don't know what your idea is, and your idea is, about your soul when it separates from this mortal body, but he preached it, you know, that this soul would float around here in space. And when Christ come back, the soul would bring that celestial body—that the soul and the celestial body would lock up here somewhere close to where the mortal body was buried. And he went on up, dismissed the folks at the grave, and he come back down there; I's sitting there on the block, and he says, 'What do you think of my preaching?' I says, 'I won't have a word of it.' And, boys—we's always been friends, you know. I says, 'I won't have a word of it.' Says, 'Let's hear from you.' Well, I begin to relate some of my experience I'd had, you know. And some visions concerning the ethereal. Well, I knew he didn't have nothing on my word to go upon, but I said, 'Brother,' I says, 'I want to bring something to, to your eyes that you've read yourself, just rehearse it.'"

He proceeded to give a long explanation of his theological point with frequent references to the Bible. He then returned to the original situation at the point when Mr. Higgins asked the fellow preacher a question: "I says, 'Now, where had He [Christ] been to get these new garments and this new body that John didn't recognize?' Said, 'Hmm.' Said, 'You got me there. I'll have to read a little more.' And that's been four years ago, and he never has mentioned that to me no more. Because he couldn't get out of it. I had him in the neck."

Divine inspiration wins again. Preaching is a competitive business, it seems. At least, theological argument is an accepted tradition within the Baptist church, and Quincy Higgins frames his arguments with other preachers as contests thus relating sacred narratives to secular ones such as practical jokes and tall tales. He wins this contest because his understanding of the Bible has come from his "visions concerning the ethereal," in other words, from divine inspiration which any human being, no matter how lowly, has the potential to have. In fact, from Mr. Higgins's point of view, formal education may be a detriment to having these visions.

Inspired visions have been a part of Quincy Higgins's religious life from the beginning; they were instrumental in his decision to become a preacher and in strengthening his faith after his mother's death.

"You said you had some visions, that—experiences. Could you tell us about those?" I asked him.

"Well, I, I, I hadn't run just exactly the race, straight path, like

I's commanded. And my mother died a shouting. Well, that put something on me, or about me, that I hadn't had. Well, for forty days, I's on my knees every day. Begging God to let me see her again. And she had features somewhat like you," he looked at Gerri. "Look on the wall up there and see her picture. But course, she done her hair up on top of her head. And when that forty days was up, I's plowing the corn over yonder at the old place. And I had a spoke to that horse that evening after dinner. I just pulled the lines. And he'd turn. Let him take his time and do as he pleased, just so he stayed in the row.

"And went on, and about three o'clock they's a whirlwind appeared somewhere in the firmament. And I went blind. I went deaf. And automatically the horse stopped. And when I come back to myself, the lines was a laying over on the cultivator. And I'd a stomped my hat in the ground, and I'd stomped the corn down in both rows. And that was my Mamma. I knowed her, Brother. You couldn't tell me with all the language you could collect, anything that'd take that away. There she was, and I knowed her, reaching down like that, with them hands, didn't have a wrinkle in them—everything was just as perfect. Looked young and tender and reaching down there. And, and I knowed, I knowed it [was] her. And that, that thrilled me more than any t'other. Well, I went—I got airborne, you know. And whenever my vision come back to me, I, the corn was up here waist—shoulder high. I'd a stomped that corn down both rows. And a stomped my hat into the ground there, where I'd plowed. Dumb and lost sight of all this world. And, Brother, that was just as certainly from heaven as you're from Ohio. That's how certain that is."

The structure of this narrative follows the traditional pattern of religious conversion narratives in the upland South (Clements 1976a, 1976b; Mullen 1982; Sutton 1977; Titon 1976, 1978, 1988). The narrator emphasizes his or her state of sin—"I hadn't run just exactly the race, straight path, like I's commanded"—and then a vision causes him to alter his life forever. Mr. Higgins's vision is similar to others reported in the Blue Ridge (Mullen 1982) in that he loses all contact with the physical world—"And I went blind. I went deaf." While he is in this trance state, he is not aware of his actions. His vision is one of spiritual perfection: he has had a ritual experience in which a liminal state has put him momentarily in contact with a higher spiritual reality, with communitas (Turner 1977; Clements 1976b). His experience is similar to that of Jesse Hatcher and Leonard Bryan; in all three cases, their lives were altered by their visions; they have been born again. This was a ritual event in Quincy Higgins's life that then becomes a ritual narrative repeated throughout his life to testify to his status as born again. Telling of this experience in his old age is a way of connecting back to his own past in order to reintegrate the experience in the present. This experience also qualifies him to be divinely inspired when he is preaching. And he had yet another vision which caused him to become a preacher. I asked him, "How did you first become a preacher?"

"Well, I didn't aim to become a preacher. Law, no, I, I was a—they's something in here that kept knocking and knocking and knocking. Well, I wasn't the man; I wanted to put it off on good men like you, and my older brother, and fellers like that. I wasn't the man. But by and by, why, I got to where I couldn't go no further. We had an awful—we lived down at the old place, and had an awful sweet little boy, second boy. He's just short and stout, and fluffy, and intelligent, and he'd come way out to the road to meet me, to get on the wagon to ride back to the house. One night my wife waked me up, and says, 'This youngun's a dying. This youngun's a dying.' Well, the very minute she got me awake, I knowed what the trouble was. Well, they's a neighbor that lived right across the hill there. And I got the lantern, I got the fire built, and the lamp lit, and I grabbed the lantern, went over after her. And she come, and she took the baby in her arms, and, and went over him and looked at him, and she said, 'Quincy, you better get a doctor here, as quick as you can. This baby's gonna die.'

"Well, I started right up, went out the road, that's on horseback. Got over down there, in a mile half, two miles of Sparta. I said, 'Lord, if you let that baby live, I'll take that Book and do the best I can.' And I went on, got the doctor, and come on back home, and I went in, and I says, 'Mamma, how's that baby?' Says, 'He's better.' I says, 'How long'd I been gone?' Says, 'You been gone about a hour. And his breath just cleared up.' You know, you're bound to acknowledge then. That there's some work in from Home Office. Law, yeah. Yeah, said, 'You been gone about an hour. And he begin to get his breath better.' And I was thrilled to death. Well, I done vowed, you know. Well, I took that Book, and I started out. And they's lots of them a crying, thinking I'd done the right thing, lots of them think we never amount to nothing. But I, I don't know of anybody that's got a, a record like mine. Not a soul. I don't know of another man in the county that's baptized four hundred. I don't know of another one that's, that's, buried four hundred and twenty-three. And went without money, and things like that. And I've got along."

Immediately after he finished this story, Mr. Higgins told the one about his rise from poverty—tying his shoes together with fencing wire—again mixing sacred and secular categories, but he had already begun this shift toward the end of the story about his vow to become a preacher. He not only became a preacher, he became one with an outstanding record, better than any other man in the county. His achievement orientation and his religious beliefs are bound together in this and in many of his narratives. He can move from the emotional and spiritual experience surrounding the near death of his son to a statement of his accomplishments as a preacher and landowner without any sense of incongruity because the spiritual dominates everything else. He believes that his material gains are a result of his spiritual gifts. This has broader implications for the study of religion in individual lives. As James Peacock says, "Religion . . . points toward the spiritual, life history toward the natural—processes through which the organism moves from birth to death." He goes on to emphasize the importance of studying the relationship between religion and life history as a means of "understanding the perennially puzzling yet fundamental relationships between collective and individual, culture and nature, structure and process, text and experience" (1984, 94). In Quincy Higgins's case, sacred narratives are part of life history, the spiritual and the natural are intertwined, and his individual life has been reinforced by his cultural expectations.

Despite the intertwining of spiritual and material concerns in his life, Quincy Higgins has some conflicts between his religious ideals and his material needs. His material values are based on his religion and his understanding of the Bible. One of his major beliefs is in helping others. He said at one point, "We want, we need people that can depend on one another. We need people that can re—can help one another." He tries to put the golden rule into effect in his own life; he told two stories about how he had helped travelers who were passing through the area. He picked up two hitchhikers who had not eaten in two days, and even though he was afraid they might attack and rob him, he took them to a grocery store and bought them something to eat. He said, "I've always felt wonderful about it." The point seems to be that he ignored his self-interest in order to do good for someone else and that he was better off spiritually for it. In another instance, he helped a stranded motorist who had no cash or credit cards by taking him to Mr. Higgins's own bank and endorsing a ten dollar check for him. He could have lost the ten dollars if the check had bounced.

I asked him, "But his check didn't bounce, did it?"

"Oh, no. No, his check never bounced. Law, no. Well, it wouldn't have made no difference to me if it had because I signed it with intentions of paying it if it did bounce. They'd just charge it to my account. And that'd been fine, that, just so they got their money. They didn't care about me, you know, and so I, I, I knowed I could pay it, and I cared for him. Law, yeah, that meant it all."

Mr. Higgins never received a thank-you note from the man, and he felt that the traveler didn't care about him. Nevertheless, Mr. Higgins cared for him, and "that meant it all." He tries to live his life by the principles of his religion, but there are still conflicts between his need to help others and his need to help himself. He is acquisitive and achievement-oriented, and in order to acquire property and money, he has had to look out for himself. The conflict, then, is between his sense of self-interest and his sense of serving others. He recognizes the conflict when he says, "I done my best for everybody else and tried to do a little for myself." He told a story to illustrate this point.

"If I—an old feller said one time—I'd kinda borrowed his wagon, you know, to—mine broke down. And I went to take his wagon back that evening—Bob Hanks was his name. I said, 'Mr. Hanks, how much do I owe you for the use of your wagon?' He says, 'Nothing t'all.' Says, 'A man lives to himself, the world's better off when he did.' And I, I've embraced that with all the grip I had. The, the— that a man lives to himself, the world's better off when he did. Well, I just wanted to help everybody else, then. I wanted be a little better off, while I's living, and after I's dead too. That there, that's just living to yourself. They's people in the country like that. That just wants all they can get without having any mercy on anybody else. Well, I've give the last dollar I had away, different times. Dollars I'd worked out. Just give it away. Well, I, I never have felt bad about it. I believe that they's, is, be, be some favoritism from beyond the reach of man. Yeah, it's fine to have nice presidents, and nice Congressmen, and, and nice county board of education, and all like that, but they's an unseen hand that's far superior to that."

The story does not exactly illustrate the point he had in mind, but it does indicate him grappling with the problem of self and others. He says he embraced the idea of a man living to himself, which seems to be a justification for isolation and self-interest, but immediately afterward he says, "I wanted to help everybody else then." This is followed by another contradiction, "I wanted to be a little better off," which seems to suggest selfish materialism except that he follows with "better off . . . after I's dead too" suggesting spiritual values. The contradictory nature of this statement continues when he identifies those who live to themselves as people who "just want all they can get without having any mercy on anybody else." He then disassociates himself from those people by saying that he has given away his last dollar. To somehow resolve these contradictions, he ends with an appeal to God, to the "unseen hand that's far superior" to human hierarchy. For a man who is very articulate in everything else he says, this is a confusing statement, but it reflects Quincy Higgins's attempt to resolve his own conflict between self-interest and serving others. This conflict is important in his life review because it is still unresolved; talking about it is an attempt to resolve the conflict with his overall world view (Butler 1964, 266).

He is a successful man in the material world, and he is a spiritual man in terms of his religious beliefs. He is also a prosperous landowner, farmer, and an active lay preacher. Mr. Higgins sees no contradiction in this since he believes that his spirituality is the foundation for his material success. His speech blends the secular and the sacred, and his narratives mix the spiritual and the material. The rhetoric of his speech and narrating reflects these dual concerns. He used the phrase "elevated in spirit" throughout his conversations with us, but the meaning changed depending on the context. The phrase has a religious meaning when he says that his neighbors' response to his funeral services made him "feel elevated in spirit." When the wealthy, educated man complimented him on his accomplishments as a land-owner and family man, and Mr. Higgins said, "That there elevated my spirit a sight," the meaning was more secular. When he was denied credit in one place but got a loan for fifteen thousand dollars in another, he said, "It's bound to elevate your spirit." The acquisition of money is the basis for elevated spirit; financial accomplishment and religion are linked together through his rhetoric.

At other points, he uses the word "elevation" without spiritual connotations to suggest his rise from poverty: "Well, wonder if you start out here working five dollars a week, and wiring your shoes on your feet with fencing wire, and reach that elevation. Now that's something to be wonderfully thought of. Ain't it?" Since the word has both these meanings, the tour he conducts of his property becomes a metaphor for his success; the landscape itself becomes symbolic. He drove us to the top of the highest mountain on his land, and we talked.

"This is pretty steep up here," I commented.

"No. Law mercy! We getting up in the land of Nod now."

"Yeah. How often do you come up here?"

"Oh, ever time some fine folks come see me."

"You bring them up here?"

"Right, bring them up here. They's an old boy works in Raleigh. . . . And he said that, that he's raised right here, and he, he—honestly, he didn't know they's such a place like this in all the world."

We were at the highest elevation on his farm, and it represents how far he has come from poverty to prosperity, and at the same time it represents his spiritual elevation, achieved through his divine inspiration and his good works. No wonder he brings all of his visitors here. His use of the word "elevation" and his taking us to the highest elevation have the same meaning; his rhetoric and his behavior are analogous. Elevation has both spiritual and material connotations, which are reinforced on this spot. Not only the stories but also the context of their telling is significant in his life review. Bringing visitors to this site in his old age is a way of showing them the accomplishments of his life.

He uses another device to elevate himself in a secular sense: his inflated language, especially his use of Latinate or Hellenic words in unusual contexts, gives a comic educated tone to what he says. For instance, in the "Amazing Grace" story, he refers to the more educated preacher as "some hypodermic, you know, from over at Fries, Virginia." I think he is aware that this might be considered incorrect usage, but as a skilled performer he also knows that this original coinage is effective in describing his attitude toward the other preacher. Like his pretended innocent bumpkin role in the Senator Scott story, this device enables him to sound knowledgeable and at the same time to make fun of the pretenses of the educated. Another example in the same story is his use of "recognization" for recognition; adding a syllable makes the word sound more impressive, thus making fun of Washington political pretensions. He also uses "rehearses" for "repeats," making the same point. This elevated language makes him seem educated and at the same time satirizes educated language. The irony is similar to Mark Twain's use of the vernacular in *Adventures of Huckleberry Finn*, "The Notorious Jumping Frog of Calaveras County," and "The Story of the Old Ram."

Another recurring rhetorical device was Mr. Higgins's use of biblical references, and here again he uses them in both sacred and secular contexts. Like Mollie Ford, he quotes the Bible in support of religious points, as when he was talking about divine inspiration and said, "He that hath not my spirit is none of mine." In other instances he mixes biblical quotes in with secular stories. He was telling a story about a Revolutionary War battle when he cited the story of Gideon from the Old Testament, and that in turn reminded him of a modern battle between Israel and Egypt. Finally, he uses the Bible to guide his actions in financial dealings. He was involved in a dispute over a loan on some land. "And the man cursed me like a dog 'cause I'd traded this note to this old man. And I had it all in there, and had my deed, and let him curse. . . . But at the same time, whenever that, they's look at these things—whenever somebody was talking and cursing back yonder in the days of old, you heared somebody a saying, 'Lay not this sin to their charge, for they know not what they doeth.'" He is cursed because of a financial transaction, but by referring to biblical times, he reminds himself not to blame the individual who cursed him.

Biblical quotes in the context of financial transactions are not unusual for Quincy Higgins; he seems to have resolved any conflicts between material and spiritual values in his life. He lives in the modern material world and deals with it every day, but his values are based on a traditional world, one in which divine inspiration is central. His narratives reflect both sacred and secular concerns: a story about a religious vision is followed by a story about his financial achievements and then by a practical joke. All of these various genres of folk narrative are unified by Quincy Higgins's point of view and the fact that they are all a part of his life story. In this they are similar to the narratives of Texas storyteller Ed Bell, who was elderly when studied by folklorist Richard Bauman. Ed Bell's stories, be they personal narratives, tall tales, or jokes, are related together by first-person narration and a connection to his life (Bauman 1987, 198). Quincy Higgins tells fictional jokes (the moonshine story), fictional tall tales, historical legends (George Washington praying), personal achievement stories, and sacred personal narratives (conversion stories, the "Amazing Grace" story), and they all are part of his life story in that they express his values and his personality; they all become part of his life review.

One of the unifying factors in his life story is his dual concern with structured society and communitas. His stories reflect his interest in the hierarchy of society and with his place in the social system; he continually refers to his relationships and encounters with people in the high bracket, with bankers, senators, professors, and so forth. In ritual terms, this hierarchy is part of structured society, the here and now, the world as it is. He is also concerned with the other world, the higher reality, the spirit realm—in ritual terms, with communitas. In communitas there is no hierarchy; it is anti-structure, an ideal realm without the strife of this world (Turner 1969, 96–97). Through his religious visions, he has experienced communitas, and through his telling of these experiences, he can ritually relive them, reminding himself and others of the higher spiritual reality. Ironically, his visionary experiences have given him higher status in the hierarchical world; he sees himself as a better preacher than others who have not been divinely inspired.

His personal view does not see these states of being as antithetical; all of his stories and comments on theology suggest that he has resolved any contradiction. The material world is contained in the spiritual world, and any secular activities, including the acquisition of property and money, are guided by spiritual principles. What has happened, I think, is that he has been able to combine the American cultural value of achievement-orientation with his fundamentalist Protestant belief in spirituality. These combined principles have guided his life, and as he looks back from the perspective of old age, they give order to his life, resolving contradictions and conflicts that may have been part of the original experience.

7

Bill Henry
Orphan and Hobo,
Learning from Life

Bill Henry started telling stories about his life before we could get
the tape recorder turned on, and he told one after another for the
next four hours. I was with another folklorist, J. Sanford Rikoon,
and we were doing fieldwork in southern Ohio for the Ohio Arts
Council. Several people had mentioned Bill Henry of Waverly as a
big storyteller, and we were not disappointed. When we interviewed
him in his living room on June 27, 1980, he was sixty–nine years
old. I interviewed him again on August 10, 1989, and he repeated
many of the stories he told in 1980. (All references are to the first
interview unless otherwise noted.) He was retired from factory work,
but, unlike Alva Snell, he did not seem to have an occupational
identity and talked very little about his work. In fact, he only told
personal experience stories about two topics in his life: his childhood
in a foster home and his hobo experiences as a young man. He has
shaped these experiences into two cycles of stories, and usually he
tells them chronologically with a transition between the two. He also
told several jokes from his vast repertoire, but these will not be the
focus of analysis here. His personal narratives are part of his life
review, and his concentration on two periods of his life reveals, from
the perspective of old age, how he perceives himself.

Because he was an orphan, Bill Henry was not certain about his
own date and place of birth; it was not until 1975 when he searched
for his birth certificate that he found out that he was born in Louis-
ville, Kentucky, in 1910. He grew up thinking he had been born in

1913 and that he was three years younger than he actually was because he had been abandoned by his parents and his records at the orphanage falsified. His mother took him to an orphanage for reasons that he did not explain in the first interview, and a foster family took him from there. During the second interview, I asked him more direct questions about his parents and the circumstances of his abandonment. He thinks that his natural parents abandoned him simply because they did not want the responsibility of a child. From what he has been able to determine, his father left his mother, and she placed him in the orphanage. She falsified the records so that it would be difficult for anyone to trace her identity. Mr. Henry met his mother for the first time after he was grown, but she did not want to have anything to do with him, even denying that he was her son.

He was taken into the foster home in 1918 at the age of eight (although in his confusion about his birthdate, he sometimes says 1920), and he stayed there until he was seventeen when he ran away because of mistreatment by his foster family. He has difficulty determining his age at any point in his life because of the wrong birthdate; he thought he was fourteen or fifteen at the time he ran away from the foster home. Shortly after running away in 1927, he started his life as a hobo traveling all across the United States for the next seven years. He worked in factories at temporary jobs during this period, but he did not start to work permanently until 1934 when he quit hoboing. He married in 1935, and he and his wife had five children, three of whom survived. He worked in different factories near Cincinnati until 1965 when he moved his family to Waverly, Ohio. He worked in a factory in Waverly until 1975 when he retired. He had been retired for five years when Sandy Rikoon and I interviewed him the first time.

As soon as we had explained our mission, he launched into the first story as we set up the tape recorder. As with Quincy Higgins and others, he projected a sense of himself as a performer.

After he told a few stories about his childhood, I asked him, "Did, did you ever recount these experiences to your own children? Did you ever tell them about what you went through when you were a kid?"

"Yeah. The boy, he wants to get all this stuff down, he wants to make a book, and often people said, 'You, you got enough stuff to make a good book.'"

"So, it's not just your kids you tell, you've told these experiences to other people."

"Yeah, other people. And they really enjoyed hearing them."

Many people think their life stories would make a book, but in Bill Henry's case others have reinforced the idea. He perceives himself as a special kind of storyteller then, one who has made his life into a series of stories, an oral autobiography. Like other storytellers discussed in this book, he uses his role as performer to attract attention to himself in his old age, to stay active and avoid disengagement. Since he is both narrator and protagonist of the stories, he is able to keep a strong focus on himself. As he mentioned, the contexts for storytelling go beyond his family.

Toward the end of the interview, I asked him, "Did you tell people about your experiences right after you got back [from hoboing]? Like where you would tell friends about where—"

"Well I'd tell a lot of them."

"What about in the years since then? Have you told many people about your hobo experiences?"

"Yeah, I told a lot of people, and they really, they really like to hear it."

"Yeah. What situations usually would it be when you would tell them about them? I mean would you be just sitting around your house or working some place?"

"Well, lot of times in different places, and down at the American Legion and Veterans of Foreign War I'd tell them. Sit around. They'd buy the drinks, you know." We laughed. "If I'd tell the stories."

He has been interviewed by newspaper and magazine reporters, which has also reinforced his sense of himself as a performer. He has had positive responses to his stories, encouragement to continue telling them, and he has had places where such performances are appropriate. He has been able to adjust to retirement and old age more easily because of his performing abilities; the transition from instrumental to expressive roles has been facilitated by his storytelling. Storytelling can be seen both as an expressive activity involving emotional interaction with others and as an instrumental public performance; Bill Henry uses storytelling to project an instrumental image of himself through the culturally defined masculine activity of hobo-

14. Bill Henry. (Photograph by the author.)

ing. Given a willing audience and enough time, he is likely to tell a
cycle of stories the way he did on the two occasions I interviewed
him. He started with the childhood foster home stories and then
switched to the hobo stories, finally ending with the jokes.

His concentration on childhood experiences in the first cycle is in
keeping with a pattern in elderly life review: "the individual must be
capable of finding and reliving parts of his/her history. And often,
the most important, charged pieces of personal history come up from
the remote past, from the numinous events and experiences of early
childhood" (Myerhoff 1978, 108). Bill Henry's childhood is especially
important because of his abandonment and orphanhood; this is the

source of an unresolved conflict that he must deal with in his life review. His actual abandonment is not part of the cycle of stories perhaps because it is too painful to talk about directly, but his foster home experiences are the basis of a long and detailed cycle of stories.

The first story he told concerns one of his earliest memories of the foster home: the setting is the farm of the family that took him in at the age of eight. He may not technically have been an orphan since his mother and father were still alive, but the circumstances of abandonment, living in an orphanage and a foster home made him what is called a "psychic or spiritual orphan" (Simpson 1987, 220). This background was not clear to us at the time of the first interview because he started telling the story before giving any prefatory material. The tape recording begins in the middle of a sentence:

"—a real milk cow. And I come running in real fast and I said, 'Boy, oh boy, oughta see what a bag Daisy's got on her.' And about that time they gave me a haymaker upside the head, and I landed on the other side of the house. Ooh, man that hurt. And that old lady [his foster mother]—I got up and I said, 'What'd I do wrong?' 'You know what you done wrong, come in here and talk like that. You don't talk that way to womenfolks.' Said, 'Now, what you said is on a gentleman cow, not on a lady cow.' Said, 'Now that is a sack on a lady cow and what you said is on a gentleman cow, and I want you to remember this on the longest day you live.' And I said I will, and I did." He laughed. "And I tell you she's a mean, she's a mean old lady. And I had told her when she got ready to die, 'When you get ready to die, I hope you have a hard time dying.'"

"You told her that?" I asked him.

"Yes, sir. And the morning I left I said, 'I don't want you to forget what I told you.' They got the lantern and lit it and throwed my shoe at me. I broke that string, you know, and put her on, and boy I had a time that morning. They all three give me a round, all big people, they were, the womenfolk, they, they were Irish and the old man was English. And when we'd go to [the field] he was a fine feller, good feller, and we'd come to the house and trouble'd start." He laughed. "It went right on that way."

I asked him, "That was in the orphanage?"

"No, that's the, they sent me back in the mountains [of Kentucky]."

Sandy asked, "Back in the—?"

"Oh, I see," I said. "I missed that part."

"1920 they sent me back there."

"Like a foster home kind of a thing?"

"Yeah, they was supposed to adopt me."

"I see."

He begins in medias res and explains any vague references later, perhaps as a means of grabbing his listener's attention and keeping it until everything is fully explained. There also seems to be a purpose in beginning with this particular story. It makes an effective introduction because it contains most of the major themes of the entire cycle of foster home stories. This story has a reference to the last story in the cycle, which is also about a confrontation: the end is in the beginning, and the whole cycle is unified as a result. When he refers to having a shoe thrown at him and breaking a string, it is not clear what he means, but the meaning becomes clear later when he returns to this incident at the end of the cycle. Bill Henry sees the cycle of stories as a unified whole, as one long story with different episodes, so that he does not have to explain details at the beginning. Their meaning will become apparent later. He counts on his audience being around for the ending in order to get the full import of the entire narrative's meaning. Sandy and I were too impatient at the beginning; Mr. Henry expected us to listen until all of the relevant details were filled in.

Many of the episodes are about confrontations with the women in the family, and the first one is typical. The women often physically attacked him, and from his point of view these attacks were unjustified. He gets hit simply because he said "bag" instead of "sack." The story implicitly makes fun of their Victorian attitudes toward sexuality, and there are underlying sexual themes in several of the other episodes. The women in the foster home and hobo stories are invariably big and strong, and they use their strength against men. His statement that his foster father was a "fine feller" when he was away from the women indicates that Mr. Henry has strong opinions about gender roles, especially what he perceives as the negative influence of women on men. As a story in the life review, this one is important because in it he is dealing with his earliest and deepest feelings about mothers. His mother had abandoned him, and his foster mother was mean to him, creating an unresolved conflict that stayed with him the rest of his life, even into old age. Other stories develop this theme in more detail.

He told another story in which the women physically abused him, and this story also comments on sexuality and gender roles.

"I was to call him Pap. And Maw. And Luly. Old-fashion girl. They're old-fashion people. Their dress was up like this," he indicated a place high up on his neck, "sleeves was here," down to the wrist, "and their dresses swept the floor. And about all you ever done, if you looked real close and looked real quick, you might see their ankles." We laughed. "A old-fashion people. So I got up on the—a box I had, wash day was Monday and got up on this wash board, this is the way you done it, and I was told to get those clothes, start here on this end of them and give them three rubs and then change and get another hold, see. Now, if I rub them six rubs and kept doing that stuff, I could rub a hole in this clothes. Well, they was standing there watching me, and I, washing on this old dress, by golly I gived that, never forgot about it, and I gived that five rubs. And off of that box I went cross the kitchen. Now they didn't push me off of the box, they gave me a haymaker upside the head, and I was, I was little, and over I went, so I'd get up and rub my head. 'Come on, come on, get on that box. Now you do what you're told to do.' Now they'd show you one time and that was it. No second, you didn't have a second time. I got up there and I went to work. I rub them three times, get with it, not just fool around there and rub easy. I rubbing three times and loosening up and get another hold and rub down three times. And then when you got through rubbing them and all, why you get that done with, why you wring them out good, and then you take them over and put them in the boiler they had. A big cast iron kettle, that's what they boiled clothes in, in the house. . . . Boy I got awful tired of that wash days, they was miserable. And every day was bad enough."

Normal family life is turned upside down: he was forced to call them "Pap" and "Maw," but there is no affection or caring between them. The usual gender roles in a family are reversed as well: the boy washes clothes and dishes and sweeps the floor, the girl does not seem to do anything except give orders to him. Again, he gives a subtle reference to sexuality when he mentions seeing the women's ankles: this satirizes their Puritan attitudes, but it also shows his sexual interest. Taken together, his childhood stories reveal Bill Henry in his old age using the life review to work out his own attitudes toward gender roles, mothering, women, and sexuality. He commented at the end of this story on how he continued some of the culturally defined women's work throughout his life.

"So I started out washing dishes, and I figured up on that the other day that I'd washed dishes, been washing dishes and doing housework sixty-three years. And I had told the wife that that was long enough for anybody to wash dishes. But then she wasn't feeling good and had maybe a bad finger or something, well I'd wash dishes. But I've taught many a young girls how to wash dishes. They didn't know nothing about washing dishes or nothing else. They couldn't even boil water without burning it."

His ambivalence toward his own assumption of a domestic expressive role comes out here: on the one hand, he declares his independence from that role, and on the other, he continues it because of his desire to nurture, to take care of his wife. Finally, he even expresses pride in his domestic ability, assuming the role of teacher to young girls in the kitchen. Unlike Jesse Hatcher, Mr. Henry has some inner conflict over his domestic expressive role in old age.

Another point he makes throughout these stories is how big the women were and how small he was. This also seems to symbolically represent a reversal of the usual gender roles. He was not big or strong enough to defend himself against these big women, and this seems to have remained a psychological theme for him throughout his life. He is five feet four and a half inches tall, and his nickname was "Shorty" when he worked in factories; he commented on his small size in the hobo stories as well. In telling stories about women beating him up, he is still attempting to cope with a childhood problem in his old age. The resolution to the foster home cycle provides a partial solution to the problem, and we shall consider it in due course.

Another pervasive theme in the childhood cycle is the hard work he was forced to do by his foster family. The previous story showed him washing clothes, but that was just one of many chores he had to perform.

"So I had to go in the kitchen every morning and get everything ready for the womenfolk. I had this coffee grinder, see, I had to grind coffee every morning, and you could set that thing, you know, to how fine you wanted it ground. So they had to have coffee every morning and hot biscuits every morning, and they killed plenty of hogs and had good ham meat and biscuits. And, and eggs, had plenty to eat. But when they wouldn't give me enough to eat, I had to go in the kitchen and wash them dishes and all this food left over, they put it in what they call a warming closet up here, raise that lid, you know, and put that stuff up there. They didn't throw it out, so of course I had to feed old Rover, he was one of my best friends. About the only friend I had around there."

One of the devices that emphasizes his bad treatment is the repetition of the verb form "had to." He had to grind the coffee, had to wash the dishes, had to feed the dog. He has no control over his own life; they determine what he is going to do, how to do it, and when it will be done. A related device is that much of the dialog in the childhood stories is in the form of orders from an adult to him. Lack of control is a major theme in the childhood cycle, and it must have had a negative psychological effect on him. Other orphans have experienced the same feeling; Eileen Simpson in writing about her and her sister's childhood as orphans mentions the "years of waiting until we could take control of our lives" (1987, 104). Bill Henry sees himself as an innocent victim just as Eileen Simpson did. As an orphan in a foster home, he did not receive any of the advantages of family life, only the work. He must have suspected that that was all he was there for, and one of his stories confirms that this was the case. The truant officer for the area was a nephew of his foster father's, and he was concerned about Bill not attending school regularly. On one visit he told Bill that he had a plan that would enable him to attend school more often.

"And we—I like for company to come in because we had all kinds of good eats and we had a lot of good old country-fried chicken, and they were good cooks, and so when company'd come in, why they'd pass this stuff around and I could take (he made an inhaling sound at this point) a good piece a chicken out. Otherwise, if there wasn't no company there, they'd dish me out what I—what they'd want me to have. And that was a wing and a neck, and you know how much eating you could get off of a wing. You could get some meat off of a wing, but that neck, you had to do a lot of picking to get much eats. And that was it." He laughed. "So, boy, they had lots of good fried chicken, and boy they passed it around; they didn't want people to know how bad they treated me otherwise.

"So I was tickled to death when company'd come in. So we'd eat, and my job was to clear up that dining room quick, get them dishes in the kitchen. And cover, put the tablecloth on and sweep that dining room and then go on in the kitchen and get them dishes washed quick. And then sweep that kitchen nice. So I cleared up the dining room, and I thought, 'Well now it's about time for them [the truant officer and his foster father] to get to talking.' They went in the front room, shut that door. There I was up the keyhole listening. Sure enough he was putting a talk to him and he said, 'Now, Uncle, I got something figured out here.' He said, 'Now that boy ought to have some education.' Said, 'I've got something, something figured out here.' 'Well,' he said, 'Let's hear it.' He said, 'You send that boy to school Monday, Tuesday, and Wednesday.' Says, 'If he can get to go three days straight, he can learn more, instead of going one day maybe in two weeks. You can't learn anything that way. And then you work him Thursday, Friday, and Saturday.' He left out Sunday because a work, he worked me on Sunday." We laughed along with Mr. Henry.

"And he snuffed through that big mustache, and he'd say (sniff), 'Dod blow it. That ain't gonna work.'" Mr. Henry laughed. "And he'd say, 'Why not, Uncle?' He said, 'I can't take a boy out of the orphans' home, and clothe him and feed him and send him to school. There's no money in it.'"

I asked, "He just wanted somebody to work around the farm, huh?"

Mr. Henry replied, "Ah, he wanted somebody to work, he could treat [me] like a mule and a dog. Back them days people didn't treat dogs too good, but later they treated dogs better than they did people. And I often wished I was a good dog."

The information about eating chicken necks seems to be a digression from the main story about the truant officer and Mr. Henry's foster father, but it fits because it characterizes his harsh treatment, which makes the foster father's statement at the end even more damning. During our second interview he again mentioned having to eat chicken necks at the foster home, showing what a vivid image it remains for him. Mr. Henry often uses digressions in his storytelling: they are not part of the main plot, but they relate thematically to the rest of the story. He also uses interior monolog to give his feelings and thoughts as a child: "and I thought." This control of point of view keeps the focus and sympathy of the listener on him. Another recurring device is the use of figurative language to describe his treatment: "he could treat [me] like a mule and a dog" in this story and "they gave me a haymaker . . . and I landed on the other side of the house" in the first story. He does not use much figurative language, and it is concentrated on violent events and his treatment in the foster home.

He is definitely aware of playing on the sympathies of his listeners by portraying himself as the abused orphan boy. He expects a sympathetic response when he says, "I often wished I was a good dog." The poor orphan child is a traditional figure: several popular sentimental ballads of the time period when Bill Henry was a child were about orphaned children (Randolph 1982, 471–72, 478–81), and Mr. Henry may have heard these. Also, there was a literary tradition that dealt with orphans' stories; the best known are Dickens's *Oliver Twist* and *David Copperfield*. James Whitcomb Riley's poem "Little Orphant Annie" was widely popular in the late nineteenth century and well into the twentieth century. The comic strip "Little Orphan Annie" began in the early 1920s and was probably familiar to Bill Henry. Thus Mr. Henry's personal narratives are influenced by traditional images.

This does not mean that the stories are imaginary; the reality of his situation was harsh; his treatment in the foster home was characterized by neglect and hard work. His sense of neglect and denial of basic nurturance is strong: his childhood experience made such a deep impression on him that it is a major theme in his life review. In his old age, he is still trying to find nurturance to offset the neglect of his childhood.

During the second interview I asked him, "What was the effect of being an orphan, more or less, of being abandoned as a child, not having a real mother? What effect did that have on your life? How do you feel about that today?"

"Well, I've had dreams and everything, and I would dream how nice it was to see other boys and kids with a good mother," he replied.

He must have had a strong sense of injustice as well, since his hard work was not rewarded. He was not fed the same food as everyone else except when a false impression was being presented to visitors. He had to feed and care for the horses as well as do household chores such as washing dishes and sweeping the floor. By listening at the keyhole, he finds out for certain what he must have known all along: he is there to work and make money for his foster father and not because "Pap" wants to provide a loving home for an orphan. His experience was typical of many orphans at this time. It was common practice to send orphans to farms to work; there were even orphan trains that took them out West. "The 'good people' who took [orphans] in . . . were looking less for foster children than for farm-hands and servants" (Simpson 1987, 143). Young Bill spent most of his time working, and hard work is a recurring theme in all of Mr. Henry's stories about his childhood.

During a pause in the storytelling, I asked him, "Did—it couldn't have been all work, I mean like on weekends or something, would people sit around and tell stories and sing songs? Or what'd they do for entertainment?"

"Well, they would, they'd visit a lot. And they had a lot of kinfolks, and they had a lot of company'd come with them, and on Sunday they'd have, sometimes they'd have twenty-five people in there and dishes, dishes, wash tubs full of dishes. And all them, you know all them that got together, you know how easy it would have been for everybody; and me, it was a killing job. I got no fun out of Sundays."

"Well what would you do if you wanted to have some fun?"

"Huh?"

"What would you do if you wanted to have some fun? Say you wanted to have some fun, what would, what could you do? As a kid growing up there?"

"Nothing."

His one-word reply is meaningful since he ordinarily is so verbose. With this kind of treatment, he had a completely negative outlook on life. The family was supposed to give him some property when he turned twenty-one, but he left before then.

"I stayed almost eight years, and I couldn't stand it no longer. They had eighty-five acres of ground laid off on me, and they had, and it was, part of it was good ground, and it had an orchard on it, and it had all kinds of coal under it. And he had, he had a coal mine under there, and we was figuring on opening up another one, you see, and, and they had plenty of oil and gas. And if I'd a lived to got that, I had it, I had it made, of course. But always said that I'd be worked to death or beat to death, and it would never do me no good. I wouldn't live till I was twenty-one."

How does a child survive under such circumstances, not just physically, but psychologically? Bill Henry used a phrase several times that indicated how he survived. In talking about using a grass sickle to cut corn and cutting himself as a result, he said, "So I learned real fast." He then said, in a way that made his statement a metaphor for his entire experience with his foster family, "So then it come to me, 'Wise up buddy, or you ain't going to be living.'" He had to learn how to get by in the face of mental and physical abuse; he had to work out strategies to survive. Since he was a small child and could not fight back physically, he had to depend on his wit. He had to use guile, deception, and verbal skills to endure. He took on the attributes of the traditional folk tale figure, the trickster (Abrahams 1968; Radin 1972), and his personal experience narratives reflect this image of himself. By telling stories in his old age about his childhood trickster exploits, he maintains continuity with that important part of his identity.

He had to sneak around behind the backs of the family members in order to get information he needed. He listened at the keyhole to find out that his foster father's only concern for him was economic. This is similar to the African-American slave trickster "Old John," who tries to stay one step ahead of his master by listening outside the plantation window every night (Dorson 1967, 126–29). Another of young Bill's tricks had to do with the family dog: "[Old Rover] was one of my best friends. About the only friend I had around there." Pap refuses to let him take the dog when he brings in the cows because the dog bites and splits their tails, and young Bill has to figure a way to take him along.

"And so he said, 'Now you're not taking that dog.' Said, 'He's got mean, and I don't want these cows' tails split.' . . . And so, they got so they'd keep Rover around the front of the house when it'd come time to go after the cows. Why they'd watch Rover and they'd say [to me], 'Get up the holler and get the cows.' Well, I'd have to go up in the briars and everything barefooted, snakes, and we had a lot of copperheads and some rattlesnakes. So I had to watch myself. So I'd run around like I was going right on, and I'd stick my head around the corner of the house, you know, and I'd go 'stz, stz, stz' and old Rover'd look around, you know, and old lady sitting on the porch, and she'd say, 'Oh no you don't, Rover.' So I'd stay around that corner of the house, and he kept such an eye on him that I had to go that time by myself. But I had to, went around, and grabbed a biscuit, you know, if they had any, and peep around the corner of the house and go 'stz, stz,' and old Rover'd look around, and I'd shake that biscuit, and he'd jump up real quick and take off, and they couldn't get him back."

We laughed.

"Yeah, boy, I had a time."

This is one of the few times Mr. Henry expressed any pleasure in his childhood recollections, and significantly, it is when he is describing a successful trick on his foster parents. Part of his childhood cycle of stories had to do with attending school, and here again he was a trickster, but this time his behavior was directed against the teacher. He had difficulty in school because he could only attend sporadically. "[Foster parents at that time] allowed their charges little time for schooling, believing . . . that it was a mistake to educate orphans above their station" (Simpson 1987, 143). If there was work to be done, his foster father would come take him out of school.

"He'd just walk up the door and say, 'Come on, William.' And most the time he [said], 'Oh, Bill, come on.' And away I went, grabbed them books, and I'd just get around and found out where all the lessons was, and the kids'd be way over in the book from the time I was there before. I'd go to my seat, and I'd sit down, and I'd start studying as hard as I could study at spelling, reading, and arithmetic, and I'd study hard as I could study, and I'd get up there, and I didn't have them lessons up past like I ought to have them; over to the corner I'd go. Stand in the corner. On one foot."

He chuckled at the memory.

"If I'd catch the teacher's head turned, I'd change feet real quick, 'cause I got tired on that one. And got tired of holding that one up. So one day she looked around, and she said—I got to go another week, and I didn't have my spelling at all. And she put on the right foot. She had, she had it in for that right foot, I'd have to stand on it. And so she turned around there and looked and I'd changed feet. And she says, 'Now, there's something funny about this. I'm sure I put you on that right foot.' Now she didn't go down to where I was and mark it on the blackboard. Up near her and she marked it on the blackboard: 'I put Bill on his right foot.'"

We all laughed at this.

"Yeah, I caught her head turned, and I changed anyhow that time. And, and she looked around too quick for me, and I didn't get changed. And boy she raised sand. Said, 'Now you're going to have to stand so much longer.' It'd be fifteen minutes most time. Sometimes ten minutes. She said, 'Now you're just going to have to stand another fifteen minutes.' Oh boy."

He chuckled again, happy in the memory of having fooled the teacher at least some of the time. This may seem like an inconsequential childhood experience, but I think it has special meaning for Bill Henry because like his other trickster stories it shows him in the unusual circumstance of being in control. The school situation is based on dominance and subordination, and there is a body of classroom folklore, jokes, and personal narratives that reflects this theme (Sullivan 1987, 39). Often in the folklore, the child is presented as a trickster in his or her relation with the teacher. The trickster tries to manipulate others through deceit so that he can be in control (Bauman 1986, 36). As I pointed out earlier, the lack of control had a negative psychological effect on Bill Henry; his foster parents and the teacher were the all-powerful oppressors, and he was the powerless oppressed. Like slaves before the Civil War, one of his few options for any kind of control was trickery, using his wits in an attempt to defeat authority. The experience of deceiving his teacher and foster parents gave him psychological satisfaction in his childhood, and telling about the experiences still gives him satisfaction in his old age. Quincy Higgins used his pranks and hoaxes to get a sense of control in old age; Bill Henry uses storytelling about trickery for the same effect. Narrating itself is a means of establishing control.

Just as slaves had more than one response to oppression, so too did Bill Henry: slaves openly rebelled at times, and so did he. He could not physically confront his adult oppressors, but he could fight his peers who treated him badly.

"Finally I gave up and I'd ask them [his foster parents] questions, why they didn't want to tell me this word, I'd ask, in my reading book. They'd say, 'Why anybody ought to know that word.' And I'd say, 'Well, I wouldn't have to go to school if I knew all this. Would I?' And they'd say, 'Now you just get smart and we'll cut a switch and wear you out.' And so I got so tired of being talked to so mean, almost got a whipping there. When I had to be punished and get whippings at school because those kids would jump onto me and make fun of me, and I had rags and looked awful in the head, and I, I could stand [it] so long, and then I'd plow into them, you know. I'd bite them, scratch them, anything, kick them in the shins. I learned that in the orphans' home. You had to fight to protect yourself. And so I'd put up with it so long, and, and the teacher'd call us in, they'd catch us in a fight, sometime two or three'd jump on me, you know, and I'd have to fight for dear life. But I had some buddies there was pretty good, and by golly they'd jump in and stop it. And well, he'd call up books, you know, they called it and you had to go in, why 'Who started this fight?' 'He did.' Yeah, the one started the fight get the whippings. And they say, 'You started the fight?' And I'd say, 'Yes, this is how it went.' I said, 'They jumped into making fun of me.' And everything. And I said, 'I could stand it so long.' And I said, 'I told them boys, "Don't you think I'd like to wear good clothes and everything like you'uns do?"'"

Not only was he an outcast in the family, he was also ostracized at school, except for the few friends he mentioned. This is similar to the experience described by Eileen Simpson in *Orphans*: "I dreaded going to school, and dreaded returning home. In neither place could I be anonymous. At school I was a dunce; at home a member of a family, but a second-class member, and in very bad standing" (1987, 69). Simpson states the orphan's lot simply and directly: "Orphans were outsiders" (68). His poor clothing marked young Bill as different at school; his foster parents did not even provide him with adequate shoes. Bill Henry often mentioned the physical discomfort associated with bare feet.

"They said, 'You get down there at the creek.' I had to go

barefooted. I only got one cheap pair of shoes a year. If I didn't take care of them and come spring them shoes give out, buddy, I had it, had to go around there barefooted in the frost; feet crack open, and the water was a lot warmer than that air and that frost. My feet would get real cold, and I'd jump in that, go down to that creek, jump in that water a little while, oh that made it worse, when I did leave. I couldn't stay in there, and when I got out of there, that cold wind'd hit those feet and they'd crack open. . . . When they did get me shoes in the fall, I'd run around in the, in the snags, you know, where they'd mold, and step on them snags and just skin my feet, stump my toes on rocks, and walk on snakes around there. . . . So they told me to, to get up in the head of the holler and get the cow, see. So I was looking up on the hills, you know, to see if I could see the cow, and old Rover was with me, but he was monkeying around, you know, he wasn't behind me in the path or in front of me that day. So I was walking along there, wasn't paying no attention to where I was walking. Great big old black snake. I stepped on that gentleman, and that was the funniest feeling. That snake couldn't see me and I was making no noise, you see, and out from under my foot he went."

His lack of shoes was just one factor that made him feel neglected and different from other children, but it took on special importance to him which becomes even more apparent in the final story of the childhood cycle. This story ties up some of the loose ends of the overall narrative, thus giving him a sense of control over it. In terms of the life review in old age, he has neatly wrapped up his orphan years in narrative form, structuring it so that he has a sense of psychological control. The neglect and extreme isolation from family and community must have left psychological scars, which the last story attempts to resolve. He survived under these conditions for eight years, and finally he could take it no longer. In telling the cycle of childhood stories, he tells the final confrontation story last, and he has built up to it by cataloging all of the abuses he suffered. When he reaches this point, there is satisfaction for the listener as well as for the narrator.

"Now, this trouble, getting back to that shoestring. Can you imagine that? And they needing me ever so bad. . . . But I left that morning, and they throwed my, the shoe at me, big frost on that morning, it was April, and they throwed that shoe at me, I had everything done in the kitchen for them, as I told you, and I had a good fire there, the fire felt good. The girl was sitting over there, she got up and dressed, she sitting over there, and she slid her feet into lowcuts she had, and hadn't been for her I wouldn't had no stockings or, you know, kids wore them days. But she'd have those old stockings, and they'd come way up here, and she wore a hole in them, why she'd throw them over at me and say, 'There, Bill, something to wear in your shoes.' Well my feet didn't stay too warm with no socks or nothing to wear, see. And so, we'd take and wash them up, you know, and take the scissors and cut off that wore place and put them on, and I had garters, of course, when I did get ahold of anything to wear, and so I'd take and fold them over a little, and the best thing about it when that foot'd get dirty, why they was way up here, and I could move them down several times, you know, and just take the scissors and cut me off a new foot, and throw that dirty foot in the fire."

We all laughed.

"Yeah, that worked out fine. And by the time I got that old stocking used up, why she'd have some more ready for me, and she was pretty good for that. So she looked over at me, and I was picking at that knot. Well, that night they told me to get in that bed and get there now, and I had to go out on the porch and upstairs, and so I—my foot out of there and you might know how hard a knot would get because that was tight squeezing because I had to get the shoe off, and I had to get going to bed. So the next morning, why I got all of that done and the fire started there in the fireplace first and then got the kitchen work done, the water, the water and everything, but I usually done that at night 'cause I didn't like going to the well in the bare feet. So she looked over at me, and I hadn't been allowed to say anything back for a long time, I hadn't said anything back, but when I did I'd get slapped across the house. I looked over at her and I said, 'This—' She's going to get up and slap the thunder out of me. And I looked over at her and I said, 'You just get up and slap it out.' Here she come, well, up went my arms like that. Couldn't slap me. She happened to think, boy you got a real nice head of hair. She settles her hand in there and started pulling that hair . . . but I backed, got up and backed over there, and oh boy that door was just right. She started to turn my head back against that door, and old-timers, you know, I don't know whether you ever hear it or not, but they'd say this is stirring up a dander. And I just thought of that, and that dress she had on up here and long sleeves, I knowed that I'd got up on that box and washed that dress many a time, and I knowed that dress was old, and I, I was pretty stout because I had to work all the time, and I had built up some muscles, and I just run through my head, 'You're bashful, you're a old-time girl, and I'm gonna make you turn me loose.' That was running through my head, you know. And I reached over and grabbed her right here and got a good hold on that dress and give her a hard jerk, and you know I tore that all open, and you ought to see a girl turn a fella loose and grab herself.

"And the old lady was sitting on the bed trying to get her clothes on. . . . So she turned me loose, and I thought I was going to get away, and the old man jumped up out of that bed, and I, I didn't get away, didn't make it. And he grabbed me by the, by the left hand by the hair of the head. And he, he was a big man, and he'd, he grabbed me and slinging me around there, and every time I'd come just right you know he'd hit me in the back." Mr. Henry hit his fist into his palm. "And he'd say (sniff), 'Dod blow it, I, I, I'll teach you a lesson.' And they had these old hickory-bottom chairs, my feet hit them and knocked them over, and finally his hold gave loose, and I made up my mind if anybody got in my way I was going to try to run right square through them, like a football player." He chuckled at the thought. "The girl got back out of my way. And I went outside, I knowed the back was open, and I went outside, and I got in the yard and I stopped. Here they all come. And she said, the old lady said, Elly Jane said, 'Get that lantern, Lully, and get it lit. He's going to have to get to the barn, he's going to have to, he's got a lot of work to do in the fields.' And I said, 'You're wasting your time getting a lantern for me. I don't need no lantern, and never going to use your lantern again.' I said, 'I, I've, almost eight years, I've been kicked and beat and worked to death and never give a kind word.' I said, 'This is it. I'm leaving.' And she said, 'Ah, now I think I've heard you said that stuff before.' I said, 'This time I'm going to tell you the truth.' So she got a hold of my shoe and throwed it at me, and I grabbed that thing and broke the string, put it on, my foot was getting cold. And so I said 'So long.' And I went up the holler and stopped at the cellar house, and I knowed where there's some bale hay wire, and it makes awful good, stout shoestrings. And I stopped out there and broke me a piece of the hay bale wire, and I got, got that shoe, boy, it kept it on."

He mentioned the shoestring in the very first story, and its meaning becomes clear in the final story of this cycle, but why he would describe the shoestring, stockings, and shoes at such length is still not apparent. The shoe seems to take on symbolic significance in terms of this event as a ritual passage from one stage of his life to another. As his earlier descriptions indicate, his feet are symbolic of the neglect and harsh treatment he received in his foster home. The family did not provide adequate shoes for him, and he suffered all of the discomforts and dangers of going barefoot as a result. I think his feet are also a metaphor for his psychological state: he had none of the protection provided by a loving family and had to face the hardships of the world alone. Thus, shoes became significant objects to him; they provided protection against the elements and symbolically gave him a sense of protection from psychic harm. No wonder he emphasizes the shoes so much in the last story. He could not leave home and go out into the world without them, and he needed the shoestring to make sure the shoes stayed on. Leaving home was a turning point in his life that has taken on ritual meaning in his life review. He rebelled against the foster family and took control of his own life; he left his childhood behind and started to become an adult. His action to save himself from his foster sister has sexual implications that relate it to the other stories that mention her. Ripping the front of her dress off keeps her from abusing him, but it is also a sexually aggressive act, establishing dominance over her. He can look back on this event from the perspective of old age and relive it through storytelling; he can assert his own independence and masculinity in old age by identifying with his young, aggressive self. He told the story again in our second interview, repeating the same important images indicating the significance the story has for him.

His next series of stories provides a transition from the childhood cycle to the hobo cycle of young adulthood. He lived with a group of men at a coal camp and learned some important lessons about life that added to his stereotyping of women.

"And so I went on up the head of the holler and over the hill and down the holler to a fella that worked in the old Cannel City, the old coal mine, the finest coal in the world was over there. And he worked over there. . . . I walked up and knocked on the door, and he come to the door, and he said, 'Jesus Christ! What had a hold of you?' I said, 'Three big wildcats.' And he said, 'I believe it.' Said, 'Don't they know I'm working in the mines? And they sent you over to get me to come work?' When he wasn't laid off, you know, why he'd come over there and work on the farm. And I said, 'No, Kelly, they didn't send me over here. I sent myself over here.' I said, 'I ain't got no home.' And he listened, he said, 'Come on, tell me more of this.' He said, 'I can hardly believe that you got up enough nerve to leave.' He said, 'You said you didn't have no home. You got a home right here.' In a little log house. Two little log houses.

"And that little log house, it was old. They had a little square window where you could stick your rifle out and shoot the Indians. And he had a big fireplace, big mantle, and Kelly said, 'Get in here and get yourself washed up.' Said, 'We're gonna eat.' And so, I got washed. He said, 'Comb on the fire mantle.' And I got the comb and was combing my hair and [got a] whole handful of hair. He's standing there watching me, and he said, 'Gee whiz, you ain't gonna have near as much hair to comb, are you?'" We laughed. "But he said, 'Now I'm gonna tell you, . . . now when we come home this evening,' he said 'I'm gonna have Uncle Oscar to work you over, see what you look like. He's a real good barber, man he could really give you a good haircut.' And so they got home why we eat supper, and he said, 'Come on, we'll go down to Uncle Oscar's.' Went down there and he said, 'Uncle Oscar, would you'—uh Oscar Boll—said, 'would you give Bill here a haircut and see what he's gonna look like?' Said, 'He looks like a wild man now.' And he, Oscar said, 'Come on, get in that there chair, my barber chair here.' Got him an old chair fixed up. And boy I come out of there and he got back and looked and said, 'By golly you're beginning to look like a human being.'" We all laughed. "And Kelly said, 'That ain't all. We'll work around and see if we can't get you some clothes to wear.' And by golly he did. He got me some pair of overalls, over Cannel City."

When Bill Henry says, "They didn't send me over here. I sent myself over here," he is asserting his independence and his new identity, verbalizing the ritual and symbolic importance of his actions in the previous story. However, his continuing isolation and fear are immediately expressed when he says, "I ain't got no home." He replaces his old family with a new one, and significantly his new family seems to be all male. He later mentioned that Kelly had a wife, but she is not evident as a character in any of the stories. His foster mother and sister had been his greatest antagonists, abusing him and providing no nurturing. In contrast, his new "father," Kelly, and Uncle Oscar are kind, caring, and immediately nurture, feed, and clothe him. His shift to a new identity is made manifest by the change of physical appearance: he is transformed from a "wild man" into a "human being." Ironically, it is males who civilize and humanize him; the females are seen as "wildcats." This seems to reverse the traditional gender roles and is another sign of his continuing interest in gender as part of his life review.

He continued to learn about women, and several of the transition stories deal with his relationships with them.

"[Kelly's] wife had a, in Cannel City, had a cousin, and they'd come over a lot of weekends and, and bring her other cousin with her, her sister, and they'd come over and they suggested that, this oldest cousin, she wanted a husband. I said, 'No, I don't want to be no husband I can tell you that.' I said, 'I don't even know if I'd like her or not.' And went on that way, and finally talked me into going two, three times with her. So little later we moved to Cannel City because he dreaded walking that two mile [there] and two mile back home after working hard all day. We went over there and got one of the coal miner company's houses. They was awful. Wasn't nothing in them houses. And so there we was sitting around there on the porch; I looked up and I seen her coming. She lived down the, up another holler. So I jumped up and took off. Said, 'Where you going?' Said, 'Your girlfriend's a coming.' I said, 'I know it.' I said, 'I tell you, I don't want to get married. And I haven't got no clothes fitting for nothing hardly. And I got no job. And I don't know if I'm even old enough to get married in the first place.' And I said, 'That'd be the worst thing that ever happened to me is to have a wife.' And I said, 'Now I'm getting out of here and I'm going to hide.'

"I run over to the next house, and I run in, you know, and that woman looked around and said, 'Why, I didn't hear you, until just right now.' Said, 'You didn't even knock did you?' I said, 'I didn't have time to knock.' I said, 'You got any place I could hide?' Said, 'What's a matter, law after you?' I said, 'No, not the law, something worse than the law.' I said, 'Girlfriend's after me.' And I said, 'I don't want to get married, nothing about it.' And she said, 'Naw, they won't come over here after you.' And she's laying on the floor looking at funny papers. And said, 'Come on and get down here, and I'll read some funnies to you.'" He laughed.

This may not be unusual behavior for a shy seventeen-year-old, but taken with the other stories about women, it has an added meaning. He had been dominated by women for eight years, and this must have affected his view of marriage and family life. In his mind, he had only been free of domineering women for a few months, and he was afraid that marriage would place him in a similar situation. He thought he was too young to get married, and the final image of the story, sitting on the floor reading the comics, indicates that he was too young. Since he did marry in later life, this story may be an indirect comment on marriage itself. From the perspective of old age and after a married life, he may still feel ambivalent about marriage, preferring the freedom that he associates with adolescence and young adulthood.

He viewed his foster mother and sister as big, strong, domineering women, and this theme occurs again in an encounter with a girl in his transition years. Right after he told the story of hiding from a girl, he told another about courting a girl he had seen with her family on their front porch.

"So one day I got enough nerve to go down there and sit, go up on the porch and talk with them. I was pretty bashful. And so this one little girl, just twelve years old, just pretty as a peach. . . . So she said, 'Now, I'm a houseworking for that lady. She pays me pretty good.' But said, 'She might fire me if she caught me with a boy.' And said, 'Now, they're having a big meeting down the railroad track.' We walked down the railroad track, down to the church down there. They had big meeting, and said, 'Now you come out and you go down the railroad, you get down there a ways, out of sight of the house there.' And said, 'Directly, I'll walk down the railroad, we'll go on to church. And before we get to that house,' she said, 'you go your way, and I'll go mine, you see.' And we got down through there, and we met one of her brothers, a walking up the railroad. And he looked at me, and he says, 'Your name's Bill, ain't it? Bill, why you want to go with a girl that young?' Said, 'She's still in diapers.' And boy, she said, 'If I get a haymaker at you, I'll settle you down!' Said, 'I'll have you to know that I'm old enough to work, and I'm old enough to go with the boys.' Said, 'I might not be thirteen yet but,' said, 'I'm still twelve.' And he said, 'Bill, she's still wet behind the ears.' And she said, 'If I get a rock, I'll hit you right between the eyes, and now you better get moving.' And by golly she went over and picked her up a rock, and he said, 'Well, I guess I'd better go.' I said, 'Yeah, I think so.' And we went on, and I went with her two or three times, and finally I quit. And I tell you, I had a lot of fun around there in Cannel City."

In telling several stories about his courting days, Bill Henry can relive his rite of passage from childhood to adulthood when he was learning to be a man and to relate with women. His masculine identity was being formed at this time so that this is a significant part of his life review. Since gender roles are a recurring theme throughout his life story, it is important that he concentrate on that time in his life when he was becoming a man as determined by the culture. Being a man is defined in terms of opposition to being a woman so that both gender roles are important in his life review. The stories about his dating focus equally on masculine and feminine roles. His view of himself is as shy and passive, interested in the opposite sex but waiting for them to make the first move. His image is closer to the traditional feminine role, and the girls, in their active pursuit of him, are closer to a traditional masculine role. In the last story, the "haymaker" the girl threatens her brother with relates her to the foster mother and sister in the previous stories. Like them, she is strong and aggressive, and in this case Bill Henry seems to admire her. He probably also grudgingly admired the women in his foster family as well, but since they used their strength against him, he could not feel very positive about them. The interesting pattern here is that Bill Henry tells stories about strong women in the childhood cycle, the transition stories, and the hobo cycle. Of all the girls and women he knew in his life, why did he select these to tell stories about? A look at one of the hobo narratives will help answer this question. The story had to do with a tough woman gangster he met in jail. She and two men were running whiskey through Georgia, and the police gave chase.

"So they took out after them, and they took off to speeding, and the guy on a Harley Davidson police motorcycle.. He had a good gun on that thing, too. And he couldn't get him to stop, and he rolled up beside of him, and there's a divider here, and they was fixing to go in under a railroad that went overhead, and he got on the running board, and that woman in there. I don't know what she had in her purse, but she hit him over the head. They usually carry a pop bottle full of pop. See, that makes an awful good weapon. But that made him duck down, and he pulled close over to this here divider, going under that, and that crushed him back against the back fender, and it killed him. And I tell you the next guy that took out after him, he got him. He was on another motorcycle. And he rolled up there, and he shot this driver in the shoulder, and he's rolling her over to put his foot out, you know, and he was sure he wasn't going to run, he shot him in that foot. He was a good, he was a good shot. And by golly they gived up. That woman never did give up. She just sat and called them everything. She just said, 'If I could get a hold of you, I would beat you till your head fell right off of your shoulders.' Oh, she was mean. And every time a jailer or anybody'd come in there, she's really mean. She was over across the hall. Good-looking woman. Mean, man she was mean. And they was going to get her and all of them for murder, for killing that guy."

Besides the woman gangster, Mr. Henry also encountered women hoboes.

"I kid the woman down there [at a nearby bar]. She liked to hear me talk about the hobo. She said, 'If you're ever taking another trip,' she said, 'can I go along?' I said, 'Yeah.' Yeah, we had girls traveling."
I asked him, "Oh you did? Did you have girls?"
"Oh yeah."
"Women hoboes."
"Yeah. They was braver than the men. They'd tell them railroad detectives off."

Tough women attract his attention and his admiration, probably because of the deep impression his foster mother and sister made on him. They took control of his life when he was eight years old and dominated him until he was sixteen. He resented and admired them; feeling powerless, he was attracted to power. On the one hand, he must have yearned for a surrogate mother to replace the one he had lost. His foster mother was at least associated with food and some minimal nurturing in his mind, and his foster sister did provide him with hand-me-down stockings. On the other hand, they both treated him badly, punishing him for the slightest infraction of the rules. They established, for better or worse, his image of women, and this stayed with him the rest of his life; he is still concerned with this topic in his old age life review. In 1989, I asked him about the domineering women in his early life and if he resented them. He did not answer directly but rather started to tell more stories about strong or mean women. He was not interested in abstract discourse about a topic; narrative is his main mode of communication, and he feels that he can best express himself through stories.

The transition stories show him becoming an independent person who could make his own decisions. He did not live with Kelly long before he struck out on his own. He first walked thirty miles to another town in Kentucky, but he was soon riding the rails with thousands of other hoboes. The hobo cycle is relevant to his life review because it presents a more masculine self-image than the previous stories in which he is usually passive and expressive in his roles. The hobo years find him out in the world, away from the domestic realm of women, fulfilling instrumental rather than expressive roles. He even talks about his shift from shyness to aggressiveness in his hobo years, saying that he would have starved to death unless he had overcome his shyness about asking people for food. He started to hobo in 1927 at the age of seventeen, and he continued this life off and on until 1934 when he went to work full-time. His pattern was to work for a while and then leave the job to go back to hoboing. Near the beginning of the hobo cycle of narratives, he defined what a hobo was.

"Well, all the hoboes had said that they didn't, they thought that was an awful bad word [bum] to say, see. And they had said there's regular bums that never worked a day in their life and didn't intend to work a day in their life. And that was the big difference between a hobo and a bum. But we'd go places and learn that if you went in this place and got a good meal of vittles, why if you could find a little rock around somewhere, why you could put that on the gatepost, and that would help the next hobo too, to tell him that you could get a good meal of vittles."

Hoboes are viewed positively and bums, negatively. This is in keeping with the way hoboes in general viewed themselves; after extensive interviews with hoboes, Kenneth Allsop spoke of the hobo's "pride and self-respect as a worker. He may have been stripped of environment, of an outlet for his limited skills, but he doggedly clung to his membership in 'the productive classes'" (1967, 50). Allsop's description of the hobo fits Bill Henry's own view of his hobo past as reflected in his stories: "He was homeless and unmarried. He freeloaded on the freight trains whose tracks he laid and whose tunnels he blasted. He lived in bunk houses or tents or jungle camps or city flophouses. He was a marginal, alienated man, capriciously used and discarded by a callous but dynamic system, yet he was proud of the mode he devised out of an imperative mobility. He was a unique and indigenous American product" (1967, ix). Mr. Henry gave the example of the hobo custom of indicating where a good meal could be had in order to show that hoboes cared for each other; they were in some sense a community.

The cycle of hobo stories contains narratives about various adventures on the road—clashing with railroad detectives, being in jail, going to trial, and working around the country. Many of these stories have the same themes and motifs found in the childhood cycle—shoes, work, learning from experience, authority figures, and Bill Henry's trickster image—thus unifying the story cycles as part of his life review. Although feet are not a significant image in the hobo cycle, he told one story that indicated his continuing fascination with shoes.

"Really I never asked too many people without they telling me too much, you know. I was afraid they'd [say] it was none of your business, which I have been told a lot of times. Just simple questions that I didn't think they'd care, but by golly they would. Guy one time, he had a good-looking pair of shoes on, and I just asked the man what a good pair of shoes like that would cost a feller, and I knew he knew, and he just said, 'I paid a lot of good money for them. Besides, it ain't none of your business.' Yeah, and I thought that was awful because I didn't think I'd talked out of the way to him."

An innocent question could have led to violence, and Bill Henry often mentioned how dangerous hoboing was. He used such phrases as "it's a tough place," "tough law," "that's a rough place," and "rough-looking country up there" to indicate how hazardous life on the rails could be. He suffered two serious injuries while riding the rails. The hazards of hoboing show that it is a culturally defined masculine pursuit; it is an instrumental activity in that it is the opposite of stationary domestic life. One of the first hobo stories he told was about the dangers of hopping a freight.

"So I got out there, you know, and here come a freight train, he's moving little bit good, too, and I picked me out a boxcar, and I thought, 'Well, now, that one, I've got to catch it.' And maybe seventy-five boxcars on that train. And I don't know what made me think that I had to have that certain boxcar. But you always catch your front end. Don't catch the back. If you miss, why you may lay down across the track and then you quit paying taxes."

We laughed.

"So I couldn't catch that and finally it come to me, 'Well, boy, you're crazy, why don't you wise up here on this? You don't have to have that boxcar. You fool around here and the train will get so fast you won't catch nothing.' So, I got back here. This front end a coming. And boy I just walked up and grabbed him as he come to me, and I got right on. And," he chuckled, "then on I learned a whole lot. But I practiced. I could catch them faster, and the other hoboes, they, I learned a whole lot from them, you know."

Like several of the stories in the foster home cycle, this one is about a learning experience, and he uses the same rhetorical device to indicate the learning process. He quotes an interior monolog: "why don't you wise up here on this?" thus making a hidden mental process obvious and emphasizing what he has learned. The consequences of not learning fast could be death. The subtext seems to be that even though he did not do well in school, he was still smart, a good learner, but he had to learn from actual experience, not from books or in an abstract way. It was a "rough country," and he had to face "tough law," and he had to be quick-witted in order to survive; the same qualities that helped him survive in the foster home helped him on the road.

Although he hoboed for most of this seven-year period, he also continued to work at various jobs, again emphasizing his instrumental masculine image. He explained why, despite having steady work, he kept leaving to ride the rails again.

"And so I'd take trips and pretty often. I'd get tired of working for nothing, and I'd take trips. I wouldn't tell them nothing. Wait till they went to church on Sunday morning and I'd take off."

Long after he quit hoboing, he worked in one factory for fourteen years, and his reason for quitting that job helps explain why he hoboed for so long.

"So I get in these factories, and they find out I didn't have any education, they just treat me any way they wanted me to be, they wanted to treat me. So I got awful fed up with that. So I give them about more than two months ahead of time warning. I could have quit right then, but I told them I'd work up till Christmas and that was it. So I happened to think, 'Well,' I told the boss, I said, 'Instead of putting me down as quitting,' I said, 'until I could get some money,' I told him, I said, 'just put me down there that you laid me off.' 'No, I couldn't do nothing like that.' I said, 'Okay, I didn't think you would help me out anyhow.' Said, 'I just thought I'd ask.' I said, 'I'll make it some way.' I said, 'I worked here fourteen years for nothing.' I said, 'I'll make it.'"

He never liked factory work, which explains why he does not have an occupational identity. He thought he was underpaid and treated badly because of his lack of education. He does not like authority figures, and his portrait of the factory boss fits this negative image: the boss was uncaring and unwilling to bend the rules to help him out. Bill Henry's independence comes out here in a way similar to the story about his leaving the foster home. "I'll make it some way" is another declaration of his independence from an institution that has dominated his life. This is another turning point story, which is emphasized in his life review: despite being subjected to the dominance of others, his core identity as an independent man can be projected in his old age. He projects a self-image as an elderly survivor of all the attempts by dominant people to subjugate him. A story about a job he held near the end of his hoboing years also paints a negative picture of a dominant boss.

"I got a job and went into a furniture company. I mean you had to work. Now that big guy'd come through. Superintendent. And if you wasn't working as fast as you could and as hard as you could, why he'd hit you on the shoulder. 'Hey old buddy, I want to tell you something. Now you either get with it or you're going to lose that job. Maybe not get fired, but just accidentally lose that job. They's fifteen or twenty . . . sometimes more, and sometimes less, standing over there at the employment office, every morning, just a begging for your job.' And I went, I worked nine hours there and come home, nobody to rock me to sleep."

This kind of treatment reinforced his attitude toward authority figures; his childhood had already given him a negative feeling toward parents and teachers, and his young adult experiences indicated that bosses would try to order him and control him in the same way. He makes a direct connection between his adult and childhood experiences when he says, "come home, nobody to rock me to sleep." He got only abuse and no nurturing as a child, and he feels that this pattern continued into his young adult life. Sandy Rikoon makes the point that "a hobo is an adult orphan, in essence a sort of 'orphan of society.' Child orphans deal with parents that might have failed them and foster parents that might exploit them. So it appears that hoboes are similarly abandoned by society (their 'parents' in a larger sense)" (1988). Since he is exploited by foster parents and factory foremen, he becomes alienated from his economic and social environment. Bill Henry's whole life became a struggle to establish independence and a sense of control, while at the same time it was a quest for nurturing, and these are still important concerns as he reviews his life in his elderly years. In the second interview I asked him if he thought that hoboes were the orphans of society, and he agreed that they were. He then told a story about telling a railroad detective who was about to arrest him, "I ain't got no home, and I'm pretty hungry." Again, rather than talking about this concept abstractly, he preferred to illustrate the concept with a concrete story.

As much as he recalls his hobo years as an escape from authority and control, he still had to confront authority figures—railroad detectives, policemen, and judges—while on the road, and he has made stories out of many of these incidents. He told us about an aborted trip to Florida and then a second trip. I asked him, "Did you make it all the way down to Florida that trip?"

"Got down to Jacksonville." He paused. "When we got out of jail."

"What were you doing in jail?"

"We crossed Georgia. They wouldn't listen to that story I had to tell, you know, when I got out of that other scrape. We got on, we got on the, me and another guy, we got on these dirt cars, and they had standards run straight up. And they tapered in this way, and we climbed in behind them standards there. And laid down on that boards. There wasn't no way of rolling off. So we just a traveling along there, just as pretty as you please, just sleeping away. Old boy reached in [when] we stopped right on the crossing. And it was five cars of police from the city and railroad detectives and sheriffs. And they just walked up, and they reached in there, and they said, 'He huh! Wake up old boy and pay for your bed.' I said, 'Who are you?' Said, 'We're the law.' Said, 'Caught you dead to right.' We'd heard about that place, Georgia. And we're the luckiest boys that ever was. They had their roads all built, and they didn't put us on a chain gang."

We all laughed at Bill Henry's turning a potentially dangerous situation into a comic story, a device he used throughout the hobo cycle, especially when describing encounters with railroad detectives and judges. Here he uses hyperbole ("the luckiest boys that ever was") and fabrication ("They had their roads all built") to make light of a terrible dilemma. Humor was one of his favorite ways of dealing with threatening authority figures, if not in the actual situation then afterwards when he narrated the event. The life review can add humor to situations that may not have been humorous as they were experienced, another means of giving a sense of control after the fact. A humorous tone runs throughout his story of facing the judge after this particular arrest.

"And they took us up to have our trial the next day, about ten o'clock, rough bunch. They got us up there and said, 'You boys guilty?' Said, 'We got five or six guys against us.' Said, 'We're bound to be guilty.' Said, 'If we wasn't, we'd have to be.' Said, 'Yes, judge, we're guilty.' Said, 'Well, I see here you boys never been caught in the state of Georgia. Never been into nothing.' Said, 'You're just traveling through.' But said, 'You're not allowed, it's against the law to ride trains.' Said, 'I'm going to give you boys $15 fine, thirty days on the chain gang.' Ooh, my goodness, that sounds terrible. So we waited a little bit for him to say something better than that. So he did, by golly. He said, 'Now I'm going to suspend this, going to turn you boys loose. If you're caught again here, I'm going to give you sixty days on the chain gang and $30 fine, and you'll do every bit of it.' And we said, 'My, Judge, we want, we thank you a whole lot and we want to promise you we'll try to be careful.'"

By telling us earlier that they were lucky and did not have to work on a chain gang, Bill Henry prepares us for a happy ending; the humorous tone throughout is consistent. They were probably frightened and meek while they waited to hear their fate, but in the story they are flippant, making a mockery of the judicial proceedings. "We're bound to be guilty. . . . If we wasn't, we'd have to be" indicates their sense that the outcome of the trial is a foregone conclusion, and their mock respect for the judge in the final statement indicates their real feelings about justice.

Several of Bill Henry's authority stories derive their humor from his role as a trickster.

"We made it up to Atlanta and got out of Atlanta and caught a freight moving out. And got to Chattanooga. And got there, and that old boy with me, he was crazy as a bat. Got there in Chattanooga, and we was waiting around there, and we thought over, cross this, quite a holler here, and on both sides of that holler was railroads, big yards. And he said, 'Now this is the train heading toward Kentucky and Cincinnati and all.' And I said, 'No, I don't believe it is.' I said, 'I think the train heading toward Cincinnati is over there.' And this big railroad running around overhead, you know. He grabbed that thing, started up the ladder, and down the ladder come a railroad detective. Couldn't get his gun 'cause he was using both hands, and he was halfway down. And he jumped off from there, and we took across that path and down in the holler and started up the other side, and he could see us good. 'Bang! Bang!' The cinders'd fly, you know, and he turned around there and hollered, 'Shoot again! You didn't hit me that time.' I said, 'Shut up, you fool, he's shooting close enough now.'"

Here again he turns a life-threatening situation into a humorous one except that, as far as we know, in this case the humor is based on something he said at the time, not later in telling the story. He is somewhat of a trickster here in that he is the weak character confronting a strong one, and he has only his verbal wit to handle the threat. Being able to respond comically in this situation makes him the hero of the narrative. The "crazy as a bat" sidekick initiates the verbal play, but Bill Henry has the last word.

He becomes a more active trickster in one of his confrontations with the police.

"That's tough law down in there, Jacksonville. They said, 'You boys ain't nothing but regular bums.' Said, 'That's the way bums act. No money, no nothing, running around, bumming up their eats.' [I] said, 'Boy we hate to hear you talk like that.' Said, 'We mooch eats.' And said, 'We're just hoboes.' 'I don't spell nothing to me; you're nothing but bums.' Took us out there and loaded us up in a what they call paddy wagon, I reckon. Said, 'Take that thing; take them up to the Georgia line and dump them off.'. . . And he got out of there, and he said, 'Go that way. Don't you come back here to Florida.' I stopped when I got about fifteen, twenty feet over in Georgia, you know. I stopped. [He] said, 'What's the matter with you. Can't you walk?' I said, 'I just wanted to tell you something.' I patted this right arm, you know, and I said, 'Old buddy, if I ever get a basket of money on that arm, carrying it on that arm, I sure as heck won't come to Florida to give to you fellers.' Said, 'Get smart and we'll take you back, put you in jail.' I said, 'You can't bother me.' I said, 'I'm over here in Georgia.'"

We laughed and enjoyed the satisfaction of the trickster getting the best of the strong oppressor. Again, the triumph is verbal because he could not confront him in terms of his strength. In telling this story in his old age, Mr. Henry can identify with his younger self, which is at least partially a creation of his older self, in order to indicate that the trickster is still part of his self-image. In another trickster story, he uses his verbal ability to avoid arrest.

"And a cinder got in under my goggle and got in that eye. I was standing in the yards up there in Indianapolis, and an old railroad detective came up and hit me on the shoulder and said, 'Old buddy, where you're going, you'll have plenty of time to pick out that cinder.' Said, 'You just got off the train, didn't you?' And I said, 'Ah, got off the train?' I said, 'You must be kidding.' He said, 'Now you're kidding me.' He said, 'I know you got off that train. I didn't see you, but you got off that train.' I said, 'Come on, let's go.' I said, 'Remember, you take and lock me up, you got to feed me, too.' And he said, 'By golly, you want to go to jail, don't you?' I said, 'Yeah, I'm just raring and pitching to go to jail.' He said, 'I ain't gonna please you that much.' Said, 'I'm gonna turn you loose.'"

We laughed.

"And he, we walked over to a street that went underneath, and there's a walkway of steps down. He said, 'How quick can you get down on that walk down there?' I said, 'Boy, you'd be surprised how quick I can get down there.' I got down there on the walk and I said, 'How'd I do? Get down here pretty quick?' And he said, 'Ah, hush up and go on.'"

He must have talked himself out of several arrests because later he said, "Boy, them railroad detectives is tough. They, they want to take you in; I'd talk them out of it." Mr. Henry's reverse psychology is similar to that of Brer Rabbit in the well-known tar baby story: "Please don't throw me in the briar patch" (AT175, Aarne 1964; Dorson 1967, 75–76). The difference is that in this particular story, the detective seems to be in on the joke; their entire exchange is part of a game they are playing. The important point though is that Bill Henry is set free; the trickster gets what he wants. Mr. Henry told the same story again in 1989, and he added references that reinforce the trickster interpretation. After he fools the detective in the story, he said, "Like the rabbit was out in the garden, you remember that?" Later he referred to the rabbit again:

"That's what I tell the railroad detective, 'I ain't got no home, and I'm pretty hungry.' And I said, 'Come on, let's go if you're going to lock me up, come on.' But I said, 'Remember, take and lock me up, and you have to feed me.' They didn't like that at all. I don't know whether you remember, if it was in your reading book or not. Old Man Gregory, or some of that bunch, old farmer, caught this rabbit, you know. He caught him, took him out. 'I'm gonna throw you in this awful briar patch.' Well that was the rabbit's home. 'Oh please, Mr. Gregory, don't throw me in that old briar patch.' That's what the Reader said."

This is a European variant of the tar baby story, one that Mr. Henry seems to have read in a grade school textbook. His reference to it here indicates that he is aware of his role as trickster and that it is a part of the self-image he is projecting in the stories.

Bill Henry plays the trickster role in the foster home stories and in the hobo cycle, and in both cases he does so in ways that are analogous to the trickster in African-American tradition. His oppressors—parents, teachers, railroad detectives, and judges—are parallel to the white slave owners in that they have or try to exercise control over his life. They have all of the power on their side, and his only weapons are wit and verbal skill. Again, the various episodes in his life story are unified as a life review. There is evidence in Mr. Henry's stories and comments that he has some identification with blacks. After riding a coal train, he commented, "I was really, coal mine dust all over me. I really looked like I was something else. But nobody called me Rastus, but I looked like him." A comic reference, to be sure, and one based on a stereotype of blacks, but still one that makes a connection between him and blacks. Also, he told a story about a black hobo that shows he sympathizes with other oppressed individuals.

"And so we hit down through Kentucky and Tennessee and down through Georgia, another trip I took to Florida. And so we got along pretty good and got down to Georgia. Well we got to Atlanta, Georgia, and trouble started, kind of. A colored boy was along. He's [a] pretty good guy. And he said, 'Do you white boys care if I walk along with you?' And we said, 'No, we don't care.' So he'd go along with us, you know, and we'd speak to them Atlanta, Georgia, people." We were interrupted at this point, and he continued the story later. As they walked down the track with the black man, people would not speak to them.

"Well, anyhow, we said to this colored boy, 'We don't know what's the matter with these people. There ain't no friendly people in Georgia?' He saying, 'No that ain't it.' He says, 'They're mad because I'm walking along with you.' Said, 'Now watch this.' Said, 'I'll drop way back. And I won't walk with you boys until we get through Atlanta, Georgia. And then I'll meet you'uns again.' He dropped back about thirty foot, back behind us. Nobody bothered him, but they wouldn't speak to him. And by golly when he dropped back there, 'Hi there. Hello.' We looked back at him and we said, 'You're right.' Said, 'I knowed I was right.'"

There is an implicit condemnation in the story of those who were not friendly because white hoboes were walking with a black man, and Mr. Henry's sympathies are clearly with the black hobo. Their bond as hoboes is stronger than any racial division that might be expected of them. Bill Henry's role as trickster is based on some of the same circumstances that faced blacks in America. He did not face racism, but he did experience prejudice because he was an orphan, poor, and uneducated. The authority figures he confronted during his life treated him badly because of his marginality.

One last trickster story shows that the trickster did not always win.

"So I told them that down at Stones, where I worked. I said, 'I went in this big fine place out there in Oklahoma, out there in the country and went in, and it was awful fine house, and I knew there's bound to be some good eats in that house.' So I told them, 'I went in and I went up pretty close, and a great big yard, and the grass did need mowing, and I got down there and pretended I was eating grass, you know. And I was watching the curtains all the time to see if they moved, so I could find out if there was anybody home.' And I said, 'I got the worst food in my life.' I said, 'There's a woman come to the door, said "Hey young man," and I thought, "Well, up boy, now I've got it. I'm going to get some eats." And I said, 'She didn't say nothing about eats. But she did say, "Young man, the grass is a lot taller in the back yard.""

The trickster gets tricked in some African-American folktales as well. Mr. Henry tells this as a personal experience narrative, but he hints that it is really a joke by quoting himself telling the story in another context. By doing this, he distances himself from the narrative, indicating that it is not a personal experience. He might not ordinarily do this, but he had been telling us stories from his own life to this point and did not want to undermine his own veracity. In 1989, he told the same story, but this time he told it all the way through as if it were based on an actual experience. His retelling of the story on different occasions is an indication that it is a performance piece and that the trickster image is one he continues to project. He also told us that he was a trickster of another sort; one of the ways he entertained people at the American Legion and V.F.W. Hall was with magic tricks he bought at a local novelty store. He had clothing that changed colors and a huge safety pin that he pretended to stick through his nose. Like Quincy Higgins's pranks, Mr. Henry's tricks and practical jokes are another attempt at gaining control within a specific social situation. They function in his old age to give him psychological control at a time of life when control has been taken away from him.

These devices and his jokes and personal life stories were all means of entertaining people and attracting attention to himself as a performer, of staying active socially in his old age when he was expected to be more passive and withdrawn. In this, Bill Henry is like storytellers studied by Linda Degh, who took personal experiences and turned them into entertainments for their communities (1985, 106; 1975). The childhood and hobo cycles of stories were used in this way, but they were also a means for him to deal with his own past, to come to grips with his emotionally impoverished childhood and to relive his greatest time of freedom as a hobo. In his old age, he still feels nostalgic about his hobo days. "And to this day, I can hear a train whistle, and that makes me feel like I ought to go on and catch that [train]." Later he said, "But I'd hear those train whistles; I was ready to go." The hobo has been romanticized in America to the point of being a culture hero (Allsop 1967, 49); the freedom and independence of the hobo image continues to have a strong appeal for people today. Bill Henry told me that he was known as "Hobo Bill," and when we were interrupted by a salesman, Mr. Henry introduced himself as "the old hobo," indicating his identity in old age as a hobo even though he has not hoboed in fifty-five years. A few years ago, he attended the National Hobo Convention and said of his experience, "I had a good time up there." Mr. Henry tends to romanticize his hobo past, thus playing on the inclinations of his listeners; they will sit and listen to a long cycle of stories because it appeals to their romantic ideals.

The cycle structure of the stories is a rhetorical device in itself, similar to what Katharine Young calls serial stories, which "carry across from one to the next certain thematic elements and thus have the property of expanding a universe or Taleworld" (1987, 101). Bill Henry expands his universe by stringing dozens of stories together based on a common period of his life, thus keeping the attention of a listener for a longer period of time. The cycle stories were in roughly chronological order, but some were out of sequence, and only a few had to be in a particular order. For instance, the "cow bag" story had to come first since it introduced the violence inflicted on him by his foster family, and the childhood cycle had to end with the story of his break with the foster family. The order of stories within the cycle seemed to depend on a stream of consciousness technique: a theme or motif in one story would remind him of another. There were digressions within stories as well as digressions between stories, but if he got off track, he would always return to his original direction, which led to the logically concluding story. For instance, he was describing the old-fashioned dresses that his foster mother and sister wore, and that reminded him of the story about washing their dresses, which fit into the sequence because it continued the theme of being abused by them. These motifemic and thematic links provided transitions between stories so that the listeners had little opportunity to ask questions or otherwise interrupt the flow of the cycle of narratives.

The hobo cycle was somewhat more loosely structured, since it covered a wider range of experiences, but here again there were recurring themes and motifs that related everything together and kept the narrative flowing. Certain stories had to come in sequence; for instance, an arrest story would come first, then a jail experience, and finally the trial. There were also digressions, though: at one point he jumped from 1927 to 1975 to tell about the search for his birth certificate, and then he went back to the hobo cycle. "We'd better get back to that," he said to provide an obvious transition. The story of the black hobo was so important that he returned to it after an interruption and a long digression about being in the hospital. "Anyhow, getting back to our train rides, I guess," was his way of shifting back to finish the story of the black hobo. During our second interview, he also tended to tell stories in a cyclic structure, but since I had more direct questions to ask him, the cycles were interrupted and it was more difficult for him to maintain the flow. He still used such phrases as "And so on it went" as transitions between stories within the same cycle. All of these devices are evidence that he thinks of these stories not as discrete narratives but as parts of a unified cycle that he prefers to tell as a whole. To make the literary analogy again, his storytelling cycles are like an oral novel, perhaps closest to works such as William Faulkner's *Go Down, Moses* or Sherwood Anderson's *Winesburg, Ohio*, which contain short stories that can stand alone but which are also thematically and structurally related. Folklorist William A. Wilson has noted the same structure in his mother's stories about her life, which he has termed the "family novel" (1990, 13).

The comparison of his oral autobiography to the novel is a revealing metaphor since the novel form itself has influenced the way we structure our life stories. "Particularly since the introduction of the novel into literature in the eighteenth century, concern with the construction of a coherent and ordered account has become the basis of the manner in which persons understand both stories and lives" (Cohler 1982, 207). The life review in the cases of some talented storytellers becomes a highly organized narrative with recurring themes and symbols to unify it. "Lives are organized in the same manner as other narratives, including historical interpretations, and are understandable according to the same socially shared definition of a sensible or followable presentation" (Cohler 1982, 207). It should not be surprising, then, that Bill Henry evokes shared meaning from his life narrative by references and allusions to such traditional folk and literary figures as the poor orphan, the trickster, and the adventurous hobo. By doing this, he is connecting with his audience on a cultural basis so that they identify and sympathize with him.

What Bill Henry has done, then, is to take control of his life by narrating it from the perspective of old age after all of the adventures have ended. Not all expressions of life review by the aged are as structured as his, not all are presented as performance pieces. Marc Kaminsky makes the point that life review is often fragmented and not organized as narrative (1984, 13), but for Bill Henry, life review is being conducted in the guise of performed stories. He has provided the structure to give meaning to the two most important periods of his life.

One of the most significant themes in the orphan and hobo cycles is the lack of control over his own life. When he was orphaned, everyone else took dominion over him; as a hobo, he was periodically subjected to the rules of others. His only means of coping with these situations were his wit and his verbal skill. He continues to use his humor and his verbal abilities to tell stories that are also a means of coping with the lack of control. He uses the same devices within the original experience and in telling about those experiences later in his life. The foster home years were the period of least personal control, and in his mind the hobo years were the period of greatest control, of freedom from the dictates of others. The two extremes of his life provide favorite topics for storytelling; his later married and occupational life are somewhere between the two extremes, and he does not tell many stories from these times; certainly he has not structured narrative cycles from his later experiences. In the second interview with him, he only talked about his factory work and his marriage in direct response to questions I asked.

For me, the second interview confirmed the interpretations I had made of his life and his stories. He continued to tell some of the same stories and to tell them in similar ways emphasizing the same themes and motifs. He is a self-conscious performer with set performance pieces, and the stories seem structured to bring about certain meanings. I wanted to get his response to some of the psychoanalytic interpretations I had made, but he would not respond to them directly; as I said above, he chose to tell stories in answer to the questions, thus leaving the interpretation up to me. This is a favorite technique of fiction writers responding to the interpretations of literary critics: why shouldn't Bill Henry use the same technique on me? One new concern was added in the second interview: he voiced a sense of regret about certain decisions in his life. "Now I often thought, well now you might be a millionaire, or more than a millionaire today if you would've took the man up. So I missed out on a lot through this life, I missed out on a lot of good things. I just know I did." This is often part of the life review for certain elderly people, to dwell on "unrealized goals" and to "make up for past failures" (McMahon and Rhudick 1967, 73), and perhaps in later years, Mr. Henry has given more thought to missed possibilities in his life. This would indicate another area where he did not have control in his life and thus make getting a sense of control even more important in his old age.

His concern with lack of control can be viewed in one sense as an identity problem. As an orphan, he was not sure who he was, and the neglect of his foster family reinforced his lack of identity. *They* determined who he was: not a son, not a brother, but an outsider. He had very little choice as to interests or hobbies or other means of developing an identity. He had no past, and he had no sense of a future. Eileen Simpson makes a similar point about orphans in general: "The regimentation and dreary routine did not provide a milieu stimulating to the development of a sense of self . . . to think of themselves as 'I'" (1987, 158). She is speaking of institutional orphans, but the same conditions prevailed in Bill Henry's foster home. His lack of a sense of self becomes poignantly clear when he talks about trying to find his birth certificate after he was an adult. "And so I went all that time till 19, about 1974, I guess it was, just about 75. My wife had wrote to Frankfort, that's where they told her to write and get me a birth certificate. To find out who I was." He chuckled at this point, but then humor is one of his ways of handling painful memories. He found out that his mother had given false information on the papers she filled out at the orphanage, which made it even more difficult to trace his background. She had abandoned him and tried to make sure he would never find her again. He eventually found his birth certificate, but of course that does not really provide an identity. Here he is in his seventies still struggling with the problem of identity, and his life review reflects that concern with who he was and who he is.

More important than acquiring his birth certificate in finding out "who he was" is his storytelling. By telling stories in his old age, he can go back over his life in order to find his identity. The narratives are in first person; "I" is repeated and emphasized throughout, reinforcing his sense of self. By telling stories about his life, he can assert his own identity as a "poor orphan boy" who survived the hardships of an abusive foster family and who finally established his right to be an individual by leaving them. He can project an identity that is still envied by many in our culture, that of a hobo, a young adventurer who lived a life of freedom. He can become the trickster hero of his own adventure tales. And finally he can express the identity that has become even more significant to him in his old age, that of Bill Henry, storyteller.

8

Matt Burnett
Childhood and Life, Old Age and Death

Matt Burnett lives on the Blue Ridge in Meadows of Dan, Virginia. He was an auctioneer all of his life, but he was forced to retire because of a heart condition. After retirement he took up toy making as a pastime, and he has been a storyteller since his youth. He tells several different kinds of stories, but he specializes in supernatural legends about ghosts and personal experience narratives about funerals and burials. Matt Burnett is a tradition-bearer in his community; when you ask for people who know stories about the old days, you are directed to his house. He knows of his reputation and has an awareness of himself as a performer.

When folklorist Alan Jabbour and I interviewed Mr. Burnett for the first time on August 10, 1978, at his home in Meadows of Dan, he began to speak as soon as the tape recorder was turned on.

"Uh, I'll tell you folks some little stories. I'm Matt Burnett, and I live here at Meadows of Dan. I'm getting a little age on me. Some of these days I'll be seventy-five years old, and uh, I been right much of a joker, I guess you'd say. And I've uh, kinda specialized in telling old stories and I've been a auctioneer and I've sang some, and uh, I live here at Meadows of Dan. And I'll tell you a few little mystery stories that I've heard about all my life."

He then proceeded to tell a local legend about an incident that took place when he was a boy in which ghosts moved objects around a house. His self-awareness as a performer is clear from the rhetorical devices he uses to introduce the legend. The pronoun shift from "I" to "you" in his very first sentence highlights the distinction between performer and audience, and the phrases "little stories," "old stories," and "mystery stories" name the genre that will be performed. By introducing himself by name, even though we already knew his name, he draws attention to his role as performer. He seems to be performing for an imaginary audience who might one day listen to the tapes we made. The frequent "uhs" in his speech indicate his anxiety about performing; he said "uh" often throughout the tape-recorded interviews (I have deleted most of these from the transcriptions in order to make reading easier). Another indication of his anxiety about performance is the repetition of words—"and, and," "kept, kept," and so forth—in the stories that follow. Despite his identity as a performer, he has some ambivalence about public performance, which becomes more apparent in remarks he made later. In his opening statement, he mentions the place name Meadows of Dan twice, thus emphasizing the importance of the locale; this is a device he uses throughout his storytelling. Also significant is the fact that he cites his age, another recurring theme in his life review. Like Alva Snell and Bob Glasgow, he sets himself up as an old-timer who is an authority on the way things used to be; this gives him special power as a performer. Finally, his reference to his job as an auctioneer is yet another way of emphasizing this role since an auctioneer is a performer.

Matt Burnett was an auctioneer for his entire life including, as he tells it, his childhood. We tape-recorded an auction and conducted a second interview with Mr. Burnett on September 16, 1978. At the auction, he was introduced to the crowd by the auctioneer in charge, Bob Gilbert.

"Ladies and gentlemen, here's my guest, one of the oldest auctioneers in the country; he's been auctioneer longer, not the oldest, but been—"

"Now wait," Mr. Burnett interrupted him, "let me say something. Now folks, I'm not a right young man, but I can, I got a good memory of things that happened a long time ago. And I've got a little history I'll tell you of myself. Sixty-three years ago today I done my first auction job. It was a small job, but I did it. Sixty-three years ago this afternoon, and I was eleven years old."

The crowd applauded, and after Mr. Burnett auctioned a few items,

15. Matt Burnett with one of his folk toys. (Photo by Carl Fleischhauer, BR8-2-20776 / 11.)

Bob Gilbert took over again. When given the opportunity, Matt Burnett presented himself as a performer similar to the way he had introduced himself on the tape recording. He again established his age and his authority to speak about the old days, and he again stressed his life as an auctioneer. Notice how he withholds until the last the fact that he was eleven years old when he conducted his first auction so that it will likely lead to applause. Later, back at his house I asked him, "Well, why don't you just tell us about, your, how you got started into auctioneering." He responded by telling a series of stories from his childhood and young adult years that constitute a life review with an occupational theme.

"Well, I'll tell you a little about this auction business that I've been doing now for, for a long time. Uh, there was an old fellow by the name of Reynolds, uh, old auctioneer in this, here in this community. People called him Len. I. D. Reynolds was his initial, and called him Len and he was a great big man, he was, I guess he weighed three hundred pounds. And I believe, I just believe that he was the best that's ever been in Patrick County. Now, he was a real talker, real entertainer, and he kept the crowd together by jokes and, and wisecracks and things of that kind. And, when I was just a little boy, oh just a little fellow, just big enough to trot along with my daddy and there'd be a sale somewhere close in the community, and uh, my dad would go, and he'd let me go and, and uh, and when we'd get there, I'd get just as close to this old big auctioneer as I could, and I'd stay there as long as, as my dad stayed at that sale, I'd stay just close to that old man as I could, well, and just look at him and watch him and listen. And I, I don't know how old I was when, when this thought first got in my mind, but I know I was just a little bitty feller, four, five, six, seven years old. And I just got it in my mind that if I ever got to be a man that that was what I wanted to do. I wanted to be an auctioneer."

The image of auctioneer Len Reynolds has stayed in Matt Burnett's mind all these years. From the description, it is clear that Mr. Reynolds was a star performer, "a real talker, a real entertainer [who] kept the crowd together by jokes and wisecracks and things of that kind." From him, Mr. Burnett learned the importance of drawing attention to himself in order to be a successful auctioneer. He learned not only techniques from him but also the role of the auctioneer, the social identity that was expected of him. The role of auctioneer is a powerful one; during the auction he has complete control of the proceedings, and all attention is focused on him. The impression Mr. Reynolds made was even stronger because it came at such an early age; as a result Mr. Burnett's account is vivid in its detail. He continued on and described how he got the opportunity to conduct his first auction.

"And I kept that thing in my mind all along, just all along, and I'd be, be out, be out playing with the other neighbor boys, and we'd have a little make-believe auction, you know. Well, maybe I'd step up on a stump, or up on a log, or up on a doorstep or somewhere, and, and well, I'd sell, maybe if I had a little pencil in my pocket I'd sell that, or sell some boy's old ragged straw hat. Just anything for a, a object to sell, you know. And it was just a little make-believe auction, and that went on for several years.

"And finally, to, to do a real job, which wasn't much of a job, it was nineteen and fifteen, this church that, that you see from here, was built in nineteen and fourteen, and, and the summer of fifteen. And they started using it in the year of nineteen fifteen, and they was some big trees, big timber, too close to that church, and they wanted them trees out from there on account of wind and sleet, you know, dangerous about blowing on the church, and the old, the old church members, they talked that thing over and they all met and, and took the old-time cross saws, cut them trees down and cut them up into firewood, and divided that amount of wood into four different sections, piled it up. Well, I don't know how long, a month or so, they agreed one third Saturday to sell that wood the next third Saturday, which would be a month, a month from that time. And they didn't advertise it nowhere except in the church.

"Well, when the, when the third Saturday in September come, after preaching, after service was over, which was a little after twelve o'clock, they, they said well we, today's set to sell the wood. And oh, they was a dozen or two of them old men and women went out to them wood piles and to see it sold. Well, I can remember some old man, I don't know, I don't remember now just which one it was, but one of them says, says, 'Who, who's gonna sell it? Who's the auctioneer?' And I was a standing right close to my dad. And my daddy and other close relatives and people around had know'd all along that I had, had this in mind, you know, and now, my dad, I can remember him a saying, saying 'Tell them, tell them you'll do it. Tell them you'll do it.' I wouldn't, I wouldn't do it, you know, and after a little, an old uncle of mine, an old fellow by the name of Castle, he was the deacon of that church out there, and he said, um, he said to the other fellows, he says, says, 'Let's let this little boy try it.' 'Let's let this little boy do it,' I believe is what he said. Now that was just exactly what I wanted to hear him say, and so I, I stepped up on that pile of wood, which was up a little height, and, and I went at it. Never, it never stung me a bit more to do that than it did to make-believe with them boys. And I went ahead and sold that wood, and, and when the thing was over, I can recall two or three or more of the old old church members, putting their hand on my shoulder and said, said, 'Son, now you're gonna make a good auctioneer, if you just keep at it.' And oh, that pleased the boy, and I've told people that that, that made my little old hat feel tighter, you know, big head."

The concrete details from this event, which happened when he was eleven, attest to the validity of Mr. Burnett's claim that he has "a good memory of things that happened a long time ago." The childhood experience was a turning point in his life; it established his lifelong occupation and thus determined many other features of his life. The vividness of his memory of this experience must be at least partially based on it being a ritual in the life cycle, an event that enabled him to pass from boyhood to manhood, from playing at auctioneer to actually being one. The play element was important though; by auctioning off pencils and straw hats with friends and pies at social gatherings, he was able to practice his profession in a nonthreatening environment, where mistakes would not have serious consequences. He also seems to have had some fears about performing in public as an auctioneer; when invited to do the church auction, he says, "That was just exactly what I wanted to hear him say"; however, he has to be pushed forward rather than going on his own initiative: "I wouldn't do it. I wouldn't do it, you know." Again we see his ambivalence about performing. But he got the kind of reinforcement he needed, and he was proud of his accomplishment then and proud in his old age as he looked back on the experience.

He apprenticed with the auctioneer who had originally inspired him in order to learn the business, and eventually the time came when Mr. Reynolds was ready to retire.

"Now, we worked at that job, six or seven hours that day, and, and it got late, late in the day, and people begin to leave and the crowd got small, and this old auctioneer said now, Mr. Campbell [the man whose property was being sold], says, says, 'People's a leaving us here; we ain't got nobody much, and, and we gotta close this, this sale out and finish it some other day.' Well, Mr. Campbell, Mr. Arthur Campbell said, said well, said, 'Can you come back in two weeks and finish the sale?' And he [Mr. Reynolds] said 'No,' says, said 'I'm gonna, gonna give it up, now,' says, 'I'm, I'm wore out and I feel bad now.' And says, 'If I don't feel better, I won't ever attempt it anymore.' And he said, 'Let that young man handle it.' And Mr. Campbell said to me, he says, 'Well, Mr. Burnett, can you come back and do it in, finish it in two weeks from now?' And I told him if that was what they wanted, that I'd do it. Well, that's what happened.

And on our way home, Mr. Reynolds said to me, he says, says, 'Matt,' said, 'I, I don't think I'll ever try it anymore.' And he says, 'You just go ahead and do it.' And I went back in two weeks and worked four or five hours longer and finished up that bid job. And that and, and then Mr. Reynolds kept, kept fading, he kept getting more feeble and more feeble, and, and I had a sale or two around his, somewhere close, I don't remember now, and he was there and I let him, I let him do a little of it. And, and he, he seemed to enjoy it, but he wasn't able to do much standing up and, and working at it then, so, so he just faded out, and from then on I, I had it all to do through this community and, and around in Floyd County and, and a big part of Patrick County. Well, I did Henry County some. Done one or two jobs in North Carolina. And I been at it now a long time."

I asked him, "You said you had a helper that you were teaching how to do an auction?"

"Uh, yeah. Now I've got a, I've got a man now that, that's been a helping me. Now you see I'm, I'm pretty well fading out now, I'm getting a little age on me, and I got a fellow by the name of Chandler . . . and he's, he's been helping me now for, I guess a couple a years.

The passing of the mantle from old retired auctioneer to young auctioneer is described twice: Mr. Burnett's taking over from Mr. Reynolds, and now Mr. Chandler's taking over from him. He seems to be aware of the irony because he uses some of the same language to describe the two events: Mr. Reynolds is said to be "fading" and Matt Burnett uses the same word to describe himself. He must also realize that his offer to let Len Reynolds do a little auctioneering after he retired is similar to Bob Gilbert's letting him auction a few items at the sale we had just come from. His narrative contrasts youth and old age: the young Matt Burnett eagerly starting out in the business is contrasted to the old Mr. Reynolds fading from active work. There is also, I think, an implicit contrast of Matt Burnett's old and young selves here, which becomes explicit in his comment in response to my question. His occupational life cycle from youth to old age is contained in the story.

During his years as an auctioneer, Mr. Burnett developed a performance style that involved telling jokes and kidding with the audience. For instance, he said that at times a husband and wife would get separated and bid against one another for the same item. When they discovered what had happened, "sometimes one of them would say, 'I'll tend to you when I get home.' And, and I'd say, 'Now, you better,' I'd say to the man, I'd say, 'You better hide the rolling pin.'" We all laughed. "'Quick as you get home,' and all that stuff, you know. Just have a laugh about it." The joke is, of course, based on a sexist stereotype as is a story he told later, and the effectiveness of the remark depends on a shared assumption with the audience about traditional views of women. The other example he gave of an auctioneer joke also expressed attitudes shared with the audience.

I asked him, "What are some of the usual kind of jokes you might crack to keep the crowd entertained? That might be one, in that situation you'd say, hide the rolling pin, but what are some other situations where you might make a little joke?"

"Uh, I, I have told an old mess a time or two. I don't, I ain't told it many times, but I have a time or two. There's a fellow, there's a man said to his neighbor, he says, he says, 'John, I'm gonna give you a ham o' meat.' 'Oh,' he says, 'You shouldn't do that.' Said, 'That's too much to give me.' 'Oh,' he says, 'You're a, a neighbor like you,' says, said, 'I'm gonna give you a ham o' meat.' 'And,' he says, 'it's a good size ham, too.' And he says, 'All right, if you wanna give me a ham o' meat, why I'll, I'll take it.' And he says, 'You'll have to cure it yourself, salt cure it yourself.' And he says well, 'That's all right I'll do it.' And, and time went on, and he never seen this neighbor. Old John never seen this neighbor. And finally one day he met up, quite a while after that he met up with his neighbor and he said, old John said to his neighbor, he said, 'I thought you's aiming to give me a ham o' meat.' And he said, 'I was aiming to give you a ham o' meat,' But says, 'You know that old hog got well.'"

We laughed.

"Yeah, that old hog got well. That hog would have died, he'd have given him one of them hams. Oh lord."

This is the kind of joke that would have been appropriate at an auction since it is brief and could be told during a lull in the proceedings to keep the crowd's attention. The subject matter is also appropriate; the auctions in this area usually involved farm property, and farmers made up a big part of the crowd. Often farmers would be buying the property of a neighbor who had died or gone bankrupt. In this context, the joke is a commentary on the relationship of neighboring farmers: they were friendly but still looked after their own interests first.

Matt Burnett's attitude toward jokes and other stories is important for an understanding of him as a performer in his old age. He refers to the jokes as "an old mess," and at another point in the interview he described his propensity for telling stories as "fooled about it." He calls his mystery legends "little stories," suggesting that they are trivial. In fact, his attitude toward storytelling in general seems to be that it is a frivolous pastime. Interestingly, he uses the same language to describe another of his pastimes. He carves children's toys out of wood and gives them away to neighborhood children or sells them to people passing by. He makes slingshots, popguns, tops that he calls "dancers," "gee-haws," miniature caskets, and other small items carved from wood. The "dancers" are made from used thread spools, and when they are spun seem to dance around the table top. The "gee-haws" have small propellers at the end of a stick with grooves carved in it. When you move another stick over the grooves in different ways, the propeller can be made to spin to the left or right. The trick is to say "gee" or "haw" when it changes direction to make it appear that you are controlling the direction through magic. Another magic trick involved two small boards that made a dollar bill appear to move from beneath one set of straps to another. All of these toys are traditional folk toys made by children or adults in the Blue Ridge and in other parts of the country.

I asked him about when he learned to make toys, "Now those, those toys that you make, the little gee-haw, that's one you learned as a kid?"

"No."

"Oh, then you learned that later?"

"No. That, that was later. I, I've not had that—I'll tell you what, about this mess that I fool with here, I always was a terrible boy for a pocket knife, and I can remember when, when I didn't, didn't have a good knife, but my daddy always kept a good knife. And he, when I was up in the—he'd let me have his knife to make little things like popguns and slingshots and things. And he always talked to me about being careful with it. And I was always a right smart fella for a knife, but after I got up old enough to go to work and so on, I, I never did do much of this sort of doings. But after this heart, heart condition took hold of me in, in sixty-five or sixty-six, the doctor said I better quit work in sixty-six, I kinda went back to that knife business."

"This mess that I fool with here" is similar to the phrases he uses to refer to jokes and storytelling. At another point in the interview he said, "I've always been a heck of a joker. I was an awful talker." We laughed at that, and he continued, "A terrible talker." He said he "was a terrible boy for a pocket knife," and he uses "terrible" and "awful" to describe his talking and storytelling. These terms can be used positively to suggest the intensity of his interest, but they also can have a comic negative connotation, which is clearly the way he is using them. He also says that he "was always a right smart fella for a knife" so that two contradictory attitudes are being expressed, and, in fact, his attitude toward toy making and storytelling is ambivalent. On the one hand, these are childish pursuits, trivial and frivolous. On the other hand, they have been parts of his life that have attracted attention to him and made him stand out in the community. He used jokes as part of his livelihood, but he no longer has that context to give them a serious purpose. The toys, stories, and jokes are not a serious business, but they give meaning to his life in his old age.

The pattern of men reviving in their old age a tradition remembered from childhood or young adulthood is widespread. Simon Bronner has studied this phenomenon among old men who carve wood, a situation similar to Matt Burnett's toy making (1985, 132). Alan Jabbour has noted how old-time fiddlers he worked with took up fiddling after retirement, having neglected it for the entire middle period of their lives. Several old fiddlers started fiddling again after stopping for twenty or thirty years: "By the time I had heard thirty versions of the story from fiddlers scattered across the Upper South, I began to realize that something bigger and more fundamental was going on. There was a larger rhythm to their life, and to their art. . . . Old age was precisely when one played the fiddle" (1981, 144). This pattern fits Matt Burnett's toy making; he whittled with a knife as a boy, but only after a heart attack forced him to retire did he have time to pursue this pastime again.

Matt Burnett's toy making is a form of folk art which serves important functions in old age. As Jabbour says:

> Folk arts comprise a deep and potent strain in the human psyche: *deep*, because folk arts express fully assimilated cultural patterns and social values for people, going beyond the level of conscious, personal cultural acquisition to a level of shared expressive identity; *potent*, because though the expressive strain in all of us may lie fallow in alien or nonnurturing surroundings, it does not die but can be tapped again a half-century later to give vent to creative and expressive potentials we might never have imagined we had. (1981, 142–43)

Matt Burnett's toy making is culturally learned; it is a part of the tradition of this area of the Blue Ridge Mountains and thus part of a regional identity. Mr. Burnett learned the tradition as a young boy; it became a part of his personal identity, and even though it lay fallow for the middle part of his life, it again became an important creative expression for him in old age.

The symbolism of the revival of childhood activities in old age represents, I think, the attempt to remain youthful in the face of a growing awareness of "fading" and becoming "feeble," to use Matt Burnett's terms. By returning to things of childhood, a person is holding on to his or her youth; the opposite end of the life cycle symbolically counters the position of old age and closeness to death.

Bronner speaks of a similar pattern among elderly wood-carvers and labels it "regression-progression behavioral complex." "Faced with adjustments to old age, retirement, death, or an alien industrial or urban environment, the carver nostalgically revives a creative behavior which helped him adjust as a child to adulthood" (1985, 139). Wood carving is a predictable activity that "eases fears of the unpredictable or threatening situation." Matt Burnett revived his childhood activity of wood carving right at the point where he became aware of his heart condition, certainly a threatening situation that produced a fear that making toys helped to alleviate.

Both Bronner and Jabbour indicate that the revival of dormant folk arts is mainly a pattern among elderly men, and this may have to do with the passage from instrumental (associated culturally with masculinity) to expressive (associated with femininity) roles in old age (Myerhoff 1978, 261–62). Matt Burnett had to give up the instrumental role of auctioneer, an occupational activity that kept him in the public realm, and retire to the domestic realm, staying home most of the time. His toy making gave him a way to recontact the outside world, and it gave him a symbolic expression of power and control.[1] Toy making as a folk craft can be seen as a life review project that "provides the artist with a new social currency. The object that embodies the past becomes a source of contemporary power for the artist. It generates audiences, stimulating interaction with grand-children, neighbors, craft connoisseurs, local historians, and, of course, folklorists" (Hufford, Hunt, and Zeitlin 1987, 42). "Tools that were once instrumental extensions of the body, now extend their makers imaginatively into the past and socially into the world" (Kirshenblatt-Gimblett 1989b, 335). Despite Mr. Burnett's feeling that toy making is trivial, its symbolic importance is so great that he must continue it.

Some of the toys provide a source of power in more specific ways: the magic tricks can be used to give him a symbolic sense of control. After reading an earlier draft of this chapter, Simon Bronner commented on Matt Burnett, "In drawing people [to him], the actions clearly place him in power. His fondness for mystery, visual riddles (the gee-haw sticks), and unusual events set him up as a font of knowledge, holding the ultimate answer" (1988a). Like Bill Henry with his magic tricks and Quincy Higgins with his pranks and hoaxes, Mr. Burnett's use of the gee-haw sticks, the dollar bill trick, and other puzzles place him in the role of trickster who, through deception, is in control of his audience. He has found in his own childhood memories a source of pleasure and power in his old age.

Matt Burnett's toys and tricks are also miniatures and as such have another symbolic value. Susan Stewart points out that miniatures represent "a nostalgia for preindustrial labor, a nostalgia for craft" (1984, 68), so that, like Bob Glasgow, Jesse Hatcher, and Quincy Higgins, Matt Burnett's life review project reveals a yearning for an idealized agrarian past. When the making of miniatures, including toys, is taken up by elderly people, it signals an attempt to return symbolically to childhood: "The world of childhood, limited in physical scope yet fantastic in its content, presents in some ways a miniature and fictive chapter in each life history; it is a world that is part of history, at least the history of the individual subject, but remote from the presentness of adult life. We imagine childhood as if it were at the other end of a tunnel—distanced, diminutive, and clearly framed" (Stewart 1984, 44).

When Mr. Burnett makes a miniature "dancer" or popgun, he, in one sense, holds his childhood in his hands; he has captured it and can return to it in his imagination. The miniature coffins he makes are an especially poignant symbol since they represent both his childhood and his old age and impending death. The toy coffins establish a link between his toy making and his storytelling since the stories are also tied to his childhood and are mainly about death and burial. The miniature toys are a means to establish continuity in his life, and they are also a means of engagement in the present. "For the adult, the miniature is an articulation of the self, and the toys they make for children are ways of influencing the development of young selves, by giving them gifts of the self" (Hufford, Hunt, and Zeitlin 1987, 60). Through his toy making, Mr. Burnett establishes relationships with children in the present, engaging them in order to pass on his own understanding of the value of childhood.

Childhood is also relevant to Matt Burnett's "mystery stories" since he learned them all as a boy. Telling them is another way of returning imaginatively to his childhood. The mystery stories are what a folklorist would call legends, and they are Mr. Burnett's favorite kind of story. He told many more legends and thematically related personal experience narratives than jokes or other fictional tales. He told only one joke and one tall tale, and these were told in response to questions and requests from me. He started out with legends, and he told them and other belief narratives throughout both interviews.

When he finished telling the first series of mystery stories, I asked him, "When did you first hear that?"

"Well, now. Here you are. Um uh. I told you that old Mister, old Uncle Rube's wife was named Annie. She was a Thompson. Her maiden name was Thompson. And, and her sister who had in her young days had married a man by the name of Monday, and this lady's name was Emmaset. She was Emmaset Monday. And when I was a boy, anywhere from four to six or eight years old, old Miss Emmaset Monday didn't live in our neighborhood, but she'd come back to visit, and she'd come to our home and spend the night. And lo, we learned that old Miss Emmaset knew these old stories. Now, that's where I got these stories from. Old Miss Emmaset Monday. We always called her Aunt Emmaset, and that's where we got all these old stories. And these things happened at her sister's home."

Just as he learned the traditional performer's role of auctioneer from Len Reynolds, he has learned the storyteller's role from Emmaset Monday. It was not just a matter of learning texts of stories but of learning the style and proper context for storytelling. The stories take on added meaning because Aunt Emmaset was the sister of the woman who is a principal character in the legends; the supernatural element is made more believable because they were told by a person who was only one remove from the events being described. Mr. Burnett later explained the usual context in which the legends would be told and gave a good sense of the appeal they had for a youngster.

I asked him, "So, did all the kids like to hear her tell these things?"

"Oh my goodness! You know they did. And you know, when she would spend the night there, we was so thrilled when we knew that, that Aunt Emmaset was gonna come to spend the night with us. Us kids was so pleased that we could hardly wait till she come and get supper over with, and, and get her at it, you know. Get her telling this."

"It was right after supper sometimes?"

"Yeah, after dark. It had to be good and dark and she'd say, we'd ask her, you know, to tell us some stories. And she'd say, she'd say, 'Turn the light down low.' She'd talk real soft and low, you know.

She'd say, 'Turn the light down real low.' And us little younguns, me and my brothers and sisters, would set down. I can remember setting down right beside her here on the floor, and she'd be a telling them things and I'd be so scared that I, that I wouldn't move at all till that light went back on. And we'd feel so scared while she was telling them stories, and she'd get about as many of them told as I've told now. She'd say, 'I believe that's about all I know.'" We laughed, and he added, "And we was really fond of that old lady."

The context for supernatural legend telling is important; the right atmosphere, dark and quiet, can add to the effectiveness of the story. Aunt Emmaset recognized this, and Matt Burnett learned it from her.

"Well, when did you first start telling them?"

"Well, I don't know now. I don't know whether I fooled about it when I was that young or not, but I can remember, way back yonder, I'd tell all such as that."

"Who'd you tell them to?"

"Well, just youngsters and anybody that would listen to me. I've always been a heck of a joker. I was an awful talker." We laughed at this, and he reiterated his point. "A terrible talker."

"Would you tell them to kids a lot? Your own children?"

"Yeah, and yeah. Tell them to my children and other children. Just everybody."

"Would you try to get the same kind of situation—dark and late at night?"

"Well, at times. If it was, if it was handy, you know. Yeah. Yeah."

"So, you've been pretty well telling those all your life, now?"

"Yeah."

He has told legends all of his life, but they have taken on added importance in old age; his forced retirement left him with more leisure time than he knew what to do with, and he took up toy making again and began to tell stories more. Although not a revival of a dormant tradition, his storytelling does function in many of the same ways as the toy making. Both activities are associated with his child-hood, and both have become significant again in old age. The legend telling, like the toy making, can be considered a part of his life review: both are ritual activities that are predictable and reassuring, establishing a connection to a time in his life when he was most secure.

Mr. Burnett's description suggests that the mystery story sessions were some of his most cherished childhood memories, and he clearly identifies with Aunt Emmaset as a storyteller, making a direct comparison between his childhood story sessions and the tape-recorded storytelling he was engaged in at the moment. Despite the frightening quality of the legends, ultimately they are reassuring: the lights come back on, the ghosts are banished, and it is sweet old Aunt Emmaset who is sitting there after all.

As a child, he believed these supernatural events actually took place, and that was part of the frightening appeal of them. As an adult, he treats the stories with more humor and incredulity, but there is still some degree of belief.

I asked him, "How do you feel about those mysteries and things like that? My—like the ones that you described that you heard when you were a boy? Noises in the house?"

"Well—"

"—and things that move? How do you feel personally about that?"

He cleared his throat and tried to explain, "Well, I, I don't know if I'd a, I'd a heared such as that, I don't know whether I'd live there or not."

Alan agreed, "Yeah."

"I might not a lived there, might not stayed there."

"Sounds pretty scary," I said.

Alan asked him, "So you've seen that place then, the Terry place."

"Oh my goodness, it's adjoining, it's adjoining us there where I was raised. I've been in the old home a many of a time. Lord yeah. Yeah."

The legends are grounded in local and family history; they are a part of a community tradition. The first legend he told when the tape started to roll was actually a legend cycle consisting of four major episodes with numerous subepisodes in each that he told one right after the other. These were the ones he learned from Aunt Emmaset and were about her sister Annie and her husband, Ruben.

"Uh, there's an old fellow by the name of Ruben Terry that lived here close to where I was raised. And, and these, mysterious things happened at his place. And, about the first thing that I can think of to tell you now, he was, in that day, was about as big a farmer as there was in this country, and he, he never, never did raise any, never did have any children, and he had to hire right much work done in harvest time and mowing season—putting up hay and stuff. And um, and it was custom them days, that, that wherever people was working for a man, that they give him his dinner. Well, on this particular day, now, the first of these stories—on this particular day, his wife was named Annie, and my daddy always called her Aunt Annie and Uncle Ruben. They was Terrys, people by the name of Terry—and on this particular day now, she was, fixing to get dinner for the work—work hand, had about two or three or four people working, and, it was in July or August, anyway, they was a apple tree over kind of the back of the orchard that was a early tree. They called them a straw-berry apple. And she needed some of these apples about preparing a dish for dinner, extra. Well, she goed across over there, and in them days more so than now, I'm sure, women wore long aprons and, for dress protection, of course, and she didn't take any, any vessel of any kind to get these apples in, she just tucked up the bottom of her apron and got a few apples in her apron. Well, she got these apples; she said she knew she got apples, and she come back to the house and emptied out her basket, er, apples into a basket, and by jingos, there was no apples there, and there was nothing but chips. Wood. Wood chips. And these chips was a kind of wood that, that wasn't any of it on that farm whatever. And she just, goes ahead and, and pours them chips in the fireplace—they had a big fireplace there, but no fire at that, that day of course.

"Well, she goes, she gives up the apple business and goes ahead about dinner, and first thing you know, right around in the room there where she's a working, an old, an old flint rock. She just, just sees it there, it—and there's nobody there but her—but that thing just appears there, right in the room where she's at. Right around in her path where she's working. Well, she picks this thing up and takes it and throws it over the yard fence, goes on back about her work. And the first thing you know, that same rock's right back in there. And she, she takes that thing up and throws it a way out down the hill. And goes on back about her work, and first thing you know, that, that blamed rock is right back there. Well, she just lets it lay there and [then] the men come in from work, and she—the well, the well where they got water was right around the corner of the house there, and, and, she always has, water, didn't have bath, bathroom places, you know, then. And she always has um, water, buckets of water, setting on a water stand in the porch, and for these men to clean up and get ready for dinner. Well, they come in, and, and got ready for dinner, and she told them about the old rock. Well, Uncle Rube says, 'I'll just take that to the back plantation when we go back to work after dinner.' Well, when, when they got through eating and got ready to go back to work, they was aiming to take the rock and it was gone. Disappeared right before their eyes, there. Disappeared.

"Well, I got a little ahead of myself there. When these men was preparing for dinner, getting cleaned up, you know, there was a long bench along there that people sat on and so on, and these three men sat down on them, on that bench, waiting for a call to dinner. Well, old Uncle Ruben had some homemade knives that he used, especially for butchering and so on, but not, not for the women folks to use. They was for butchering and so on. And when they get through with them knives there was a certain shelf in that porch close to where that water bucket was that these knives was always kept on from year to year, you know. Well, them men, when they got up to go to dinner, and when they sat down at the table to eat, they, they heared a little noise in the porch, and, and Uncle Ruben, I reckon, got up and went out to to see that, see what that was, and three of these butcher knives had left that shelf and had come over and stuck up in the wall, right beside of each, where each one of them men was sitting, just drove up in the wall. And nobody, they knew that there was nobody outside there to throw them knives whatever. And there's, there was that now."

This ended the first major episode. There are many indications here that this is a set performance piece. Near the beginning, Matt Burnett says, "The first thing that I can think of to tell you." This serves as an opening marker to again remind the listener of the performer (I) audience (you) relationship. He also refers to "mysterious things" in order to make it clear that this story is a supernatural legend. Shortly thereafter he says, "The first of these stories . . . "; this statement prepares the listener for a series of tales. The episode ends with the phrase "there was that now," which is a formulaic closing. Like Alva Snell, he frames the story as a past event by such phrases as "them days," "them days more so than now," and "didn't have bathroom places, you know, then." Here, he emphasizes his knowledge of the past, which the listener may not have. As with the toy making, telling stories about the past is a means of asserting power; in the legend telling, he has an authority which a younger person lacks.

He uses concrete details throughout in order to ground the story in reality. He tells us that it was July or August, that the apples were strawberry apples, and that it was an old flint rock. None of this information is necessary for the story, but it is important in order to establish the reality of the event; he uses concrete details for verisimilitude. This is a typical rhetorical strategy for magic belief legends (Mullen 1978, 23–42). Another related legend device is the use of specific settings and proper names. Mr. Burnett establishes both at the beginning of the story: "an old fellow by the name of Ruben Terry that lived here close to where I was raised." Also effective in this way is his statement later in the story, "And my daddy always called her Aunt Annie and Uncle Ruben." Not just proper names are used but names which indicate that these people were known by his father, thus making the story seem even more factual. Some of Mr. Burnett's rhetorical devices were not to make the story believable but to make it more effective. At the climax of each subepisode, he uses different devices to enhance the supernatural meaning. When the apples turn into wood chips, he says "by jingos"; when the flint rock disappears, he repeats "disappeared" for emphasis; and when the knives fly across the room, he uses parallelism, saying "stuck up in the wall" first and then "drove up in the wall" the second time. Finally, he arranges the order of the subepisodes to make them more effective. He seems to be apologizing when he says, "Well, I got a little ahead of myself there," but actually he has moved the most exciting incident, the knives sticking in the wall, to last place in the story.

Linda Degh has pointed out that the "legend does not have a polished style, its frame and form do not coordinate narrative elements into a logical chain" (1972, 73), but Matt Burnett's legend telling is the exception: it is coherent and unified, using various rhetorical devices to make the stories succeed as stories. These are set pieces for him, and his performance of them is an indication of how important they are in his life. There is an element of belief here, which is a defining factor in making them legends, but they are told more to entertain than to convince. These two functions, however, are interrelated in that the more convincing they are, the more entertaining they are. They are meant to frighten, and this is better accomplished if they are believable. The rhetorical devices that support belief are also devices to make the legends more entertaining, thus engaging the audience more effectively.

All of this analysis has been based on one major legend episode, but remember there are three more episodes in the same narrative.

"Well, they was a basement onto this, onto this one room building that they, that these old people lived in. But in years, years after, years later, off just a few, four, five steps from this one-room building, they put up a right nice framed house, had a bedroom or two, and so on. But they seldom ever used that, except for company. Well, this one-room house that they lived in, and stayed in most of the time, had a basement in it. And at night, long about time these other things was happening, at night they could hear somebody down in that basement, sawing—like using a handsaw. And said they could actually hear the board drop when he'd saw it off. Well, after he sawed off a little while, he'd, it'd sound like he was nailing, nailing these boards up. And then, after a little, he would cut another board or two and nail that up. Well, the old people, I guess they took them a light or lantern or something, and had to go outside and around below the house to go down into the cellar; and they go down in there, and there's no sign of anybody—anything, no plank, no nothing in there. But they knew they heard that noise right, right under them there. But they couldn't, couldn't see any sign of anything at all. And that was another one of the mysteries.

"Well, the old people would sit out at night, of course when it was cool and nice in the summertime. They'd sit out on that kitchen porch there, and right in the, right out [of] the blue, a woman would appear, right up in the front yard, in front of this big house, a woman and a little, small child, dressed in white would, would just come right out of the blue, they'd just, they was just there. And they'd walk out to, walk up maybe, and just like turning off a switch it was gone. Well, they'd go back and sit down, and, and of course, they'd talk about such a thing, happening, and first thing they know, just like a flash, that thing was right back there, that little kid a playing around this, this lady standing around there. Well, they'd take to go to it again and that thing would disappear. Well, that, that was the last of that then.

"Well, this big house was, was you might say it was used more for guests, company. And there was an old Primitive Baptist preacher, now these old people, old Mr. Terry and his wife was old Baptists, and this old friend the Baptist preacher, his name was Matt Blanchard, and I, and I was named after that man, and, and they put him up there to sleep in that big house, and of course, he was up there by hisself, and Mr. Ruben and his wife back in the other house and it's like I tell you, the two buildings was about ten or twelve feet apart, but a nice board walk from one to the other. Well, in the night, old man Blanchard said that he know'd what he's talking about, that he could hear somebody up, upstairs, like they was a slipping, moving things, like moving the trunk or moving the beds or moving something round over the floor upstairs, just like, noise of that kind. Well, he said, first thing you know, something come, come rolling down them steps, said, said it sounded like, well, maybe like, I believe they said he described it like maybe something like a pretty good sized pumpkin or some something of that sort. [It] just come bump, bump, bump, down that steps and his bed, was kindly, kindly under the stairway there. This noise comes bumping down the steps and out on the floor. Well, that was the last of it. He took that all right and, and, and that was the last of that noise. And then, after a while, he, I don't know whether he slept any or not, I don't guess I would, and after a while, he said that something, seemed like with long arms, just reached right under, between him and the cover, and all the cover disappeared off of him. Just completely. There he was with no cover, no nothing, up there in the dark. And that, that went on there for seconds or minutes, or ever so long, him laying there without any, any cover or anything, up there in that dark room. And, he said he knowed, just felt them arms go under him and raise that cover off of him. Well, he gets up and goes, gets his clothes on and he goes down and sets up, the rest of the night, down where the other people's at. Yeah boy. And," he snapped his fingers, "that's the last of that, that part of it."

He arranges these major episodes like the subepisodes so that the most exciting incident, the actual contact with a ghost, comes last.

In fact, the episodes are ordered in such a way that they build in intensity; for instance, the sight of the ghosts comes right before the contact with a ghost. He sets off the episodes by ending each with a variation of the same formula: "that was another one of the mysteries," "that was the last of that then," and "that's the last of that, that part of it." He signals the end of the entire cycle by adding a snap of the fingers to the formula. Notice that Mr. Burnett never uses the terms "ghost," "spirit," or "supernatural"; he tells the stories in an almost matter-of-fact way. I think this is more effective because it leaves the listener to supply the explanation of the noises, the moving objects, the disappearances, the woman and child in white, and the "something" that grabs the preacher. These are all common motifs in ghost legends (Jones 1959), and the preacher in a haunted house is the basis of legends and tales (Abrahams 1970, 179–82), but the motifs have been put together in this case to make a legend cycle that is particular to a place and a group of people and thus close to Matt Burnett's life, especially to his childhood.

This narrative and the other belief narratives he tells are all linked together by the common theme of death—in the preceding legend more specifically with a concern for an afterlife, a spirit world that can be detected through noises, moving objects, and apparitions. The others are concerned more with mortality and the physical fact of death, especially with funerals and burials.

"Uh," Mr. Burnett cleared his throat as he began, "I uh, start this sometime by telling folks that, that I saw a man that had been dead in this cemetery up here for ten years. He'd been dead ten years, but I saw him. Yeah, I saw him. He was right there. He'd been dead ten years, but he was yet there. The way that happened, there was an old fellow by the name, by the name of Langen. There used to be a family of Langens that lived right back in this community and they was pretty wealthy people. Well-to-do folks, the older ones was, and plum on up, I guess. Now, this old man's name was Stepco, called him Stepco Langen. That was his name, but most people for short would call him Step, Step Langen. And him and his wife, of course, sometime before, maybe in their last days, they, they agreed between one another that they would love to be buried in the same grave, even though one might be gone quite a while first, but they did want to be buried, when the last one went, they wanted the other one, the grave opened up, and both of them buried in one big grave. Well, that's what happened. This old lady, this old man, died in nineteen five, and in nineteen fifteen, his wife died. And, of course, now, this request was carried out.

"And my daddy was always a fellow that helped dig graves. And he helped dig that grave, or them graves, and, and when they, when they got that old man's grave opened up and throwed out, all the dirt throwed out, throwed out of the box, off of the box—now them days, they didn't have nice caskets like they do now, no sir. Yep, they had, most everything was a nice homemade coffin; they didn't say casket then, they'd say coffin. And they was fellows in the country that, that could make a nice one, out of some kind of first-class lumber, you know. Well, he was buried in that kind of a outfit, and, and this coffin was always placed in a nice, homemade, new box. Large box. Well, when they got them graves dug, all the dirt throwed off of, off of that box, my daddy and another fellow was 'n there cleaning it off nice, and I don't know how come these, these men to do it, fellow by the name of Schyler over here, but his nickname, I guess, was Babe; they always called him Babe Schyler. And, my dad and Babe Schyler was in there, and they cleaned that, lid of that box off right nice.

"And there was other men on the bank around there, and I was a little old boy, and there's something said about they's a gonna open that up. That was it. This lid was screwed, put on with screws, you could just tighten it with your finger, half a dozen of them, yeah. Well, they took them loose and laid that lid to that box back against the bank, and, and that homemade coffin, it is, the lid opened down to here, you know, but it didn't hinge back and lay back. You took out some screws and lay that lid back, just like you would the box lid. So, they took that off too, and that uncovered the old man down to his belt, you might say. And them old coffins was made—" (There was some nervous laughter at this point.) "—was made with a glass, with a glass over their face, down to their waist. A glass. And when they, they took that lid off of that coffin, that glass was broke all through to pieces. That glass was shattered into no telling how many pieces, and, but it just hadn't fell out. Just, it hadn't fell out on him. It was just, it was just broke just as though he had give it that—" Mr. Burnett made a motion of thrusting his fist up.

Realizing the implications, I exclaimed, "Oh no!"

"—and it looked just like that was just about the way it was broke."

"Like he had tried to break it."

"Like he—"

"Trying to get out?"

"Yes sir. And I, honestly now, I can just see that. That glass was broke all to pieces, and, and that, all down in there, on him, face and all, was a, a mold, old white-looking blue, white-looking mold, standing up in there. And you know when, when that lid was took off, they, the, the men said, that air caused that mold to kinda go away. . . ."

"And you saw that?"

"I saw that. I got, I was right down, just right down, a peeping right down there, a little young'un, you know."

"How old were you?"

"Well, uh, ele—uh, eleven years old."

This is a personal experience narrative and not a legend, but it contains a legend motif and continues the death themes of his legend cycle except that instead of being concerned with the spirit world, it is about the end of physical life. This is the kind of story that could become a legend, and there are certainly buried alive legends already in circulation (AT990, "The Seemingly Dead Revives," Aarne 1964; Motif S123, "Burial Alive," Thompson 1955).[2] Like his view of the legend cycle, Matt Burnett sees this story as a performance item; he starts out saying, "I uh, start this sometime by telling folks," which refers to other performances of the same story. As with the legends, he emphasizes the factuality of the event by repetition—"I saw him. Yeah I saw him. He was right there . . . but he was yet there"—and by establishing a specific setting and using proper names and concrete details. The details dwell on some of the physical facts of death and burial, the kind of coffin and the white mold on the body. These vivid details must come from the impression that seeing a decaying corpse had on an eleven-year-old boy. Eleven was also the age when he first conducted a real auction, so that this year in his life took on added significance as a rite of passage from childhood to adulthood. Children often do not have an understanding of the concept of death. "Only gradually does [a child] recognize that there is a thing called death that takes some people away forever; very reluctantly he comes to admit that it sooner or later takes everyone away, but his gradual realization of the inevitability of death can take up until the ninth or tenth year" (Becker 1973, 13). At the crucial age of eleven, seeing a corpse from the grave was part of young Matt Burnett's passage to an adult awareness of mortality. Confronting the physical fact of death must have been traumatic for him, especially in his awareness that the man may have been buried alive.

Like the legend telling and toy making, the telling of this personal story connects childhood and old age. He recalls his first youthful confrontation with death at a time in old age when he is getting closer to the end of his own life. Psychologically, dealing with death is an important issue for the elderly; they talk more about it than other age groups, and they feel growing fear and anxiety as others their own age die (Kalish 1985, 154–55). Matt Burnett seems to have an almost morbid fascination with death; most of the stories he told were about funerals, burials, wakes, and ghosts. He only told three stories—a joke, a tall tale, and a hunting story—that did not have death as the subject. The death legends and personal experience stories seem to project some of his worst fears about death.

How does one deal with these fears through narrative? The answer to this can only come from looking at all of Matt Burnett's stories about death. He tells another story that treats the problem of live burial from another perspective.

"Occasionally now I tell a story about a—now back, back when I was a boy, I can remember, back when I was a boy, they, they wasn't such a thing in this country as, as a funeral home. Plenty of them now, in all, all towns and places, funeral homes around us here. Back when I was a kid, they wasn't no funeral homes, and, and when a person died, especially in, in warm weather, hot weather, they was buried just as quick, they was shrouded and buried just as quick as they could get them dressed and, and get that grave dug. Even if it was before twelve the next day they was buried. And I heard of one, one lady that died and they was hustling around to— supposedly died—and they was a hustling around to get her buried, and, and men a digging the grave and there was, it had growed up between the house and grave, and, and some men was chopping that off and clearing out a way to carry this casket up to the graveyard, and, and the women at the house [were] dressing this lady, getting her ready.

"Well, by nine or ten o'clock the next morning they, they had her ready, and they had the grave ready, and they had the road chopped out up, up to the graveyard—growed up place. Well, there's no ambulance, nothing of that kind to carry anybody to the graveyard, they just, just carry them by hand. Now, the way they done that, I, I know about that, I've seen it done. They would go to the woods and they'd cut three, three sticks about four or five foot long and about that big—stout—and put them three sticks across, under this coffin, and three men on each side, and carry that, that coffin to the graveyard. Well, this lady, they got everything ready, and, and they started to the graveyard with her, and, and by jingos, I said she was supposedly dead, you know, they, something happened that, you know, and, and they was going ahead on it to the graveyard, carrying that casket, and her husband and little children, and neighbors and friends, following close behind. Well, they got on up there where them stumps was cut off, cut off tolerable high, and, and one of the men stumbled, stumbled over a, a stump and fell, and, and, and everybody dropped their holds and that casket hit the ground pretty hard. And they got her up, got the casket up then, and went on to the grave, and when they got up there they opened the casket for the last, last view. By jingos, that jolt had, had [made] that lady come to. Yes, laying in there alive."

We laughed in disbelief.

"Yeah boy. Well, they got her out of there, and, and just, just as soon as they saw she was alive, they just opened up the thing, you know, and she just crawled out. And," Mr. Burnett laughed, "she went to the house and, and fixed dinner for the men that—" We all laughed here. "—that had dug her grave." We were roaring by this point.

"Well, and, and the thing, the thing is, she went on back about her work you know, well, in a certain length of time, she, she passed away again. Well, they got everything ready, they was going right up through that same row of stumps, this old husband a following along behind, you know, and children and neighbors and friends, trailing along, great trail, and they got up there pretty close to them stumps, and the husband said, hollered real loud, said, 'Hey, fellas, watch out for them stumps!'"

We all laughed harder than ever.

Mr. Burnett tells this story after a series of legends and personal experience narratives dealing with the same topic, and he uses legend devices in the telling of it; in other words, he tells it as though it really happened. He refers again to his childhood at the beginning; he gives historical information about funeral and burial customs of that time; and he establishes setting and concrete details. In this case, however, all of the legend devices serve to set up a hoax. He wants us to think it is another true story in order to make the impact of the punch line of the joke even more effective. Here again, he uses deception as a means of symbolically keeping control of the situation. This narrative is a "humorous anti-legend" (Degh 1971, 296–98; Vlach 1971, 95–140); it uses legend devices but undermines the expectations of that genre when at the punchline the actual genre is revealed: it is all a joke. Mr. Burnett has some problems carrying out the hoax though; he says early in the story "supposedly died" and later repeats "I said she was supposedly dead," which, of course, gives away the plot twist. I think he does this because he feels uncomfortable deceiving us; up until this point, he has been telling us true stories and has established a relationship of trust. Even though he knows the joke depends on a deception, he cannot quite hoax us completely. Coming after the personal narrative about the man who was buried alive, this story comments on and plays with the same theme, but treating it comically reduces the anxiety associated with death. Matt Burnett can manipulate his audience and at the same time deal with his own psychological fears about death and burial.

There is another level of meaning in the story; it is a sexist joke. The humor depends on the stereotypical relationship of a husband and wife: the wife is not wanted by her husband, but he has trouble getting rid of her—she will not even stay dead. This meaning is not revealed until the punch line, but it is then obvious that she was a burden on him. Another sexist element occurs when she rises from the grave and immediately fulfills her traditional role by fixing dinner for the men who had dug her grave. Mr. Burnett, in telling this story, is also fulfilling a traditional role, perpetuating a culturally masculine point of view. He does give the woman's perspective in a story he told immediately after the coming-back-to-life tale.

"And there's another, another man died and supposedly, you know, and, and they got everything ready, and, and, and from the time," he laughed, "from the time he was passed out, plumb on up till they took him to the grave, they noticed sweat on him, you know. He was sweating. Though he was in his coffin, he was sweating. And they'd keep that wiped off, and, and when they took him to the grave, the last viewing of the corpse, and the lady, the man's wife, walked up to the, to the casket to look at him the last time. And she had on one of these long aprons like I mentioned to you, and by jingo that man was a sweating and sweating like everything, and she just wiped the sweat off of him and slammed that lid, and just as quick as she could." We laughed, and he ended the story, "She was afraid he'd come to."

She took the sweating as a sign of life and wanted to get him underground as soon as possible. This balances the previous story in showing that women may also want to get rid of their husbands, but both stories present a negative view of marriage. These two are humorous stories about death, but they are similar to other more serious stories he told in their emphasis on physical details about corpses.

"And another thing, now this grave that I was telling you about, it, it's right in the cemetery right here at this church, right up there at the highway. And another thing that took place there, I wasn't in to that, wasn't at that grave digging till—I was working that day and never come in till late in the evening, and I went out there; they was yet digging, and there's an old fellow, Scott, an old fellow by the name of Joe Scott, he was a, he was a old man. And he had told people that when he, when he died that he wanted to be buried in the cemetery at Meadows Church, right beside of his grandfather, which had been dead no telling how many years. Well, that was remembered, and when he died, fellows went in to dig the grave, and, and, and there's no, no tombstones there, just old gray rock, like a lot of graves is now, just gray rock setting up there at the old man Scott's grave. And, and the men that went there to dig the grave, they wasn't sure, just what grave that the old grandfather's grave was, you know.

"So, old Mr. Joe Scott, that had died and was to be buried there the next day or something, he had a brother that lived just a mile or so right back over there, and somebody proposed that they go after Mr. Winfield, his name was Winfield Scott. Somebody said, 'Go after Mr. Winfield, and he'll know where, where his old grandpa's grave is at.' So, they went and got him, brought him over there, and he said, 'Well, right here is grandfather's grave.' Showed them which grave it was. Well, they went to digging, and about half of that grave dug real easy, and the other dug normal, kindly—kinda solid and hard like. But about half of it went down just real easy. Well, they, they said they discussed, as they went on down there digging, that they might be going down in the grave, that half. Maybe them stones had been misplaced and moved, set up wrong, and that was what, what had happened. They had been tore down and set back up the wrong place.

"And when I got out there that evening, they was, they was nearly done. That grave was nearly deep enough. And, and they got to finding something down in there that looked like he had been buried so long, you know, that everything was gone. And they got to finding something that looked like rotten wood, in, mixed in with the dirt. And they, they sent for old man Scott to come back out there, talked with him about that thing. That they wa—they was afraid they was going down half the width of that grave in another grave, and sure enough it was. Well, old man Scott come back out there, and, and he was there when I come in from work and went out there. And there was a fellow by the name of Yates down in there at work, with a shovel, and they was, they was talking that, that, they was afraid they was hitting another grave. And old man Scott said well, said, 'Just keep on digging,' says, 'There won't be no harm done. That's no harm.' And this fellow Yates was just a setting his foot on that shovel and throwing the dirt out. And once in a while, somebody say that this, this looks like clothing, rotten clothing, you know, in with that dirt. Sure enough it was. After a little, this fellow Yates says, says, 'Here's that old head.'"

We laughed at this point.

"Said, 'Here's his head.' That old man Scott says, says, 'Well, lay it out up here.' And he laid that thing out up on the bank, just got his shovel under it and laid that little skull, skull out up on the bank. And there wasn't anything to it except, except the top of his head.

And all in the back of his head there was gone. You know, just a little turtle, turtle shell of a looking thing. Well, old man Scott he took his cane and he turned that thing over and over and looked at it, punched it around. I broke off a splinter about eight or ten inches long off of a rail that was laying there, and I gouged the, took that little old skull, I gouged the so-called brains and dirt and stuff out of the top of that little skull, and cleaned it out right good. And old man Winfield says, 'Well, put it back in there, cover it up.' Says, 'Just make the grave bigger and we'll bury brother Joe be—beside of him anyway.' And that, that's the way that story went."

Like the other personal experience narratives, this one uses many legend devices, and it is obviously thematically related to them. The detailed description of the skull has the effect of emphasizing mortality: this is the fate of all of us, to have our "so-called brains" mixed with "dirt and stuff" in the grave. It reminds me of the treatment of mortality in many British and Anglo-American ballads. In "The Unquiet Grave" (Child 78) the corpse speaks to her mourning lover, "My breast it is as cold as clay,/My breath smells earthly strong;/And if you kiss my cold clay lips,/Your days they won't be long" (Friedman 1963, 33). In "The Wife of Usher's Well" (Child 79) corpses return to their mother's home but are called back to the grave by the gnawing worms within them (Friedman 1963, 36). In these ballads and in Matt Burnett's story the moral is for humans to recognize and accept the physical fact of death, a point that is made through the explicit gory details about the dead body.

Another of his personal experience stories also deals with a corpse, but in this one, the treatment is humorous. I had heard the story from Mr. Burnett before but had not recorded it, and therefore I asked him to repeat it.

"Oh me. Well, well, that was a, an old neighbor here, that was years ago. There was an old man lived here close to us, he had lost his wife years ago and he lived, and he had two girls that never did marry, and, and them girls lived there with their father in an old log house just across the back of my farm here. And that old man got old and feeble, and, and finally one morning, I don't remember that we knew he was sick or any worse than usual, but anyway the news come out over in this community that old man Will had died. His name was Will Cochran, and he was known by the people around here as Big Will, and he had a cousin that lived on little ways from him down there, a slim, slim, fellow, and his name was Will, and they called him Little Will. This old fellow was Big Will and the other fellow was Little Will. And so the news come out over through here that Big Will had passed away.

"Now we went over there, and the other few neighbors had gathered in, and, and I remember there was half a dozen fellows or more sitting out in the yard, some of them was setting on a pile of wood, sticks of wood and so on, out in the yard, and," he laughed, "they'd two fellows that I think they said that sit up with the old fella till he died the night before, and one of them was a fella by the name of Runnels, Tilton Runnels, and the other one was a fella by the name of Bill Metcalf. And Bill was about as tall a man as you ever see. And Tilton was about as short a man as you ever see, and, and he, he had a nickname that people called him from part of the town, because he had such short little legs, they called him Skillet, Skillet Legs, you know." Mr. Burnett laughed again. "That was Tilton's nickname, Skillet.

"And so when we got there, they was Bill and Tilton was shaving old man Will to get him ready. Now they dressed him, them days, they dressed them at home and put them in the homemade coffins and buried them like that, instead of the funeral homes taking care of these jobs. And, and," he laughed, "Will and Bill and Tilton was a trying to clean the old feller up, to get him ready to, to be put away, and they had to shave him. And you could hear that old dull razor scrape, scrape that man's face just about like scraping a hog. I guess that razor was dull, and maybe the lather wasn't good, and I don't know how lather works on a dead person no-how. Don't know. But anyway, that old razor was a sounding off. And Bill was an awful wicked fellow and they was, they said they was drinking beginning of that day. And, after Little Bill said, said to Skillet, he said, said, 'By God, Skillet, bear down, I says, he's dead, it won't hurt him.'"

Here again we have the mortality theme in the physical description of the corpse, but this time it is treated comically. As with the shift from a serious legend about being buried alive to a humorous anti-legend about revival from death, this story balances the other corpse story. Corpses are reminders of the inevitable end of every individual, but life goes on, the living can even make fun of the dead body. In this story, a community ritual provides the means for dealing with death; the men are gathered to prepare the body for burial and engaged in the traditional drinking behavior associated with wakes. The story is morbid and funny at the same time. The fear of death is controlled within a community context; a circle of friends is together interacting in ways, drinking and joking, that are reminders of their ongoing vitality in the face of death. One of the rhetorical devices that Matt Burnett uses to reinforce this theme is the reference to nicknames—"Big Will," "Little Will," and "Skillet Legs." This gives the story a comic quality, and it also imparts a communal base, a sense of place. These are all men who know each other, and they are known to the storyteller as well. There is a comic warmth in his references to them that counters the coldness of the death theme. Mr. Burnett laughs throughout the telling of the story.

Names are an important device in most of Matt Burnett's story-telling. In every legend and personal experience story he cites people by name and he also usually gives place names. In the joke and the humorous anti-legend, he does not use names. The legends and personal stories are belief genres, and the use of names helps to make them more believable; the joke and anti-legend are fictional genres that do not require this, although the anti-legend could use names as part of its hoax function. Jokes as fictional folk tales are distant, and the legend and personal narrative are more immediate. As Degh points out, the legend reacts "sensitively to local and immediate needs" so that it "is more local than the tale, more likely to develop local patterns" (1972, 73). Thus, Matt Burnett's use of proper names and place names localizes the legends and the personal narratives, and it goes beyond this to give a sense of community, a place he has lived all of his life, people he has known since childhood. This takes on added importance because of the recurring theme of death: the community context helps the individual to face death and mortality. The topics of Mr. Burnett's stories—funerals, burials, wakes—are community rituals that help people survive the loss of family and friends and to reckon with their own inevitable deaths.

These meanings are especially significant to the storyteller himself. Since the time Matt Burnett first learned of his heart condition, he has had to be more aware of mortality than other people ordinarily are. As he has gotten older, he has increasingly seen himself as "feeble" and "fading." As psychologist Jean Wertheimer has pointed out: "In the face of these limited perspectives, the aged individual is compelled in concrete terms to be aware of his or her mortal condition. This awareness, furthermore, is attended by the feeling that death has already begun, that it has long since begun" (1983, 250). Matt Burnett's personal way of coping with old age and death is to return to childhood pursuits, to toy making and to telling stories he either learned as a child or ones based on childhood experiences. The rituals of storytelling and toy making are what Wertheimer calls "'mechanisms of permanence' which through fantasy suspend the irresistible passage of time" (1983, 253). Ritual mechanisms of permanence function to give the individual a sense of being outside of time and as such are "attempted defenses against death." When he is telling stories or making toys, Matt Burnett imaginatively returns to childhood, thus defending himself against death.

Psychologists often view these mechanisms as pathological regression, as obsessive attempts to control stress (McCaslin 1987, 161); however, in Matt Burnett's case these rituals seem positive for his mental health. Psychologist Peter Blos speaks of "regression in the service of development" in adolescence (1967), and Erik Erikson applies this concept more broadly to "a search for the solution of a (literally) *age-specific conflict*" (1982, 63). Erikson's point, then, is closer to Butler's theory of life review in which the old person goes back over his or her life in order to resolve conflicts (1964, 266). If Matt Burnett's return to childhood behaviors is, indeed, regression, then it is in the service of development since it enables him to apply activities from the past to his present situation. His ritualized storytelling and toy making may be similar to "regressive" behavior in psychological terms, but they are also "progressive" in that they paradoxically enable him to face the future by drawing on the past (Bronner 1985, 139). As with all of the elderly people examined in this study, Matt Burnett's old age exemplifies the themes of continuity and engagement. He has maintained continuity with his own past and engaged people in the present through his toy making and storytelling.

NOTES

1. This discussion of power as asserted through folklore is informed by the concept of praxis as defined by Simon Bronner (1988b). See also Bronner 1986.

2. See also Baker 1982, 49–50; Hessing and Elffers 1986–87, 115–26; Rose 1978, 4–8; and Solomon and Solomon 1981, 18.

Conclusion:
Engagement and Continuity

There is a great distance both geographically and socially between Mollie Ford who was discussed in the first chapter and Matt Burnett who was described in the last. An eighty-four-year-old black woman isolated in a hollow along the Ohio River in southern Ohio may not seem to have much in common with a seventy-four-year-old white retired male auctioneer living on the Blue Ridge Parkway in Virginia, but they share something besides old age. Mollie Ford and Matt Burnett both have a desire to engage other human beings, to talk with them, interact with them, to pass on to them what they see as important from their lives. They and all of the other seven people discussed in this book want human contact in order to establish continuity with their own past lives and with the future lives of those who will listen to them. They see themselves, in Mollie Ford's terms, as "stepping stones, the teachers to teach you all." Mollie Ford states this purpose more explicitly than the rest, but it underlies all of their stories and all of their folklore. They share this life theme, but they are all different in the ways it is expressed in their life stories.

Mollie Ford is a folk teacher who uses biblical stories, figurative language, and sermon techniques to impart her wisdom to the next generations. Jesse Hatcher has a strong sense of continuity with the past, and he engages people from his community by telling them about the old folk remedies, traditional canning recipes, and the history of his church and of his people back to slavery times. Mamie and Leonard Bryan are less self-conscious about themselves as performers in a continuum, but they dwell on the past, and their stories contain values that they see as necessary for living properly in the present and future. Bob Glasgow sets himself up as an authority on the past—the history of his family back to the Revolutionary War and farmlife in the nineteenth century, especially the building techniques for houses and barns; he becomes the curator in a living museum in order to engage people in his life and his stories. Similarly, Alva Snell has a strong awareness of himself as the old fisherman talking about his occupational past so that younger people can see what it was like. Quincy Higgins takes visitors on tours of his farm, appropriating any setting to tell jokes, legends, and stories about his life. Bill Henry concentrates on his own life story and engages listeners by emphasizing two major narrative cycles, his orphan and hobo years. Matt Burnett is different in that his own life story is secondary to supernatural legends and narratives about death and burial, but these stories are thematically related to the major concerns of his old age.

Certain themes run through the life stories of several of the nine. Religion is a major concern of Mollie Ford, Jesse Hatcher, Leonard and Mamie Bryan, and Quincy Higgins. This does not mean that religion is not important to the other four people, but they did not emphasize it as much when they talked about their lives. For instance, Bob Glasgow was a religious man; he mentioned his beliefs several times, but it was not a major theme in his conversation on the various occasions I talked to him. The five religiously oriented people had differences among themselves: Jesse Hatcher's religion was quiet and contemplative; Quincy Higgins's was expansive and acquisitive; Leonard and Mamie Bryan's was both personal and communal, connecting them to each other and to their church group; Mollie Ford's was idiosyncratic and evangelical. For all of them, religious beliefs were an important source of identity in old age. Most of them had a conversion experience that had given them a new self, which was then their core identity for the rest of their lives. Telling of their religious experiences was a ritual occurrence, reliving the original ritual through narrating it, reestablishing the link between their present selves and the new selves after conversion.

Ritual involves repeated patterned activity, symbolic enactments which dramatize abstract conceptions (Myerhoff 1984, 305); in both its sacred and secular forms, it is found in the lives of the nine people in this study. For Bob Glasgow, giving visitors a tour of the house and barn on his farm was a ritual event in which he asserted his identity and his connections with the past. Quincy Higgins's repeated trips to the highest point of land on his property was a secular ritual for him, symbolizing his achievements in life. Matt Burnett's toy making has symbolic value for him, linking him to his childhood, and Jesse Hatcher's preserving of food is a ritual that links him spiritually with his wife. Bill Henry's telling of stories about his childhood and youth is a ritual experience in which he takes listeners back with him to his past, projecting his core identity. Storytelling is a secular ritual for all nine people; by telling stories about their lives, they connect the present moment, the speech event, to the past experience, the narrated event (Babcock 1984, 65), thus establishing a strong sense of continuity. Barbara Myerhoff says that "ritual states enduring and even timeless patterns, thus connects past, present, and future, abrogating history, time, and disruption" (1978, 164–65). William Faulkner recognizes this in his fiction; his stories about Ike McCaslin, Sam Fathers, Uncle Buck and Uncle Buddy, and Mollie and Lucas Beauchamp in *Go Down, Moses* provide a fictional analogy to the real-life stories of Mollie Ford, Jesse Hatcher, Mamie and Leonard Bryan, Bob Glasgow and the rest. For fictional and factual characters alike storytelling is a ritual process—healing, correcting, connecting, resolving.

Interconnectedness as a central theme in life stories is related to ritual, and it also has sacred and secular expressions (Myerhoff and Simic 1978, 232). The interconnectedness of human beings is an important element in communitas, an ideal of unstructured and undifferentiated society, which some people experience fleetingly through religious ritual and others through secular ritual (Turner 1977, 96–97). For Mollie Ford, Jesse Hatcher, the Bryans, and Quincy Higgins, interconnectedness is based in their religion, but for Bob Glasgow and several others, it is not. Interconnectedness meant living in harmony across racial lines for the elderly black people; they all stressed the importance of equality in the sight of God and the immorality of racial hatred. Quincy Higgins believed in helping others as a religious value, but he did not emphasize overcoming racial differences as an issue in human oneness. Mr. Higgins and Mr. Glasgow were alike in stressing the importance of neighbors and community interconnectedness, but Mr. Glasgow's views seemed to have more of a secular base. Matt Burnett indirectly supported the ideal of community; with his constant references to local place names and nicknames, he created a sense of place and community in his stories and legends. Bill Henry's strongest sense of community was not connected to place but to a group, to the hoboes that he traveled with during his young adult life. Also, for Alva Snell community was not necessarily associated with place but with his occupational group, commercial fishermen. For Mollie Ford, Jesse Hatcher, and the Bryans, interconnectedness was on a spiritual level, all humanity joined together in harmony; but for Quincy Higgins, Bob Glasgow, Matt Burnett, Bill Henry, and Alva Snell, interconnectedness suggested links within a specific community or group. Whichever way it was viewed, connections between human beings were important for all of them as elderly people. They resisted isolation and sought human contact whether in broad spiritual terms or in a more immediate secular context.

A consciousness of division, strife, and disharmony was also apparent in their narratives and conversation. The blacks recognized racism as a social reality that they confronted daily, and several of the white people talked about class distinctions and antagonisms. These themes suggest the opposite of communitas; they refer to what Victor Turner calls "society as a structured, differentiated, and often hierarchical system of politico-legal-economic positions with many types of evaluation, separating men in terms of more or less" (1969, 96). Mollie Ford, Jesse Hatcher, and the Bryans related personal experience narratives about their contacts with racist behavior. Alva Snell told stories that showed his contempt for upper-class yachtsmen, who were contrasted with hardworking fishermen. Bill Henry's stories painted a negative picture of authority figures—factory bosses, railroad detectives, and judges—who used their superior positions to make life difficult for the little man. Quincy Higgins has more respect for authority, but his stories deflate people higher on the social scale—ordained ministers, professors, senators, and bank presidents—while inflating himself as the representative uneducated poor boy who has made good. Bob Glasgow's only resentment against another group came out in his story about almost losing his farm to an unscrupulous lawyer.

Achievement orientation was another recurring life story theme based in structured society and hierarchy. Achievement suggests high and low, more and less, and competition against other humans. Bob Glasgow, Quincy Higgins, and Alva Snell told stories that projected this value; they worked hard all of their lives to achieve success, which was defined in different ways for each one. Alva Snell wanted to be the top producer among all the commercial fishermen in his region; he succeeded in this goal and seemed to be satisfied with it in his old age. He acquired enough money to live comfortably and to travel when he wanted; he did not seem to want a great deal of property or material possessions. Quincy Higgins and Robert Glasgow are farmers and as such needed to acquire land in order to be successful; Mr. Higgins acquired property worth a hundred thousand dollars, but Mr. Glasgow because of difficulties beyond his control could never duplicate the level of prosperity his grandfather had achieved. The result is that Quincy Higgins tells stories about his own rise from poverty to prosperity while Bob Glasgow tells stories about his grandfather building the showplace house and barn still standing on his property. Both men emphasize achievement and social status in their narratives.

Some of the stories told by the elderly people in this book are about communitas and some are about structured society; taken together they illustrate Turner's point that "for individuals and groups, social life is a type of dialectical process that involves successive experience of high and low, communitas and structure, homogeneity and differentiation, equality and inequality" (1969, 97). Quincy Higgins's stories about his achievements, Bob Glasgow's about his grandfather's achievements, Alva Snell's about competition, and the Bryans', Mollie Ford's, and Jesse Hatcher's stories about racial inequality are all set within structured hierarchical society. Mr. Higgins's stories of his conversion and his calling to be a preacher, Leonard Bryan's about his conversion, Jesse Hatcher's healing, Mollie Ford's preaching about racial equality, and Bob Glasgow's stories of communal cooperation all aspire to the ideal of communitas. Each individual moves back and forth from structured society to communitas, as does the culture as a whole.

Most of the stories the nine elders told projected their ideals and positive values, but in a few particular performance situations stories that had contradictory functions were told. As Richard Bauman has pointed out, narrative "may . . . be an instrument for obscuring, hedging, confusing, exploring or questioning what went on, that is, for keeping the coherence or comprehensibility of narrated events open to question" (1986, 5–6). This did not happen often with the nine storytellers since they were trying to make the past coherent and comprehensible to their listeners, but when it did happen the situations involved hierarchy or the manipulation of identity. At times Quincy Higgins kept his listeners off balance by pulling pranks on them that were similar to the ones he tells stories about. He is demonstrating his superiority to his listeners and to the people he has previously tricked; therefore, his storytelling performance is a reminder of status and hierarchy. Leonard Bryan tells some stories that explore and question his former actions, thereby negotiating his identity as an ongoing process. In at least some cases the storytellings, which seem divisive or questioning, are ultimately aimed at the goal of resolution and interconnectedness. When Mollie Ford, the Bryans, and Jesse Hatcher tell stories about racial hatred, there is an implicit contrast between social reality and a higher spiritual ideal, between structured society and communitas. When Leonard Bryan questions his past actions, it is in an attempt to resolve them with his present point of view.

The ways in which elderly people talk, their rhetorical strategies, indicate certain similarities. Their purposes are often the same: to hold the attention of younger listeners so that lessons can be communicated and self-esteem can be enhanced. All nine used narratives to attract and maintain attention; they turned their life experiences into entertaining tales, or they drew directly upon tradition for legends, tall tales, and jokes to accomplish the same purpose. In performance terms, they enhanced experience with a display of their language competence, subjecting themselves to the evaluation of their audiences (Bauman 1984, 11). All nine used many of the same devices as part of their storytelling: repetition and parallelism, recurring metaphors and images, biblical references and allusions, shifts of tone and pitch, and quoted dialog which dramatized significant scenes. Most of their stories were set off by markers at the beginning and end, and the rhetorical devices were then clustered within this frame. Significant points of value tended to have even denser clusters of devices to emphasize their importance, such as Mollie Ford's shift of pitch and style to make her point about human oneness, or Quincy Higgins breaking into song in the middle of a story to make his point about divine inspiration. These devices are used by performers of all ages, but there was one strategy that may be more prevalent among elderly storytellers. Many of them tended to establish a greater dis-

tance between the narrated event, what took place in the past, and
the storytelling or speech event, the present situation in which the
story is being told (Babcock 1984, 65). They used such repeated
phrases as "in them days" and "back then" to emphasize the great
gulf between yesterday and today. This rhetorical device relates
directly to one of the recurring content themes about the past.

Six of the elderly men tended to view the past as an idealized
golden age. Bob Glasgow, Alva Snell, and to a lesser extent Jesse
Hatcher, Quincy Higgins, Bill Henry, and Matt Burnett all looked
on the past as being superior to the present. For Bob Glasgow, the
golden age was associated with an agrarian ideal of the nineteenth
and early twentieth centuries, a time of hard work, abundance, honesty, self-reliance, and a balance between individual achievement and
communal cooperation. Alva Snell's golden age was associated with
occupational life during his years as an active fisherman which, like
Mr. Glasgow's ideal time, featured hard work, abundance, and self-
reliance. There was more emphasis on individual achievement since
competition with other fishermen was fierce, but cooperation was
necessary among the crew on his boat. Jesse Hatcher tended to idealize
his childhood and youth, but this was tempered by the recognition
of the racial inequities of the time. His golden age, like that of Mr.
Glasgow and Mr. Snell, is characterized by hard work and abundance,
but his is unique in emphasizing a closeness to nature, which comes
out when he talks about folk medicine and foodways. He suggests
that modern people have lost these qualities of life because we "run,
run, run." Quincy Higgins's emphasis on traditionalism also has some
overtones of the golden age; for him religious conviction and divine
inspiration are associated with traditional life, which is being eroded
by the forces of modernism. Bill Henry's golden age is more narrowly
defined in terms of his own life; he romanticizes his hobo years as
his time of greatest freedom and comraderie. Nothing since has
equaled it for excitement and adventure, which he sees as the stuff
of good storytelling. Matt Burnett views his childhood as a kind of
golden age; this was the time of security of family and close community, the time when he heard Aunt Emmaset tell her ghost stories
and when he first learned to make wooden toys. For all these men,
storytelling is a way of keeping the golden age of the past alive in
the present.

Interestingly, the two women, Mollie Ford and Mamie Bryan,

idealized the past the least. Mollie Ford talked about the hardships her mother encountered as a rape victim and of her own hardships as a child without a permanent home. Mamie Bryan presented a more realistic view of her courtship than her husband did; he idealized their love, but she suggested that she was too young to know any better. She also talked about the hardships of taking care of the farm and children while he was away working in the mines. Women present a more realistic view of marriage than men (Bernard 1972); more research needs to be conducted on the personal narratives of elderly women in order to see how widespread this pattern is and what the causes of it are.

Traditional gender roles were significant in the ways some of the elderly people adjusted to old age. The concepts of expressive and instrumental roles (Myerhoff 1978, 261–62; Zelditch 1955, 313–14), and the culture/nature dichotomy (Ortner 1974, 72–73) help in ana-lyzing gender roles among the elderly. The women tended to make better adjustments to old age because their expressive roles remained the same: Mollie Ford's role as teacher was within a domestic realm and included a strong component of nurturance. She was no longer able to actively carry on this role, but her ideals and her impulse to teach remained strong. Mamie Bryan's expressive roles of wife and mother were still functioning for her in her 80s, but in some ways she had taken on more instrumental roles because of the unique circumstances of her marriage. She gained power in the relationship because her husband was away for such long periods of time, and she ended up asserting herself in old age more than she had in her young adult life. Jesse Hatcher became more expressive in his old age as he gradually took over certain domestic tasks from his ailing wife. He was better prepared to do this than most men because he already had a propensity toward nature, defined culturally as more feminine, rather than toward the more masculine realm of culture. Bill Henry had carried out certain expressive domestic roles all of his life, but he was ambivalent toward them and tended to emphasize his instru-mental masculine role of wanderer in his life review. The other men seemed to resist the shift to expressive roles associated with old age and tried to maintain at least the semblance of instrumental behavior. Matt Burnett told stories and made toys within the domestic realm, but he used them to maintain contact with the outside world. Alva Snell was retired but projected a strong male occupational identity.

One of the underlying concepts that unifies the study of folklore in the lives of these nine elderly people is identity. Their stories, their beliefs, their customs, all project some cultural and individual identity. How each individual views herself and how she wants others to view her determines what themes occur in the stories, how the story is structured, and the way it is performed. The descriptions of beliefs and customs also reflect the self-image of the person. Jesse Hatcher's conversation about folk medicine and foodways reveals his self-image as a spiritual creature within the context of nature. Bill Henry's stories about his hobo adventures project an image of a youthful self, even as he tells them in his old age. Continuity and identity are related then; the core identity is formed through life experiences and then maintained throughout old age. All of the old people in this study are examples of what Sharon Kaufman calls "the ageless self" (1986). For instance, Quincy Higgins was a performing personality during his youth, as his courting story attests, and he is still a performing personality at age seventy-eight.

This does not mean that identity is static; a core identity is maintained, but its development is dynamic and continues to be dynamic throughout old age. Reinterpretation takes place as part of the process of the continuity of identity. A previously quoted passage from Sharon R. Kaufman is relevant here. "The sources of meaning which themes integrate are continually reinterpreted in light of new circumstances. A person selects events from his or her past to structure and restructure his or her identity. Thus, themes continue to evolve from and give form to personal experience—making identity a cumulative process" (1986, 149–50). We saw this in the case of Leonard Bryan: his belief that women should not be preachers had to be altered when his daughter became a preacher. His story about her telling him of her calling shows him reinterpreting his own identity; he becomes less of a dogmatic fundamentalist and more of a supportive father as the story is told down through the years. Telling the story helps to maintain continuity with the past, but it projects a changing identity in the present. Mamie Bryan's stories about her courtship and her life on the farm project an identity of a woman without much control over her own life, but her later identity as primary parent and protector of the homestead comes out strongly in her conversations about their children, about planting by the signs, and selling of the farm land. Identity is complex at any one moment, and even more complex when viewed over a period of time from the perspective of old age.

Identity, continuity, and engagement are all related together through ritual. Telling stories, using folk medicines, planting by the signs, and singing hymns in church are ritual activities. These activities are patterned behavior, linking the present to the past, reinforcing a sense of continuity. When an old person tells a story about his or her own life, he is not only projecting an identity, he is also engaging a listener in the sharing of a ritual, thus attempting to project continuity into the future through that listener. When Bob Glasgow tells the story about the abundant farm dinner he had as a youth, there are many levels of meaning. He is projecting his identity as a product of that time and place, as an honest, direct, independent farm boy who is still within the eighty-seven-year-old man. He is establishing continuity with the past for his own sake, as a ritual reminder of that ideal time of life, and as a reminder of security in the face of changes which threaten him and his values. And finally, he is engaging another human being in the ritual of storytelling in order to pass on those values and that image of a better time with the underlying hope that the listener will take some of those values into his own life. Sociologists have pointed out the lack in contemporary American life of respected "tribal elders" who can help the young to adjust through rituals of initiation (Sennett 1975, 195–96), but there are elders in the United States who use personal ritual to provide knowledge and understanding to those who follow, and we have looked closely at nine of them. In one way or another, Mollie Ford, Jesse Hatcher, Leonard Bryan, Mamie Bryan, Bob Glasgow, Alva Snell, Quincy Higgins, Bill Henry, and Matt Burnett are all using ritual to connect the generations every time they tell a story.

They are exceptional—elderly people who live in communities where they have various degrees of contact with younger generations, contact that has been denied to many of the elderly in modern American society. They are not representative of all old people but of a certain kind, the ones who want to stay in contact with ongoing life and who have the health, imagination, and performance abilities to do so. There are many others out there like them, old people eager to talk and to tell stories; the rest of us should pay attention, should listen.

References

Aarne, Antti. 1964. *The Types of the Folktale: A Classification and Bibliography.* Translated and enlarged by Stith Thompson. 2nd rev. ed. Helsinki: Suomalainen Tiedeakatemia Academia Scientiarum Fennica.

Abrahams, Roger D. 1968a. Introductory Remarks to a Rhetorical Theory of Folklore. *Journal of American Folklore* 81:143–48.

———. 1968b. Trickster, the Outrageous Hero. In *Our Living Traditions,* edited by Tristram Potter Coffin, 170–78. New York: Basic Books.

———. 1970. *Deep Down in the Jungle: Negro Narrative Folklore from the Streets of Philadelphia.* Chicago: Aldine.

———. 1972. Personal Power and Social Restraint in the Definition of Folklore. In *Towards New Perspectives in Folklore,* edited by Americo Paredes and Richard Bauman, 16–30. Austin: University of Texas Press.

———. 1976. The Complex Relations of Simple Forms. In *Folklore Genres,* edited by Dan Ben-Amos, 193–214. Austin: University of Texas Press.

Allen, Barbara. 1989. Personal Experience Narratives: Use and Meaning in Interaction. In *Folk Groups and Folklore Genres: A Reader,* edited by Elliott Oring, 236–43. Logan: Utah State University Press.

Allsop, Kenneth. 1967. *Hard Travellin': The Hobo and His History.* New York: New American Library.

Amoss, Pamela and Stevan Harrell, eds. 1981. *Other Ways of Growing Old.* Stanford: Stanford University Press.

Atkinson, John W., ed. 1958. *Motives in Fantasy, Action, and Society: A Method of Assessment and Study.* Princeton, N.J.: D. Van Nostrand.

Babcock, Barbara. 1980. Reflexivity: Definitions and Discriminations. *Semiotica* 30:1–14.

———. 1984. The Story in the Story: Metanarration in Folk Narrative. In *Verbal Art as Performance,* edited by Richard Bauman, 61–79. Prospect Heights, Ill.: Waveland Press.

Baker, Ronald L. 1982. *Hoosier Folk Legends.* Bloomington: Indiana University Press.

Bakhtin, Mikhail. 1981. *The Dialogic Imagination,* trans. Caryl Emerson and Michael Holquist. Austin: University of Texas Press.

Baldwin, Karen. 1985. "Woof!" A Word on Women's Roles in Family Storytelling. In *Women's Folklore, Women's Culture,* edited by Rosan A. Jordan and Susan J. Kalčik, 149–62. Philadelphia: University of Pennsylvania Press.

Barker, Addison. 1957. Weather Lore in *Blum's Almanac,* 1844–1950. *North Carolina Folklore* 5:11–19.

Barthes, Roland. 1979. Toward a Psychosociology of Contemporary Food Consumption. In *Food and Drink in History,* edited by Robert Forster and Orest Ranum, 166–73. Baltimore: Johns Hopkins University Press.

Bauman, Richard. 1984. *Verbal Art as Performance.* Prospect Heights, Ill.: Waveland Press.

———. 1986. *Story, Performance, and Event: Contextual Studies of Oral Narrative.* Cambridge: Cambridge University Press.

———. 1987. Ed Bell, Texas Storyteller: The Framing and Reframing of Life Experience. *Journal of Folklore Research* 24:197–221.

Bauman, Richard and Joel Sherzer. 1974. *Explorations in the Ethnography of Speaking.* Cambridge: Cambridge University Press.

Bausinger, Hermann. 1958. Strukturen des alltäglichen Erzählens. *Fabula* 1:239–54.

Becker, Ernest. 1973. *The Denial of Death.* New York: Free Press.

Belden, Henry M. and Arthur Palmer Hudson, eds. 1952. *Folk Ballads from North Carolina* and *Folk Songs from North Carolina,* vols. 2 and 3 of *The Frank C. Brown Collection of North Carolina Folklore,* edited by Newman Ivey White. Durham: Duke University Press.

Ben-Amos, Dan. 1972. Toward a Definition of Folklore in Context. In *Toward New Perspectives in Folklore,* edited by Americo Paredes and Richard Bauman, 3–15. Austin: University of Texas Press.

Bendix, Regina. 1989. Tourism and Cultural Displays: Inventing Traditions for Whom? *Journal of American Folklore* 102:131–46.

Blos, Peter. 1967. The Second Individuation Process of Adolescence. *The Psychoanalytic Study of the Child* 22:162–86.

Boatright, Mody C. 1958. The Family Saga as a Form of Folklore. In *The Family Saga and Other Phases of American Folklore,* edited by Mody C. Boatright, 1–19. Urbana: University of Illinois Press.

———. 1961. *Folk Laughter on the American Frontier.* New York: Collier Books.

Bernard, Jesse. 1972. *The Future of Marriage.* New York: World Publishing.

Botkin, B. A., ed. 1945. *Lay My Burden Down: A Folk History of Slavery.* Chicago: University of Chicago Press.

Brewer, D. C. and W. D. Weatherford. 1962. *Life and Religion in Southern Appalachia.* New York: Friendship Press.

Briggs, Charles L. 1984. Learning How to Ask: Native Metacommunicative Competence and the Incompetence of Field Workers. *Language in Society* 13:1–28.

———. 1985. Treasure Tales and Pedagogical Discourse in *Mexicano* New Mexico. *Journal of American Folklore* 98:287–314.

Bronner, Simon J. 1985. *Chain Carvers: Old Men Crafting Meaning.* Lexington: University Press of Kentucky.

———. 1986. *Grasping Things: Folk Material Culture and Mass Society in America.* Lexington: University Press of Kentucky.

———. 1988a. Personal correspondence.

———. 1988b: Art, Performance, and Praxis: The Rhetoric of Contemporary Folklore Studies. *Western Folklore* 47:75–102.

Brown, Linda Keller and Kay Mussell, eds. 1984. *Ethnic and Regional Foodways in the United States: The Performance of Group Identity.* Knoxville: University of Tennessee Press.

Butler, Robert N. 1964. The Life Review: An Interpretation of Reminiscence in the Aged. In *New Thoughts on Old Age,* edited by Robert Kastenbaum, 3–18. New York: Springer.

Caldwell's Illustrated Historical Atlas of Adams County, Ohio. 1880. Newark, Ohio: J. A. Caldwell. Rpt. 1977. Evansville, Ind.: Unigraphic.

Camp, Charles. 1982. Foodways in Everyday Life. *American Quarterly* 34:278–89.

———. 1989. *American Foodways: What, When, Why and How We Eat in America.* Little Rock, Ark.: August House.

Child, Francis James, ed. 1965. *The English and Scottish Popular Ballads.* 5 vols. New York: Dover.

Chudacoff, Howard P. 1989. *How Old are You? Age Consciousness in American Culture.* Princeton, N.J.: Princeton University Press.

Clark, Margaret and Barbara G. Anderson. 1967. *Culture and Aging: An Anthropological Study of Older Americans.* Springfield, Ill.: Charles C. Thomas.

Clements, William M. 1976a. Conversion and Communitas. *Western Folklore* 35:35–45.

———. 1976b. Faith Healing Narratives from Northeast Arkansas. *Indiana Folklore* 9:15–39.

———. 1983. The Folk Church: Institution, Event, Performance. In *Handbook of American Folklore,* edited by Richard M. Dorson, 136–44. Bloomington: Indiana University Press.

Clifford, James and George E. Marcus, eds. 1986. *Writing Culture: The Poetics and Politics of Ethnography.* Berkeley: University of California Press.

Cochrane, Tim. 1983. Isle Royale Commercial Fishermen's Authority Stories: An Indication of Changing Environmental Perception. Paper presented at the annual meeting of the American Folklore Society, Nashville.

Cohler, Bertram J. 1982. Personal Narrative and Life Course. In *Life-Span Development and Behavior,* edited by Paul B. Baltes and Orville G. Brim, Jr., 205–41. New York: Academic Press.

Crapanzano, Vincent. 1980. *Tuhami: Portrait of a Moroccan.* Chicago: University of Chicago Press.

Csikszentmihalyi, Mihaly and Eugene Rochberg-Halton. 1981. *The Meaning of Things: Domestic Symbols and the Self.* Cambridge: Cambridge University Press.

Cumming, M. Elaine. 1964. New Thoughts on the Theory of Disengagement. In *New Thoughts on Old Age,* edited by Robert Kastenbaum, 3–18. New York: Springer.

Davis, Arthur Kyle. 1970. *Traditional Ballads of Virginia.* Charlottesville: University of Virginia Press.

Dégh, Linda. 1972. Folk Narrative. In *Folklore and Folklife: An Introduction,* edited by Richard M. Dorson, 53–83. Chicago: University of Chicago Press.

———. 1975. *People in the Tobacco Belt: Four Lives.* Canadian Centre for Folk Culture Studies, Paper 13. Ottawa: National Museum of Canada.

———. 1985. When I Was Six We Moved West: The Theory of Personal Experience Narrative. *New York Folklore* 11:99–108.

Dégh, Linda and Andrew Vazsonyi. 1971. Legend and Belief. *Genre* 4:281–304.

Dolby-Stahl, Sandra K. 1985. A Literary Folkloristic Methodology for the Study of Meaning in Personal Narrative. *Journal of Folklore Research* 22:45–69.

Dornbusch, Charles H. and John K. Heyl. 1958. *Pennsylvania German Barns.* Allentown, Pa.: Schlechter's.

Dorson, Richard M. 1959. *American Folklore.* Chicago: University of Chicago Press.

———. 1967. *American Negro Folktales.* Greenwich, Conn.: Fawcett Books.

Dundes, Alan. 1983. Defining Identity through Folklore. In *Identity: Personal and Socio-Cultural, a Symposium,* edited by Anita Jacobson-Widding, 235–61. Uppsala: Uppsala Studies in Cultural Anthropology 5.

Erikson, Erik. 1959. *Identity and the Life Cycle.* New York: International Universities Press.

———. 1982. *The Life Cycle Completed.* New York: W. W. Norton.

Evans, Nelson W. and Emmons B. Stivers. 1900. *A History of Adams County, Ohio*. West Union, Ohio: E. B. Stivers. Rpt. 1980. Evansville, Ind.: Unigraphic.

Faulkner, William. 1942. *Go Down, Moses*. New York: Random House.

Fischer, David Hackett. 1977. *Growing Old in America*. Oxford: Oxford University Press.

Friedman, Albert B. 1956. *The Viking Book of Folk Ballads of the English-Speaking World*. New York: Viking Press.

Fry, Christine L., ed. 1980. *Aging in Culture and Society*. New York: Bergin.

Fry, Christine L. and Jennie Keith, eds. 1980. *New Methods for Old Age Research: Anthropological Alternatives*. Chicago: Center for the Study of Urban Policy.

Gennep, Arnold van. 1960. *The Rites of Passage*. Chicago: University of Chicago Press.

Genovese, Eugene D. 1974. *Roll, Jordan, Roll: The World the Slaves Made*. New York: Pantheon.

Gilmore, Janet C. 1986. *The World of the Oregon Fishboat: A Study in Maritime Folklife*. Ann Arbor: UMI Research Press.

Glassie, Henry. 1966. The Pennsylvania Barn in the South: Part Two. *Pennsylvania Folklife* 15:12–25.

———. 1971. *Pattern in the Material Folk Culture of the Eastern United States*. Philadelphia: University of Pennsylvania Press.

———. 1974. The Variation of Concepts within Tradition: Barn Building in Otsego County, New York. In *Man and Cultural Heritage: Papers in Honor of Fred B. Kniffen*, edited by H. J. Walker and W. G. Haag, 177–235. Baton Rouge: School of Geoscience, Louisiana State University.

———. 1982. *Passing the Time in Ballymenone*. Philadelphia: University of Pennsylvania Press.

———. 1985. Artifact and Culture, Architecture and Society. In *American Material Culture and Folklife: A Prologue and Dialogue*, edited by Simon J. Bronner, 47–62. Ann Arbor: UMI Research Press.

———. 1986. Eighteenth-Century Cultural Process in Delaware Valley Folk Building. In *Common Places: Readings in American Vernacular Architecture*, 394–425. *See* Upton and Vlach 1986.

Goffman, Erving. 1959. *The Presentation of Self in Everyday Life*. Garden City, N.Y.: Doubleday.

Gopalan, Gopalan V. and Bruce Nickerson. 1973. Faith Healing in Indiana and Illinois. *Indiana Folklore* 6:33–97.

Gowans, Alan. 1986. The Mansions of Alloways Creek. In *Common Places: Readings in American Vernacular Architecture*, 367–93. *See* Upton and Vlach 1986.

Grant, Jacquelyn. 1982. Black Women and the Church. In *But Some of Us Are Brave: Black Women's Studies,* edited by Gloria T. Hull, Patricia Bell Scott, and Barbara Smith, 141–52. Old Westbury, N.Y.: Feminist Press.

Gumperz, John J. and Dell Hymes, eds. 1972. *Directions in Sociolinguistics.* New York: Holt, Rinehart, and Winston.

Gutmann, David. 1977. The Cross-Cultural Perspective: Notes toward a Comparative Psychology of Aging. In *Handbook of the Psychology of Aging,* edited by James Birren, 302–26. New York: Van Nostrand.

Halpert, Herbert. 1985. Remarkable Sight and Hearing in the Lying Contest. *New York Folklore* 11:161–76.

Hand, Wayland D., ed. 1961, 1964. *Popular Beliefs and Superstitions from North Carolina,* vols. 6 and 7 of *The Frank C. Brown Collection of North Carolina Folklore,* edited by Newman Ivey White. Durham: Duke University Press.

———. 1976. *American Folk Medicine: A Symposium.* Berkeley: University of California Press.

———. 1980. *Magical Medicine.* Berkeley: University of California Press.

Handler, Richard and Jocelyn Linnekin. 1984. Tradition, Genuine or Spurious. *Journal of American Folklore* 97:273–90.

Hareven, Tamara K. 1978. The Search for Generational Memory: Tribal Rites in Industrial Society. *Daedalus* 107:137–49.

Havinghurst, Robert J. 1968. Disengagement and Patterns of Aging. In *Middle Age and Aging: A Reader in Social Psychology,* 161–72. *See* Neugarten 1968.

Hawes, Bess Lomax. 1984. Folk Arts and the Elderly. In *Festival of American Folklife Program Book,* edited by Thomas Vennum. Washington, D.C.: Smithsonian Institution.

Hessing, Dick J. and Henk Elffers. 1986–87. Attitude toward Death, Fear of Being Declared Dead Too Soon, and Donation of Organs after Death. *Omega* 17(2):115–26.

Hofstadter, Richard. 1961. *The Age of Reform: From Bryan to F.D.R.* New York: Alfred A. Knopf.

Hubka, Thomas. 1986. Just Folks Designing: Vernacular Designers and the Generation of Form. In *Common Places: Readings in American Vernacular Architecture,* 426–32. *See* Upton and Vlach 1986.

Hufford, David. 1977. Christian Religious Healing. *Journal of Operational Psychology* 8:22–27.

———. 1983. Folk Healers. In *Handbook of American Folklore,* edited by Richard M. Dorson, 306–13. Bloomington: Indiana University Press.

Hufford, Mary, Marjorie Hunt and Steven Zeitlin, eds. 1987. *The Grand Generation: Memory, Mastery, Legacy.* Washington, D.C.: Smithsonian Institution.

Hutslar, Donald L. 1981. The Ohio Farmstead: Farm Buildings as Cultural Artifacts. *Ohio History* 90:221–37.

Jabbour, Alan. 1981. Some Thoughts from a Folk Cultural Perspective. In *Perspectives on Aging,* edited by Priscilla W. Johnston, 139–49. Cambridge, Mass.: Ballinger Publishing.

Jolles, Andre. 1965. *Einfache Formen, Legende, Sage, Mythe, Rätsel, Sprüche, Kasus, Memorabilen, Märchen, Witze.* Tübingen: M. Niemeyer.

Jones, Louis C. 1959. *Things That Go Bump in the Night.* New York: Hill and Wang.

Jones, Loyal. 1977. Studying Mountain Religion. *Appalachian Journal* 5:125–30.

Jones, Michael Owen, Bruce Giuliano, and Roberta Krell, eds. 1981. Foodways and Eating Habits: Directions for Research. *Western Folklore* 40:vii–137.

Joyce, Rosemary O. 1983. *A Woman's Place: The Life History of a Rural Ohio Grandmother.* Columbus: Ohio State University Press.

Joyner, Charles. 1984. *Down by the Riverside: A South Carolina Slave Community.* Urbana: University of Illinois Press.

Kalish, Richard A. 1985. The Social Context of Death and Dying. In *Handbook of Aging and the Social Sciences,* edited by Robert H. Binstock and Ethel Shanas, 149–70. New York: Van Nostrand Reinhold.

Kaminsky, Marc, ed. 1984. *The Uses of Reminiscence: New Ways of Working with Older Adults.* New York: Haworth Press.

Karp, David A. and William C. Yoels. 1982. *Experiencing the Life Cycle: A Social Psychology of Aging.* Springfield, Ill.: Charles C. Thomas.

Kaufman, Sharon R. 1986. *The Ageless Self: Sources of Meaning in Late Life.* Madison: University of Wisconsin Press.

Keith, Jennie. 1977. *Old People, New Lives.* Chicago: University of Chicago Press.

Kertzer, David and Jennie Keith, eds. 1984. *Age and Anthropological Theory.* Ithaca: Cornell University Press.

Kirshenblatt-Gimblett, Barbara. 1989a. Authoring Lives. *Journal of Folklore Research* 26:123–49.

———. 1989b. Objects of Memory: Material Culture as Life Review. In *Folk Groups and Folklore Genres: A Reader,* edited by Elliot Oring, 329–38. Logan: Utah State University Press.

Kniffen, Fred B. 1986. Folk Housing: Key to Diffusion. In *Common Places: Readings in American Vernacular Architecture,* 3–26. *See* Upton and Vlach 1986.

Kotre, John. 1984. *Outliving the Self: Generativity and the Interpretation of Lives.* Baltimore: Johns Hopkins University Press.

Labov, William. 1972. *Language in the Inner City*. Philadelphia: University of Pennsylvania Press.

Labov, William and Joshua Waletzky. 1967. Narrative Analysis: Oral Versions of Personal Experience. In *Essays on the Verbal and Visual Arts,* edited by June Helm, 12–44. Seattle: University of Washington Press.

Langness, L.L. 1965. *The Life History in Anthropological Science*. New York: Holt, Rinehart, and Winston.

Langness, L.L. and Gelya Frank. 1981. *Lives: An Anthropological Approach to Biography.* Navato, Cal.: Chandler and Sharp.

Lawless, Elaine J. 1988a. *God's Peculiar People*. Lexington: University Press of Kentucky.

———. 1988b. *Handmaidens of the Lord*. Philadelphia: University of Pennsylvania Press.

Lévi-Strauss, Claude. 1969a. *The Elementary Structures of Kinship*. Translated by J. H. Bell and J. R. von Sturmer. Edited by Rodney Needham. Boston: Beacon Press.

———. 1969b. *The Raw and the Cooked*. New York: Harper and Row.

Levine, Lawrence W. 1977. *Black Culture and Black Consciousness: Afro-American Folk Thought from Slavery to Freedom*. New York: Oxford University Press.

Lewis, C. S. 1958. *The Allegory of Love: A Study in Medieval Tradition*. New York: Oxford University Press.

Lloyd, Timothy. 1982. On Landscape. Paper presented at the annual meeting of the American Folklore Society, Minneapolis.

Lloyd, Timothy C. and Patrick B. Mullen. 1990 *Lake Erie Fishermen: Work, Identity, and Tradition*. Urbana: University of Illinois Press.

Lowenthal, David. 1975. Past Time, Present Place: Landscape and Memory. *The Geographical Review* 65:1–36.

Manney, James D., Jr. 1975. *Aging in American Society: An Examination of Concepts and Issues*. Ann Arbor: Institute of Gerontology.

Marcus, George E. and Michael M.J. Fischer. 1986. *Anthropology as Cultural Critique: An Experimental Moment in the Human Sciences*. Chicago: University of Chicago Press.

McCaslin, Rosemary. 1987. Defenses. In *The Encyclopedia of Aging,* edited by George L. Maddox, 160–62. New York: Springer Publishing.

McClelland, David C. 1961. *The Achieving Society*. Princeton, N.J.: D. Van Nostrand.

McCulloh, Judith. 1975. Uncle Absie Morrison's Historical Tunes. *Mid-South Folklore* 3:95–104.

McMahon, Arthur W., Jr., and Paul J. Rhudick. 1967. Reminiscing in the Aged: An Adaptational Response. In *Psychodynamic Studies on Aging:*

Creativity, Reminiscing, and Dying, edited by Sidney Levin and Ralph J. Kahana, 64–78. New York: International Universities Press.

McMillan, Wheeler. 1974. *Ohio Farm.* Columbus: Ohio State University Press.

Meinig, D. W. 1979. *The Interpretation of Ordinary Landscapes: Geographical Essays.* New York: Oxford University Press.

Morin, Francoise. 1982. Anthropological Praxis and Life History. *International Journal of Oral History.* 3/1:5–30.

Mullen, Patrick B. 1978. *I Heard the Old Fishermen Say: Folklore of the Texas Gulf Coast.* Austin: University of Texas Press.

———. 1981. Two Courtship Stories from the Blue Ridge Mountains. *Folklore and Folklife in Virginia* 2:25–37.

———. 1983. Ritual and Sacred Narratives in the Blue Ridge Mountains. *Papers in Comparative Studies* 2:17–38.

Myerhoff, Barbara G. 1977. We Don't Wrap Herring in a Printed Page: Fusion, Fictions and Continuity in Secular Ritual. In *Secular Ritual,* edited by Sally F. Moore and Barbara G. Myerhoff, 199–224. Amsterdam: Van Gorcum, Assen.

———. 1978. A Symbol Perfected in Death: Continuity and Ritual in the Life and Death of an Elderly Jew. In *Life's Career—Aging: Cultural Variations on Growing Old,* edited by Barbara G. Myerhoff and Andrei Simic, 163–205. Beverly Hills: Sage Publications.

———. 1979. *Number Our Days.* New York: Simon and Schuster.

———. 1984. Rites and Signs of Ripening: The Intertwining of Ritual, Time, and Growing Older. In *Age and Anthropological Theory,* edited by David Kertzer and Jennie Keith, 305–30. Ithaca: Cornell University Press.

Myerhoff, Barbara G. and Andrei Simic, eds. 1978. *Life's Career—Aging: Cultural Variations on Growing Old.* Beverly Hills: Sage Publications.

Neugarten, Bernice L., ed. 1968. *Middle Age and Aging: A Reader in Social Psychology.* Chicago: University of Chicago Press.

Neumann, Siegfried. 1966. Arbeitserinnerungen als Erzählungsinhalt. *Deutsches Jahrbuch für Volkskunde* 12:179–90.

Ortner, Sherry B. 1974. Is Female to Male as Nature is to Culture? In *Woman, Culture, and Society,* edited by Michelle Z. Rosaldo and Louise Lamphere, 67–87. Stanford: Stanford University Press.

Passin, Herbert and John W. Bennett. 1943. Changing Agricultural Magic in Southern Illinois: A Systematic Analysis of Folk-Urban Transition. *Social Forces* 22:98–106.

Peacock, James L. 1984. Religion and Life History: An Exploration in Cultural Psychology. In *Text, Play, and Story: The Construction and Recon-*

struction of Self and Society, edited by Edward M. Bruner, 94–116. Washington, D.C.: American Ethnological Society.

Peck, Catherine L. 1988. Your Daughters Shall Prophesy: Women in the Afro-American Preaching Tradition. In *Diversities of Gifts,* 143–56. *See* Tyson, Peacock, and Patterson 1988.

Perdue, Charles L., Thomas E. Barden, and Robert K. Phillips, eds., 1976 *Weevils in the Wheat: Interviews with Virginia Ex-Slaves.* Charlottesville: University Press of Virginia.

Portelli, Alessandro. 1981. The Time of My Life: Functions of Time in Oral History. *International Journal of Oral History.* 2/3:162–80.

Preston, Dennis. 1982. 'Ritin' Fowklower Daun' Rong: Folklorists' Failures in Phonology. *Journal of American Folklore* 95:304–26.

Radin, Paul. 1972. *The Trickster: A Study in American Indian Mythology.* New York: Schocken Books.

Randolph, Vance. 1982. *Ozark Folksongs,* edited and abridged by Norm Cohen. Urbana: University of Illinois Press.

Rapaport, Amos. 1969. *House Form and Culture.* Englewood Cliffs, N. J.: Prentice-Hall.

Ricoeur, Paul. 1979. The Model of the Text: Meaningful Action Considered as a Text. In *Interpretive Social Science: A Reader,* edited by Paul Rabinow and William M. Sullivan, 73–101. Berkeley: University of California Press.

Rikoon, J. Sanford. 1988a. *Threshing in the Midwest, 1820–1940: A Study of Traditional Culture and Technological Change.* Bloomington: Indiana University Press.

———. 1988b. Personal correspondence.

Robinson, John A. 1981. Personal Narratives Reconsidered. *Journal of American Folklore* 94:58–85.

Rose, Lionel. 1978. Popular Precautions against Premature Burial. *Folk Review* 7(11):4–8.

Santino, Jack. 1978. Characteristics of Occupational Narratives. *Western Folklore* 37:199–212.

———. 1989. *Miles of Smiles, Years of Struggle: Stories of Black Pullman Porters.* Urbana: University of Illinois Press.

Schrager, Samuel. 1983. What is Social in Social History? *International Journal of Oral History* 4(2):76–98.

Schreiber, William I. 1967. The Pennsylvania Dutch Bank Barn in Ohio. *Journal of the Ohio Folklore Society* 2:15–28.

Sennett, Richard. 1977. *The Fall of Public Man.* New York: Alfred A. Knopf.

Shuman, Amy. 1986. *Storytelling Rights: Oral and Written Communication among Urban Adolescents.* London and New York: Cambridge University Press.

Simpson, Eileen. 1987. *Orphans: Real and Imaginary.* New York: New American Library.

Smith, Barbara Herrnstein. 1980. Narrative Versions, Narrative Theories. *Critical Inquiry* 7:213–36.

Solomon, Jack and Olivia Solomon. 1981. *Ghosts and Goosebumps: Ghost Stories, Tall Tales, and Superstitions from Alabama.* University: University of Alabama Press.

Sopher, David E. 1979. The Landscape of Home: Myth, Experience, Social Meaning. In *The Interpretation of Ordinary Landscapes: Geographical Essays,* 129–49. *See* Meinig 1979.

Stahl, Sandra. 1977a. The Oral Personal Narrative in Its Generic Context. *Fabula* 18:18–39.

———. 1977b. The Personal Narrative as Folklore. *Journal of the Folklore Institute* 14:9–30.

Steward, Dana, ed. 1984. *A Fine Age: Creativity as a Key to Successful Aging.* Little Rock, Ark.: August House.

Stewart, Susan. 1984. *On Longing: Narratives of the Miniature, the Gigantic, the Souvenir, the Collection.* Baltimore: Johns Hopkins University Press.

Sullivan, C. W. III. 1987. Johnny Says His ABCs. *Western Folklore* 46: 36–41.

Sutton, Brett. 1977. In the Good Old Way, Primitive Baptist Traditions. *Southern Exposure* 5:97–104.

———. 1988. Speech, Chant, and Song: Patterns of Language and Action in a Southern Church. In *Diversities of Gifts,* 157–76. *See* Tyson, Peacock, and Patterson 1988.

Sydow, Carl Wilhelm von. 1948. *Selected Papers on Folklore.* Copenhagen: Rosenkilde and Bagger.

Thompson, Stith. 1955. *Motif-Index of Folk-Literature.* Rev. ed. Bloomington: Indiana University Press.

Titon, Jeff Todd. 1978. Some Recent Pentecostal Revivals: A Report in Words and Photographs. *Georgia Review* 32:579–605.

———. 1980. The Life Story. *Journal of American Folklore* 93:276–92.

———. 1988. *Powerhouse for God: Speech, Chant, and Song in an Appalachian Baptist Church.* Austin: University of Texas Press.

Titon, Jeff and Ken George. 1978. Testimonies. *Alcheringa: Ethnopoetics* 4:69–83.

Toelken, Barre. 1979. *The Dynamics of Folklore.* Boston: Houghton Mifflin.

Turner, Victor. 1977. *The Ritual Process: Structure and Anti-Structure.* Ithaca: Cornell University Press.

Tyson, Ruel W., Jr., James L. Peacock, and Daniel W. Patterson, eds. 1988. *Diversities of Gifts: Field Studies in Southern Religion*. Urbana: University of Illinois Press.

Upton, Dell and John Michael Vlach, eds. 1986. *Common Places: Readings in American Vernacular Architecture*. Athens: University of Georgia Press.

Vlach, John M. 1971. One Black Eye and Other Horrors: A Case for the Humorous Anti-Legend. *Indiana Folklore* 4:95–140.

Watson, Lawrence C. and Maria-Barbara Watson-Franke. 1985. *Interpreting Life Histories: An Anthropological Inquiry*. New Brunswick: Rutgers University Press.

Wertheimer, Jean. 1983. The Mechanisms of Permanence Time: Support for a Psychodynamic Hypothesis of Psychological Aging. *Journal of Geriatric Psychiatry* 16:245–55.

Wilson, William A. 1990. In Praise of Ourselves: Stories to Tell. *Brigham Young University Studies* 30:5–24.

Wolfe, Charles, ed. 1981. *Children of the Heav'nly King: Religious Expression in the Central Blue Ridge*. Record Album AFC L69 L70. Washington, D.C.: American Folklife Center, Library of Congress.

Wolfson, Nessa. 1976. Speech Events and Natural Speech: Some Implications for Sociolinguistic Methodology. *Language in Society* 5:189–209.

Yates, Frances A. 1966. *The Art of Memory*. Chicago: University of Chicago Press.

Young, Katharine Galloway. 1987. *Taleworlds and Storyrealms: The Phenomenology of Narrative*. Dordrecht, The Netherlands: Martinus Nijhoff.

Zeitlin, Steven J. 1980. An Alchemy of Mind: The Family Courtship Story. *Western Folklore* 39:17–33.

Zelditch, Morris. 1955. Role Differentiation in the Nuclear Family: A Comparative Study. In *Family, Socialization and Interpretation Process*, edited by Talcott Parsons and Robert F. Bales, 307–51. Glencoe, Ill.: Free Press.

Index

A Note on the Author

Patrick B. Mullen is professor of English at the Ohio State University and author of *I Heard the Old Fishermen Say: Folklore of the Texas Gulf Coast,* and co-author of *Lake Erie Fishermen: Work, Identity, and Tradition.*